THE TRUMPETS WILL SOUND

THE TRUMPETS WILL SOUND

The Story of the
Royal Military School of Music,
Kneller Hall

by
Gordon Turner
and
Alwyn W Turner

PARAPRESS LIMITED
TUNBRIDGE WELLS · KENT
in association with
DROIT MUSIC LIMITED

First published in the UK by
PARAPRESS LTD
12 Dene Way
Speldhurst
Tunbridge Wells
Kent
TN3 0NX

ISBN: 1-898594-38-4

A catalogue record for this book is
available from the British Library

Design and typesetting by
Vitaset, Paddock Wood, Kent

Printed in Great Britain by
Biddles Ltd, Guildford and King's Lynn

CONTENTS

ACKNOWLEDGEMENTS

This book would have been impossible without access to the Diary and the archives at Kneller Hall, and we must express our profound gratitude to the Commandant, Colonel Tim P B Hoggarth, for the co-operation and support he has shown by making these documents available to us. In the same context, we must acknowledge the contributions of Major (retd) Roger Swift and Lieutenant-Colonel (retd) Rodney Bashford in maintaining the archives and records at the School.

Our thanks are also due to Ms Elizabeth Imlay, our editor, to Mr Ian Morley-Clark for his help with the publishing, to Mr Jack Tulip for taking many of the photographs of the School for the book, to Mr Toby Jessell MP for his assistance, and to Sir Malcolm Arnold for his kind words in the Foreword.

Finally we must register the deep debt that students of military music owe to the late Mr William Tanner, whose work in compiling lists of bandmasters and directors of music provides an invaluable source of information.

PICTURE CREDITS

We would like to thank the following individuals and institutions for providing the pictures used in this book: Bandmaster John Brigden, Mr Michael Farnham, Mrs B Housman, Captain John Huggins, Mr Matt, the Public Archives of Canda, Radio Times, Richmond & Twickenham Times, Col Nigel Roberts, the Royal Military School of Music, Mr Dick Tulip, Mr Jack Tulip, Maj (retd) Gordon Turner, Mr Vic Webster, Mrs Dolly Young and Mr Jerry Young.

FOREWORD

by Malcolm Arnold

Getting old is not one of the most memorable things in life except that from time to time people can be very kind to you and honour you in the most unexpected of ways; and one of the most rewarding of the honours that I have been privileged to receive was the invitation to write a Foreword to this book by Gordon and Alwyn Turner on that wonderful musical academy Kneller Hall, The Royal Military School of Music.

The title, *The Trumpets Will Sound*, is particularly nostalgic to me for it was as a trumpet player that I first made my mark in the wonderful world of music. I began a love affair with the instrument when I first heard the great American jazz trumpeter, Louis Armstrong, and I continued my infatuation with the instrument through the Royal College of Music and into the chair of the principal trumpet with the London Philharmonic Orchestra. Wind instrumentalists in general, and trumpeters in particular, are a funny lot who have to be masochistic by nature for, as my trumpet mentor the legendary Ernest Hall used to tell me 'when you put that mouthpiece to your lips you're on your own, there's just no place to hide.'

During my years as an orchestral musician I was constantly meeting and working with first class wind players who told me that they had learnt their craft at the Royal Military School of Music, Kneller Hall, as a result of which, although I had never been to the School, I built up a very healthy respect for an establishment that was capable of producing a seemingly endless stream of fine artists. One or two talented pupils can be a stroke of good fortune for any music college, but the plethora of polished performers coming from Kneller Hall could only have resulted from instruction of the very highest of standards.

Then in 1948, although I deserted my first love – the trumpet – and became a professional composer, I still continued my life long affair with wind instruments with a number of compositions written specifically for wind combinations, which gave me a great deal of satisfaction; not the least of these was my adaptation of 'Colonel Bogey' which was featured so prominently in David Lean's wonderful theatrical film *Bridge On The River Kwai*. I think that scene in the jungle when that tattered, unruly, pathetic crowd of men, apparently without any hope, suddenly become proud soldiers as they start to whistle that wonderful march, is incredibly moving. As any old service man will tell you, nothing is quite so inspiring as marching behind, and to the stirring sound of, a military band.

So I was particularly pleased when in 1957 I was invited to play a role in the Kneller Hall Centenary, and to mark the occasion I wrote a march for a military band, 'HRH The Duke of Cambridge' – in honour of the founder of Kneller Hall, the Duke of Cambridge, who was then Commander-in-Chief of the British Army. It was given its first performance on the 28th of June 1957 by the Band of the Royal Military School of Music under the direction of – if my memory serves

Sir Malcolm Arnold presenting a prize to Std BM Jerry Young (J. YOUNG)

me right – Rodney Bashford; and I am proud to think that my original autographed score of the work is still held by Kneller Hall. It was during that association with the School, when I really got to know the dedicated tutors who achieved such a consistently high standard of performance from their pupils that I fully realized the extent of the contribution made to music by Kneller Hall.

Then, more recently, the School decided to name student classes after modern British composers and honoured me yet again, by naming one class after me. At the time I felt that the particular students of the class named after me might not perhaps feel quite as honoured as I did. However, that question was resolved in the most gratifying way when in February of this year Lieutenant-Colonel Rodney Parker invited me to a concert given by the Band of The Royal Yeomanry, combined with the Pipes, Drums and Dancers of the Scots Guards, in the Anvil Concert Hall, Basingstoke, and during the interval Rodney introduced me to the members of the 1989 Royal Military School of Music Class – the 'Malcolm Arnold Class' – all of whom most graciously assured me of the pride they felt in being 'Arnold Class' students.

So you can see that my associations are neither recent nor half hearted and are, to me, one of the most important elements of my life. Long may the Royal Military School of Music flourish and continue to provide the world of music with musicians of the very highest standard. A Kneller Hall book is well overdue. I congratulate Gordon and Alwyn Turner for undertaking the task of producing this volume and I know that it will be a highly successful testament to a great musical legend.

Malcolm Arnold
Norfolk, May 1996

CHAPTER 1

WHITTON
HALL

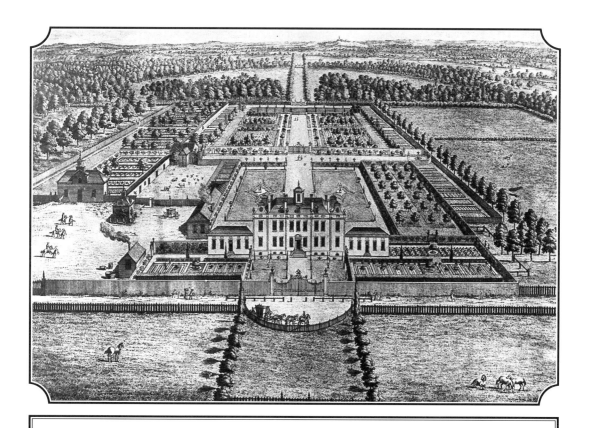

ENGRAVING BY KIP OF WHITTON HOUSE (RMSM)

When Godfrey Kneller decided to acquire a country estate in 1709, his intention was not simply to move into more spacious premises, but to make a public statement about his status in society.

It was a statement he felt fully entitled to make. Ever since he had first established himself thirty years earlier with a portrait of Charles II, he had enjoyed an unbroken spell of success. His reward for that portrait had been his appointment as official court painter, and he had held on to his position ever since, despite the upheavals of James II's brief reign and of the Glorious Revolution of William and Mary. He was still the incumbent artist when he died in 1723, having survived yet another abrupt change in the succession with the advent of the Hanoverians.

Although posterity may have paid less attention to Godfrey Kneller than it has to some other British court painters, such as Holbein, Van Dyck, Gainsborough and Landseer, his contemporaries harboured no such reservations. During his four and a half decades as the most famous painter in the country, there was scarcely a personage of note who did not sit for Kneller: monarchs, members of the court and of the aristocracy were joined by the great figures of the restoration world – including Pepys, Newton, Congreve, Wren – and by foreign kings, most notably Louis XIV and Peter the Great of Russia.

There was little in Kneller's childhood to suggest such a glittering future. He was born Gottfried Kniller in 1646, the third son of the town surveyor of Lübeck in northern Germany. His father was a keen amateur portraitist, his enthusiasm so contagious that two of his sons were to become professional artists, despite their early training in other fields. In Gottfried's case this training was aimed at the army – he studied mathematics with particular reference to fortifications at Leyden University. It was here that his talent and love for art finally overcame his desire for a military career and, having completed his university course, he embarked upon the difficult path to becoming a painter.

Over the next ten years he was fortunate enough to benefit from the instruction of some of the most spectacular talents in Europe. In Amsterdam he studied under Ferdinand Bols, a pupil of Rembrandt, and possibly even under the great man himself; Rembrandt was then in the last years of his life, but his influence is clearly discernible in Kneller's early works. In Rome his teacher was Giovanni Bernini, another genius nearing the end of his life. Equally adept at sculpture, painting and poetry, Bernini was predominantly an architect, and it was in this discipline that he taught Gottfried.

By the time he arrived in London in 1676, therefore, with an introductory letter to a successful German merchant in his pocket, the newly anglicized Godfrey Kneller could boast the best artistic apprenticeship that Europe could offer. He also had one other talent that was paradoxically both to make his reputation and to damage his long-term stature as a painter: an ability to turn out work at an astonishing pace.

When, following a portrait of Charles II's illegitimate son, the Duke of Monmouth, he was offered the chance to paint the King himself, it was at a time when Charles was already sitting for the resident court artist, Sir Peter Lely. To the amazement of all present, Kneller had finished his portrait whilst Lely was still daubing the background pigment onto his canvas. This speed of execution and facile production was to become characteristic of his work, and was to lead him into temptations that would ultimately provide his detractors with their chief criticism; 'Where he offered one picture to fame,' wrote Horace Walpole, the premier gossip of the 18th century, 'he sacrificed twenty to lucre.'

In his own time, however, Kneller could do little wrong. The early influence of Rembrandt was put aside in favour of more established court styles, as he concentrated on becoming the biggest fish in the smallish pond that was English art; it was an endeavour that resulted in unqualified triumph. In Europe there were those who refused to take him seriously, but in Britain he was showered with honours: he was knighted by William III in 1691, and became the first painter to be given a baronetcy, courtesy of George I in 1715.

His position in 1709 was thus unarguable. He was the most significant painter in Britain, feted and celebrated like no other. What could be more natural than that he should want a country seat to confirm his status?

In his search for a suitable site near enough to London to enable him to continue his work, but expansive enough to reflect his stature, Kneller's eye alighted upon Whitton, near Twickenham, then little more than a hamlet. Nearly a hundred acres of land were purchased in 1709, and work began that year on constructing the house that was eventually to bear the portraitist's name.

There was an existing building on the site, constructed some time between 1635 and 1646 by Edmund Cooke, but no pictures have survived, and it is unclear how extensive the establishment was. For the purposes of the 1664 Hearth Tax, however, the house was assessed as having 20 fireplaces, suggesting a substantial property. Subsequent owners included Charles Pitcairne, Sir Thomas Mack and Henry Kempe, before Kneller bought the property and demolished the old building.

Facade stone 1848 (J TULIP)

❄

There is some uncertainty surrounding the architecture of Kneller's new house. Whitton Hall, as it was then known, was an expansive country seat in the manner of the period, complete with formal gardens and deer park. What remains doubtful is who was actually responsible for the design of the compact and very stylish nine-bay building that can be seen in Kip's engraving.

Strong circumstantial evidence, however, suggests that Sir Christopher Wren might have been partially responsible for the work. Undoubtedly, a man of Kneller's status would have insisted upon one of the great architects of the time, and Vanburgh, Hawksmoor and Talman have been ruled out on design grounds, leaving Wren – or at least one of his school – as the most likely candidate. There even survives an elevation originating from Wren's office, though probably drawn by Robert Hooke, which bears a remarkable resemblance to the first version of Whitton Hall.

It is true that Wren built very few country houses in his later years, but his friendship with Kneller, and the fact that they occupied much the same place in society as the established elder statesmen of their respective professions, makes his involvement feasible. Also perhaps significant are the portrait of Wren executed by Kneller in 1711, the year when the building was completed (in part-payment for services rendered?) and the similarity in the two men's background: like Kneller, Wren had studied architecture for a short while under Bernini.

In this latter context it is even possible that Kneller himself – as a sometime architectural student – may have made a serious contribution to the design. He certainly had a major part to play in the interior decoration of the place, though he also called in his contemporaries Verrio and La Guerre for assistance.

Whoever was ultimately accountable for the architecture, there is no question that Whitton Hall answered Godfrey Kneller's desire to consolidate his social standing. George

Vertue wrote of the artist that 'with glorys & Honours heap'd on him he built himself a fine Palace at his Country seat at Whitton about 8 mile from London, where he has purchast an Estate & lives in the sommer visited & courted by all People of Honour & distinction.'

Such a lifestyle suited Kneller, a man whose talent was exceeded only by his vanity and by his love of luxury and flattery. Surrounded by his own works and by those of Rubens, Rembrandt and Van Dyck, he received visitors, continued his painting and played the part of the country squire for all he was worth. He also threw himself into local society, becoming the Church Warden of Twickenham parish – notwithstanding his rumoured lack of faith in Christianity – and a Justice of the Peace.

In this latter role he acquired a reputation as something of a maverick. When a soldier charged with stealing a joint of meat from a butcher was brought before him, Kneller had no hesitation in accepting the defendant's claim that the temptation of the wares on display was more than a hungry man could bear; the soldier was discharged, and the butcher severely reprimanded. On another occasion he refused to hear any evidence at all in an argument over which of two parishes was responsible for a pauper – he simply ascertained which was the richer, and decided that was where the man belonged. He was also known to tell disputants to go away and sort their problems out themselves in the nearest alehouse.

But even such a pillar of society was vulnerable to the rising crime wave of the 18th century, and in 1718 Kneller was attacked whilst travelling to London by some of the many highwaymen who plied their trade on Hounslow Heath. Fortunately he was robbed of just £20 and a gold watch, a loss he could bear with little discomfort. Indeed, he survived even the financial collapse of the South Sea Bubble two years later, in which he lost £20,000; when he died in 1723 he still managed to leave a fortune amounting to an income of some £2000 per annum. He also, of course, left Whitton Hall.

The chief beneficiaries of his will were his widow, Lady Susannah Kneller, and his daughter, Agnes, the two other principal residents of the house.

Agnes, interestingly, was not actually Lady Kneller's child; her mother was a Mrs Voss, who ran a fashionable coffee shop in St James' Market, off the Haymarket, in Charles II's time. Also a German, Mrs Voss was married to a Quaker, but Kneller bought her from her husband for an unknown sum in order to acquire her services as mistress. The relationship lasted for some years, and Mrs Voss appears to have mixed freely in society under the name of Mrs Kneller; she also helped him with his business affairs.

Agnes was born in the early to mid 1680s, and was both acknowledged and accepted as Kneller's child. Even after Kneller's marriage in 1703, she continued to live with her father and later moved with him and her step-mother to Whitton. Her son, to whom the inheritance passed, adopted his grandfather's name, becoming Godfrey Huckle Kneller; his descendants have continued to keep the name alive.

Two days before Godfrey Kneller died, the poet and close family friend, Alexander Pope, visited him. Pope later wrote of this final encounter:

> The next word he said was this 'By God, I will not be buried in Westminster.' I asked him why not? He answered 'they do bury fools there.' Then he said to me 'My good friend where will you be buried?' I said 'wherever I drop; very likely in Twitnam.' He replied 'so will I' then proceeded to desire I would write his epitaph.

Pope did indeed write an epitaph for his friend, though in retrospect he called it 'the worst thing I ever wrote', and it can still be seen in Westminster Abbey, where Kneller was the first – and, so far, the only – painter to have a monument erected:

> Kneller, by Heaven and not a master taught,
> Whose art was nature and whose pictures thought;
> Now for two ages having snatched from fate
> Whate'er was beauteous, or whate'er was great
> Rests crown'd with Princes' Honours, Poets' Lays,
> Due to his merit and brave Thirst of Praise;
> Living, great Nature fear'd he might outvie
> Her works; and, dying, fears herself may die.

Portrait of Mrs Knight, mistress of Charles II, by Godfrey Kneller, hanging in Officers' Mess (RMSM)

Following his death-bed request, however, Kneller was not buried in Westminster. In fact his final resting-place has never been successfully identified. He died in his London home, but his body was immediately taken down to Whitton for interment; it is believed that he was laid to rest somewhere within the grounds of his country house, where presumably he still lies.

❋

The widowed Lady Kneller continued to live at Whitton Hall until her own death in 1729. Her step-grandson, Godfrey Huckle Kneller, had by then married Mary Weekes of Donhead Hall in Wiltshire, and had moved to his wife's home. Whitton Hall was therefore sold and subsequently acquired a series of owners.

The first of these was a Mr Ride, of whom nothing is known. He was followed in 1758 by Sir Samuel Prime, a successful lawyer who had been made a King's Serjeant twenty years earlier and was still practising. Prime enjoyed a reputation in the legal and social worlds he inhabited as being something of a bore; always impeccably dressed in old-fashioned clothes and wearing strong scent, he was said to have no sense of humour and to speak extremely slowly.

It was perhaps this latter trait that was responsible for the enormous lengths of his legal speeches. On one occasion, it is reported, he took three hours to make his point on a particularly hot day in a crowded court-room. A small boy, who had climbed into the rafters to hear the case, fell asleep with the tedium of the argument, and tumbled from his perch, causing Prime to be charged with responsibility for a case of near-manslaughter; he was fined three dozen bottles of wine.

Despite this dullness of manner, Prime was a generous host and Whitton Hall was known for its hospitality during his residency, just as it had been during Kneller's time. It was a tradition that continued after his death in 1777, when his place was taken by his son, also called Samuel Prime.

Between them, the two Primes made substantial changes to the house and grounds. What internal refurbishment was carried out is not known, but certainly the high walls surrounding the estate and various nearby buildings were demolished to make the house handsomer in prospect, whilst further land was bought to extend the property.

Following the death of the younger Samuel Prime, the hall was again sold. It was occupied by the Reverend Fisher and then by Mr Charles Calvert.

The son of a brewer, Calvert was born in 1768 and inherited half the family firm in 1802. He expanded the business sufficiently to become the Whig MP for Southwark within a decade, serving through to his death in 1832. Like Kneller before him, he sought to confirm his improving position in society by purchasing a significant country house. Whatever modifications the Primes had made to Kneller's original home, it seems certain that it was Calvert who was largely responsible for re-shaping the building towards the structure that can be seen today.

The work was entrusted to Philip Hardwick, an architect whose biggest project was the magnificent entrance to Euston Station, an undertaking almost as significant and reflective of its age as Wren's design for St Paul's had been; sadly, his masterpiece has not survived, having been destroyed by the British Transport Commission. Under his superintendence, the two single-storey wings at either end of Kneller's house were removed and new extensions added: a drawing-room at the south-east end and a dining-room at the south-west, together with an 85-foot long conservatory.

Kneller Hall (RMSM)

The extent of the transformation was difficult to ascertain at the time, for Calvert was reluctant to allow access to outsiders; when Brewer was compiling his *History of Middlesex*, for example, he applied for and was refused permission to inspect the house for inclusion in the work, and instead had to confine himself to a sarcastic comment on Calvert's 'modesty' in not flaunting his wealth. Fortunately, however, a full record survives of the property as it stood at the end of his occupancy, in the form of a set of details dating from when it was auctioned in 1841.

On Calvert's death of cholera in 1832, a dispute arose over his inheritance, the details of which have been lost with time. It appears that Calvert left the house and land to one Edward Godfrey, and that the will was then contested by his widow, Jane Calvert. Little is known of Mrs Calvert, save that she was much younger than her husband and that they married when he was already an old man; it seems possible that his will had already been drawn up in Godfrey's favour and was never amended. In any event, the dispute went to the Court of Chancery, and it was on the orders of this body that the property was offered for sale by auction, the proceeds presumably to be split between the two parties.

The auction particulars, issued by Messrs Driver of Richmond Terrace, Westminster, give a complete picture of what was by now called Kneller Hall, together with a map showing the extent of the land and the shape of the estate. In addition to the 'capital and noble mansion known as Kneller Hall', there were stables, coach houses, a wood yard, a melon yard and kitchen gardens, together with extensive Pleasure Grounds which were:

most tastefully disposed in Lawns, Parterres, and Plantations of Lauristinus and other Plants, in the highest state of perfection and luxuriancy; they are laid out to produce the most beautiful effect; amongst which must not be overlooked the various Belts, interspersed with Gravel Walks, the beautiful and extensive Lake, with the Bridges from one Islet to another, the Rustic Boat House, the Water Fall, the Pavilion – and though last, not least – the picturesque Groups of Trees scattered about the Park like Grounds.

These features in the grounds are also thought to have been constructed by Charles Calvert. The auctioneers conclude that 'the whole now forms a Residence remarkably well adapted for a Nobleman, Minister of State, or Family of distinction.'

Kneller Hall: the grounds (RMSM)

Certainly the property would have been suitable for such a personage, but it is uncertain who the actual purchaser was. It is believed that Jane Calvert remained in residence until her death some time around 1845, but there is a gap in the records, during which the owner of Kneller Hall cannot be identified, between the 1841 auction and 1847.

In that year the property was purchased by the Committee of Privy Council on Education. It is possible that the house had lain empty for the previous few years, for when the new owners came to occupy it, they discovered that it was in very poor condition, with the walls crumbling and the timber dilapidated. Another re-build was ordered, this time under the architectural direction of George Mair, with the work being the responsibility of the builder, John Kelk (later Sir John Kelk of Albert Memorial fame).

The single-storey wings of Calvert's era were kept, but refaced and raised a further two storeys, whilst the centre of the house was demolished and rebuilt; it too was raised from the two storeys of Kneller's original to the current three storeys. The single turret that had adorned Kneller's house was replaced by the distinctive twin turrets of today, and the colonnade – in imitation of the then fashionable Woollaston Hall – was erected. The resulting edifice is what can still be seen: an imposing Jacobean construction of red facing brickwork, adorned with Bath stone dressing and a Portland stone plinth.

There is one further area of confusion; what had been advertised in 1841 as an estate comprising 102 acres appears to have been reduced by 1847 to barely half that size. What happened to the remainder is not clear.

In Chancery.

JANE CALVERT, WIDOW, and OTHERS,.... PLAINTIFFS.

EDWARD GODFREY, and OTHERS .... DEFENDANTS.

———o———

THE KNELLER HALL ESTATE,
WHITTON, MIDDLESEX.

SPECIFICATIONS
OF A HIGHLY VALUABLE
IMPROVABLE ESTATE,

Free of Great Tithes, and exonerated from the Land Tax,

PART FREEHOLD AND PART COPYHOLD,

But being held under the Manors of Isleworth Sion and Isleworth Rectory, may be considered EQUAL TO FREEHOLD, the Quit Rents and Fines being small fixed Sums.

Most eligibly situated only Eleven Miles from London, in a beautiful part of the

COUNTY OF MIDDLESEX,

Being at Whitton, a short distance from Twickenham, and in the

PARISHES OF ISLEWORTH AND TWICKENHAM;
COMPRISING

A CAPITAL AND NOBLE MANSION,
KNOWN AS KNELLER HALL,

Replete with every accommodation, and appropriate for the Occupation of any Family of the first distinction; most pleasantly seated in Park-like Grounds, with all the Appendages of Ornamental Pleasure Grounds, Beautiful Lake, Luxuriant Plantations, Lawn, Parterres, Walks of great variety, Conservatory, Grapery, Greenhouse, Entrance Lodge, a Good Farm House and Homestead, Gardener's Cottage, a well inclosed Kitchen Garden, and sundry Parcels of Rich Meadow Land, containing with about Seven Acres of highly productive Arable and Garden Ground,

A TOTAL AREA
OF
102 A. 3 R. and 15 P.

———o———

Which will be Sold by Auction,

By MESSRS. DRIVER,

AT THE AUCTION MART, BARTHOLOMEW LANE,
On Thursday, the 29th of July, 1841, at 12 o'Clock,
IN ONE LOT.

(Pursuant to an Order of the High Court of Chancery, and with the approbation of Samuel Duckworth, Esq., one of the Masters of the said Court)

To be viewed by applying on the Premises. Particulars with Plans annexed may be had at the Master's Chambers, in Southampton Buildings, Chancery Lane; of Messrs. Vandercom, Comyn, Cree, Law, and Comyn, Solicitors, No. 23, Bush Lane, London; at the King's Head, Twickenham; the Pigeons, Brentford; Star and Garter, Richmond; at the Auction Mart, Bartholomew Lane; and of Messrs. Driver, Surveyors and Land Agents, No. 8, Richmond Terrace, Parliament Street.

J. Shuttleworth, Printer to Her Majesty, 3, Chapel Place, Poultry.

SPECIFICATIONS.

---◆---

KNELLER HALL AND ESTATE, MIDDLESEX.

---o---

This very valuable Property is most eligibly situated in the Parishes of Twickenham and Isleworth, in a beautiful part of the County, only about eleven miles from London, two from Richmond, and one and a half from Hounslow.

The MANSION HOUSE is known as KNELLER HALL, being formerly the residence of the eminent painter, Sir Godfrey Kneller, whose pencil, or that of his Pupil, is now visible on the Walls and Ceiling of the principal Staircase, in nearly their pristine beauty; it afterwards became the property of the Prime family, from whom the late Charles Calvert Esq., M.P. for South-wark, purchased it, and who laid out a considerable sum in building a most noble Drawing Room, spacious Dining Room, and a beautiful Conservatory, 85 feet in length communicating therewith, sparing no expence in laying out the Pleasure Grounds in the very best taste, and the whole now forms a Residence remarkably well adapted for a Nobleman, Minister of State, or Family of distinction.

The ESTATE is exonerated from the Land Tax, and as the Great Tithes are the property of the Vendor, they will be included in the Purchase, as well as the various Fixtures in and about the Premises, the Clock, and the Brewing Utensils.

THE MANSION

Is a Substantial BRICK BUILDING, the roof partly slated and partly covered with a lead flat: it is approached from the road by a neat Lodge, with a handsome Carriage Drive, skirted by Plantations, and the House is entered through the Conservatory, and contains

ON THE UPPER FLOOR, Six Servants' Apartments and a Closet.

ON THE ONE PAIR FLOOR, a Boudoir with ornamented Ceiling, having four Medallions in alto relievo, an enriched Cornice and handsome carved Chimney-piece, Morning Room with Panel Ceiling and Statuary Chimney Piece, Day and Sleeping Nurseries, Seven Bed Rooms, two Anti-Rooms and Three Dressing Rooms, and Water Closet.

A Principal STAIRCASE, which is very spacious, and ornamented with Wainscot Balustrades, the Ceiling and Walls being supposed to be Painted by Sir Godfrey Kneller or some of his Pupils; there is also a secondary Staircase.

ON THE GROUND FLOOR—A capital Entrance Hall, 25ft. by 19ft, approached from the Conservatory, a most splendid and lofty Drawing Room, 40ft. by 26 ft, having enriched Ceiling and Cornice, picked out with Gold, carved Statuary Chimney Piece, and decorated with Scagliola Corinthian Columns and Pilasters; a noble Dining Room, 32ft. by 21ft., and an elegant Conservatory, 85ft. in length, communicating with these two Rooms, and heated with hot water; a Bow Breakfast Room, Anti Room, Gentleman's Room, with Water Closet therein; a small Anti Room and Bed Room, Study, Housekeeper's Room, Butler's Pantry, Second Footman's Room, Two large Closets in Corridor, with Two Store Rooms over, Servant's Hall, capital Kitchen, Scullery, and a good Water Closet, and Pantry near the Back Entrance from the Court Yard.

IN THE BASEMENT—Two Arched Wine Cellars, a Knife Place, Bottle Apartment, and various Ale and Beer Cellars.

AN INCLOSED YARD, with covered Colonnade, leads to the following Domestic Offices, viz., Washhouse, Larder, and Dairy, with good Laundry, and Three Servants' Apartments over, also a Brick and Slated Coal House.

THE DETACHED OFFICES are in an enclosed Paved Court Yard, and situated at a convenient distance from the Residence; they comprise a Brick and Tiled Stable for Six Horses, and Three Coach Houses for Six Carriages, with convenient Loft over, and adjoining is a Modern brick and Slated Building, containing a Harness Room, and a spacious Apartment intended for a Stable, but which is not completed, with Granary and Loft over.

Also a detached Brick and Tiled Brew House.

KNELLER HALL.

Kneller Hall c.1850 (TURNER)

The building was opened in January 1850 as an institution for training schoolmasters who were to teach the children of paupers and criminals; as Kneller Hall Training College (swiftly renamed from its original title of Kneller Hall Normal School), it was intended to provide accommodation for 100 students, in addition to the masters. This provision was clearly a trifle optimistic, for there were initially a mere four student teachers resident; by April 1852 this had risen considerably, but the establishment was still operating at less than half-capacity, with just 46 students.

The ideas behind the College were inspired by the work of the great Swiss reformer and educationalist, Johann Pestalozzi, and were characteristic of the liberal evangelism sweeping Britain in the 1840s. The first Principal was Frederick Temple, with Francis Turner Palgrave as Vice-Principal, both of whom, as we shall see, were later to acquire greater fame in other fields.

From the outset, the College faced hostility from many quarters. The government was unhappy (as ever) with the expense of the undertaking, the Church was unhappy that

Self-portrait by Godfrey Kneller, hanging in the Officers' Mess
(RMSM)

non-Anglicans were admitted to its course, and – most importantly – the entire project was way ahead of its time. The concept of training those who would become teachers in workhouse schools was admirable, but unfortunately the levels of pay and conditions in those institutions were so appalling that few qualified men were ever likely to be tempted to devote their lives to such a profession. Many graduates of Kneller Hall did go on to teach in workhouses – perhaps feeling a sense of moral obligation – but when the College was closed, most soon made their way into more mainstream schools, where teachers enjoyed some respect and some more appropriate reward for their endeavours.

Furthermore, Kneller Hall was unable to provide much practical experience; though 24 local children were brought in for the students to teach, the situation of these pupils was entirely unlike that of those in workhouses, where class sizes were much greater and the absence of parents placed different demands on their schoolmasters.

Frederick Temple was aware from the outset that the odds were stacked against him. As early as 1852, he was writing that 'Politics are looking very black for me. My work is really in danger.' By May 1855 the pressures had become too much; knowing that the end was approaching fast, he resigned his post, and the College was closed. He wrote to a friend that month: 'They have accepted my resignation. They have not, however, the audacity to propose to carry on Kneller Hall without me. They are going to make it a barrack or a lunatic asylum or something of that kind.'

Dr Temple was not too damaged by the failure of his project; he was later to become Headmaster of Rugby, Bishop of Exeter and ultimately Archbishop of Canterbury, in which latter post he was followed some years later by his son, William Temple. And his Vice-Principal, Frank Palgrave, went on to be Professor of Poetry at Oxford and to edit *The Golden Treasury*, the volume that was for many generations of schoolchildren the definitive anthology of English verse. (Its status as a classic was re-affirmed in 1996 with a paperback reprint of selections from the work.)

Meanwhile the building had again come vacant. It was of course now owned by the government, and it was from another department of state that the first serious approach came for a new use.

✳

Officials of the War Department were at the time actively engaged in seeking new premises for a guards barracks in London, and their preferred choice was the Royal Military Asylum. Nowadays situated in Dover, and known as the Duke of York's Royal Military School – after its founder, George III's son who had served as the Commander-in-Chief of the Army – the Asylum was then located in Chelsea. If this prime site was to be acquired for the Guards, however, the problem presented itself of what to do with the children of the Asylum. It was to this problem that Kneller Hall seemed to be the answer.

An enquiry to the Council of Education met with an encouraging reply, and investigations were undertaken. The Medical Officer of the Asylum Dr J G Balfour, was charged with ascertaining the conditions at Whitton; his report, however, was deeply unfavourable, concluding that Kneller Hall was not 'an eligible place for the boys of this Institution'. It was, he reported, far too damp, and 'from the great tendency to scrofulous diseases among the children of soldiers, it is a point of vital importance that the site of any Institution in which they are to be received should be dry and thoroughly drained.'

Similar doubts were voiced by the representative of the Registrar General's Department, Dr Farr, who pointed out that Whitton fell within a high-risk area, where 'the mortality is at the rate of 21 in 1000 annually'.

These conclusions must have been disturbing enough to the War Department, but when a financial report assessed the cost of converting Kneller Hall to be £33,000, the Treasury too began to express its concern. This figure seems excessively high, since the purchase and complete re-development of Kneller Hall by the Education Committee just a few years earlier is reported to have cost just £40,000, but it was accepted to the extent that the proposed move of the Asylum in 1856 was postponed.

A vague suggestion was made that funds might be made available the following year. It was not to be, for by then the Commander-in-Chief of the British Army had come up with his own scheme for utilizing Kneller Hall.

CHAPTER 2

A NEW BEGINNING

THE DUKE OF CAMBRIDGE (RMSM)

George, Duke of Cambridge, was the son of Adolphus, tenth child of that most fecund of monarchs, George III. Born in Hanover in 1819, he was for a few months the heir presumptive to the throne of the United Kingdom, until the birth of his cousin, Victoria, placed the succession beyond his grasp. When he was nine years old he was made a colonel in the Hanoverian Guards, though this was strictly an honorary position, and his military career did not really commence until 1836; it ended some 59 years later, when he was finally forced to retire as Commander-in-Chief of the British Army at the age of seventy-six.

History has long cast Cambridge in the role of the original Colonel Blimp, an old-fashioned soldier who opposed every innovation that might change his beloved army. It is certainly true that in his later years he fought a series of desperate, doomed rearguard actions against the reforms of Gladstone's Liberals – resisting such progressive measures as the abolition of the sale of commissions and the introduction of khaki – but within the service he was always held in high regard, seen as a doughty champion against political interference. And in his first decade as Commander-in-Chief he was himself a reformer, responsible particularly for two major institutions that have survived to the present: the Staff College at Camberley (following an initiative by his uncle, Frederick, Duke of York) and the Royal Military School of Music.

During the Crimean War, Cambridge led the First Division, comprised of Guards and Highlanders, and served with distinction at Alma and Inkerman. He revealed no great genius for battlefield command, but he did win universal praise for his courage and commitment, and he was undoubtedly well liked by his men; a sergeant in the 63rd Foot wrote that: 'No officer was more truly beloved by the Army than was the Duke, from his constant attention to their welfare, his identity with them in their sufferings, and his ready acquiescence in anything likely to add to their comforts.' And Florence Nightingale pointed out that his 'manner is very popular, his oaths are popular, with the army.'

He was invalided out of the campaign shortly after Inkerman, but not before he had attended perhaps the most significant parade in the history of British military music.

At a Grand Review in Scutari to celebrate Queen Victoria's birthday in 1854, before the General Staff of the allied forces, the massed bands of the British Army struck up the national anthem. The result was deeply humiliating – not only did the individual bands play different arrangements, they even played in different keys.

The cacophony that ensued must have been a particular embarrassment to the Duke of Cambridge. He was the senior member of the royal family present, he prided himself – as a lover of opera – on his appreciation of music, and he was by far the youngest of the divisional commanders in the British army, perhaps therefore more sensitive to being shown up in public than his rather elderly colleagues. It is believed that the parade at Scutari was the point at which he decided something needed to be done about the state of military music.

To understand what went wrong on that fateful day in the Crimea, it is necessary to look back to the early evolution of British military bands.

Drums had been part of the army since at least the battle of Halidon Hill in 1333, and trumpets, fifes and bagpipes had been gradually introduced over the years, but these were all essentially battlefield instruments, valued for their military rather than their musical function. It was not until the Restoration era that hautboys – an early incarnation of the oboe – were authorized for the two senior regiments of foot-guards, and not until 1749 that we find the first reference to what is recognizably a modern band. An advertisement appeared in a local Sussex newspaper that year for a concert to be given on 29 December by the Band of The Buffs, though how long this ensemble survived is unclear, since an inspection of the regiment in 1785 noted that there was 'No Band'.

More durable was the Band of the Royal Artillery, raised in Germany in 1762 during the Seven Years' War. This band, which is still extant, was inspired by the hugely successful Prussian army, a force that boasted bands capable of playing wind instruments on the march and string instruments on parade, and was originally recruited from German musicians. Likewise both the Grenadier and Scots Guards took on Germans in the mid-18th century to replace serving British bandsmen.

There was thus an early presumption in favour of continental musicianship: the Prussians had shown the way forward and their lead was respected, especially at a time when the monarchy was itself still more Hanoverian than

English. For a century or so, the received wisdom was that British musicians were inherently inferior to their European counterparts; when in 1820 the Commanding Officer of the 15th Hussars requested permission of his Colonel, the Duke of Cumberland, to recruit a band, the son of George III replied: 'It will be utterly impossible to form a Brass Band as these instruments require Germans who alone can play the Trumpet as it ought to be played.'

Such an attitude was a little extreme – most British regiments of the time had begun to employ British bandsmen – but it was not unprecedented; musicians aside, foreign bandmasters were at a premium and would remain so for some time.

The major problem was the attitude of the central authorities. The politicians of the War Department – ever conscious of financial restrictions – were reluctant to accept that bands might be of any significance in the armed forces, notwithstanding the sterling service rendered by bandsmen during the Napoleonic wars, and there was no attempt to institute musical training. The size of bands was kept under tight control, and the only bandmasters to receive a salary directly out of central funds were those of the Royal Artillery and the Royal Military College. For the rest, the officers of each regiment were responsible for taking on whomsoever they saw fit; bandmasters were recruited and paid on an entirely private basis, and more often than not were either foreign or civilian, or both.

Despite their irregular nature, some of the bands of the first half of the 19th century reached very high standards, and managed to attract the cream of the country's musicians. This was particularly true of the Guards and the Artillery, who enjoyed the stability of being permanently based in London. The Coldstream Guards, for example, were conducted for seven years from 1818 by Thomas Lindsay Willman, the principal clarinettist with the Philharmonic Orchestra, whilst in the mid-century the 2nd Life Guards benefited from the leadership of Henry Cooke, who was principal oboist with the same ensemble as well as being a professor at the Royal Academy of Music. Individual musicians also frequently doubled up in the leading orchestras of the day, including such famous names as William Winterbottom, who came from one of the greatest dynasties in military music and who played trombone in Michael Costa's orchestra for many years before becoming a bandmaster in the Royal Marines.

For the regiments of the line, however, who were constantly on the move between Britain and the outposts of Empire, it was more difficult keeping hold of quality players. The peripatetic nature of army life and its accompanying hardships held little appeal for civilians. It was expected and accepted that a posting abroad would result in the resignation of the bandmaster, and his transfer to a regiment lucky enough to be stationed at home.

The consequence was that when the Crimean War took Britain back into full-scale armed conflict after forty years of peace, large numbers of bandmasters sought other appointments. Typical of many was Henry (formerly Heinrich) Schallehn, a German who had been appointed bandmaster of the 17th Lancers in 1845; declining to accompany the regiment to the Crimea, he became instead conductor of the Crystal Palace Band, pursuing a civilian career before re-entering our story.

Those enlisted bandsmen who went to war in 1854 were therefore in the unhappy position of being musically leaderless; of the twenty or so regiments who paraded at Scutari, no more than four could boast a bandmaster. In any event, music was not considered to be a priority – the bandsmen were there primarily as soldiers, not musicians, and the casualties sustained give a good indication of why civilian bandmasters were none too keen to get involved: the Charge of the Light Brigade cost the 4th Light Dragoons ten musicians, whilst the Band of the Rifle Brigade saw its strength reduced from 45 to just 16 during the campaign. In such circumstances, it is perhaps not surprising that the Scutari review was such a disaster.

There was, moreover, another factor contributing to the chaos that day. The decentralized structure of British military music had ensured that there was no standard instrumentation for bands, or indeed any universally acknowledged tuning. This had long been a problem and there were some who recognized the need for uniformity. Chief amongst them was Carli Boosé, the Bandmaster of the Scots Guards and – needless to say – a German.

In 1845 he produced the first-ever British publication of a military band arrangement, a selection from Verdi's opera *Ernani*. So enthusiastically was it received that Boosey & Co. provided the funds to establish a periodical entitled *Boosé's Military Journal*, an endeavour that was soon imitated by other publications: one under the editorship of Charles Godfrey, bandmaster of the Coldstream Guards, and another edited by Adam J Schott of the Grenadier Guards. The fact that all three foot guard bandmasters were now publishing their own arrangements, and that they all used essentially the same instrumentation, exerted a powerful influence on other bands.

Even so, the process of standardization was not undertaken with any degree of urgency, and the discordant tuning at Scutari demonstrated that there was still a long way to go.

What made the humiliation of that parade even more difficult for the British to endure was the fact that the French bands who had been sent to the Crimea maintained an extraordinarily high level of musicianship. The cause was not hard to discover – in 1836 France had founded the Gymnase de Musique Militaire, a central college of music designed to raise standards throughout the army. In 1852, shortly before the Crimean conflict, there had even been published a training manual, Albert Perrin's *Organization of Military Bands*, to further this aim.

The lessons were not lost on the more influential figures in the British band world. Two men in particular campaigned for reform: James Smyth, Bandmaster of the Royal Artillery, who wrote to the authorities at Horse Guards to point out the superiority of the French bands, and the aforementioned Henry Schallehn, who had booked some of the French ensembles to play at Crystal Palace, and who went a stage further, circularizing a memorandum entitled 'The British Military College of Music'.

Their arguments were straightforward. No-one doubted anymore that, at their best, British musicians were capable of matching their European rivals, but the opportunities for bandsmen were so limited that few regiments could achieve any continuity; as Mr Schallehn's memo pointed out: 'The numbers of trained performers in this country being small, they are soon able to obtain increased renumeration by buying their discharge.' What was needed was better training, better pay and conditions for serving musicians (civilian bandmasters enjoyed far superior rewards and treatment to those of enlisted men), and a promotion structure to give some career prospects to the talented.

The main thrust of those calling for change was that a central institution should be created. Apart from anything else, argued Mr Schallehn, a music college would enable bandsmen to 'acquire a unity of style in playing together, not attainable by any other means.' Just a few years earlier the first-ever public concert by British massed bands, at

Chelsea in 1851, had ushered in a new era. There was a growing desire on the part of military musicians to take their trade to the public, a dawning awareness of the potential social role of bands; massed band events were clearly a part of that future, and common standards an essential pre-requisite.

By the mid-1850s, then, there was a sense of dissatisfaction with how military music had previously been structured; throughout the upper echelons of the hierarchy, pressure was building for reform. What was needed was a man with the power, influence and inclination to make the break with the past.

In 1856 that man was found. The death in that year of Lord Hardinge enabled Mr Schallehn's former commanding officer in the 17th Lancers, the Duke of Cambridge, to realize his greatest ambition and to become Commander-in-Chief of the British Army.

Cambridge was at the time just thirty-seven years old, and there is little doubt that he achieved his position as a result more of being the cousin of the Queen than of being the most qualified man for the job. This was, however, far from unprecedented and the post had even become something

The earliest surviving photograph of Kneller Hall pupils, 1880 (RMSM)

of a tradition in the royal family: to Cambridge's credit he was older and had served longer in the army than either his uncle, the Duke of York, who had been similarly promoted at the age of twenty-eight, or his great-great-uncle, 'Butcher' Cumberland, who had been a mere twenty-four when he reached the highest rank. And unlike either of his two kinsmen, his principal concern was to develop the ways of the Army, rather than to revolutionize them.

It was entirely in character that one of his first acts was to take up the suggestions of those who wanted to improve British military music. Where Cumberland had been strongly biased toward the martial traditions of Germany, and York had been anxious to keep the growth of music under tight control, Cambridge had a genuine understanding of the contribution that military bands could make to what was now the most powerful nation in the world.

On 25 September 1856, just two months after his appointment, he wrote to all the regiments of the army to suggest the establishment of what was termed a military music class. Displaying an intelligent sense of priorities, he emphasized that his intention was 'to relieve Regiments from the great expense now consequent upon the necessity of employing professed musicians, civilians, as masters of bands.' Indeed his principal concern was to convince his constituency of the savings involved:

> A preliminary outlay of £500 or £600 would be necessary for the supply of musical instruments; and it is calculated that £1,000 per annum would be afterwards necessary to maintain the class, including the salary of a Director, the necessary professors, copying and arranging music, etc., repair of instruments and other incidental expenses.
>
> There are now 112 Battalions of Infantry and 26 Regiments of Cavalry, exclusive of Artillery, Sappers, Military Train and 10 Colonial Corps.
>
> If every Regiment would pay an original subscription of £5 and £8 per annum for the Fund, ample provision would be made for all expenses.

Though 'no immediate benefit could be expected from the institution', the far-sighted understood that officially trained bandmasters would ultimately reduce the financial burden then shouldered entirely by regimental officers. Civilian bandmasters at the time received a salary of anything up to £360, and the accounts of the 13th Hussars from 1814 show that officers were expected to contribute between six to eight guineas each for their band. In this context,

Cambridge's proposal was really very modest, particularly since the service being bought under the existing system was so often unsatisfactory.

There were, of course, those who were less than impressed. The proprietorial attitude that many officers displayed towards their bands was reflective of a wider culture, in which nothing could be more distasteful than professionalism; a gentleman did not buy his commission in expectation of financial reward, indeed he considered it both inevitable and proper that he should pay his own way. Regimental independence was jealously cherished, and the possession of a private band was an important part of the social life of the Officers Mess.

Though the reception was thus somewhat mixed, it was sufficiently encouraging for Cambridge to move on to the next stage of his plan: the acquisition of Kneller Hall. At the time the Royal Military Asylum still had designs on the property, and a Horse Guards letter to the War Office dated 4 November 1856 was careful not to tread on anyone's toes, merely asking for temporary accommodation and enquiring:

> whether the Secretary of State for War would have any objection to allow accommodation for about 50 men and boys at Kneller Hall to be used for this purpose during the time that arrangements are being made for transferring the Royal Military College.

Kneller Hall, the drive in the 19th century (RMSM)

Kneller Hall, the lake in the 19th century (RMSM)

No objection was found, and it was decided that the West Wing of Kneller Hall would be more than sufficient for the purposes required. On 4 December 1856 a circular from Horse Guards announced that approval for the scheme had been received from all Commanding Officers (a statement that somehow lacked the ring of veracity), and that the opening of the military music class was anticipated on 1 January 1857.

The Duke of Cambridge's reputation for obstructive tactics in the face of necessary change is nowhere better refuted than in this schedule of activity. The gestation period, from initial suggestion to implementation of the most radical upheaval in the history of British military music, was expected to take barely three months. In the event the logistics of the operation slightly delayed the programme, but on 5 January 1857 Frederick Temple handed over the building to the War Office, and on 3 March the doors were opened for the first military music class.

CHAPTER 3

EARLY
YEARS

THE SCHOOL BAND c.1880 (RMSM)

The first class that assembled in March of 1857 comprised 85 pupils – seventeen of them bandboys – drawn from a total of some 48 regiments. If this suggests a relatively broad platform of support for the new initiative, it should be noted that the Foot Guards and the Household Cavalry sent just four students between them (two drummers and two boys), and that neither the Artillery nor the Engineers provided a single musician for training. It appears that whilst the line regiments may have seen the necessity for Kneller Hall, those units with long-established bands of their own had yet to be convinced of the need for change.

One of the few accounts of what everyday life was like for those pupils who did attend in the early years comes from an 1894 article in *The British Musician*, written anonymously by a musician who had been a student at Kneller Hall between 1859 and 1861. Reflecting on his time at the School, he wrote that a typical day began at six o'clock when the students, sleeping in two-man dormitories, were woken by reveille. Breakfast was not until eight o'clock, with the intervening period occupied by a country walk. Three and a half hours' morning practice was followed after a one o'clock lunch by a further two and a half hours' practice. Tea was at five and then there was another period of practice until seven o'clock, at which point the instruments were locked up in the stores for the night.

This basic pattern appears to have changed little during the remainder of the century, though in 1891 a new timetable was adopted which allowed a half-hour break in morning and afternoon, and a two-hour lunch period, with the evening meal being moved back to six o'clock. Even with these breaks, however, the normal day still included more than eight hours' work. An account from the '90s also suggests that as time went on more attention was being paid to physical fitness, with early-morning cross-country runs having replaced the pre-breakfast walks.

On their return from the run, the students would call in at the store to collect their rations to take to the cookhouse. One day those in odd-numbered rooms would have a roast meal whilst the even-numbers had boiled beef and carrots; the following day the positions would be reversed. Though three quarters of an hour was allocated for tea, there was no further food available, just whatever was left over from lunch and anything that could be bought from the pub over the road, where for example a halfpenny could buy a portion of jam.

In the early years the daily routine was broken up by a twice-weekly afternoon performance in the grounds, when the public were invited to come to listen to the students' band play. As the experience and reputation of the School grew, however, this became a more formal affair. During the summer, public concerts were given on an island in the middle of the lake, with visitors paying a penny for a programme and a chair which they could place where they wished. This was the origin of the successful summer concert series that has become so much a part of Kneller Hall life.

Just how established these performances had become is seen in the *British Bandsman & Orchestral Times* of June 1888, which reported the first of that year's Kneller Hall Military Promenade Wednesday Afternoon Concerts. The programme – the earliest that has survived – gives some indication of the work then being performed:

Choral	Sebaste	Stainer
Overture	Die Zauberflöte	Mozart
Selection	Die Meistersinger	Wagner
Song	The Harmonious Blacksmith	Handel
March	Schiller	Meyerbeer
Overture	Mignon	Thomas
Selection	Henry VIII	Saint-Saëns
Walzer	Brautleider	Gung'l
	God Save The Queen	

Several features are immediately apparent from this choice of material. First there is the complete absence of British military works – only Sir John Stainer, the choral composer, represents British music, whilst the Hungarian bandmaster, Joseph Gung'l, is the sole march-writer featured. There is also the remarkable fact that of the eight composers whose work was performed, four were then still alive, whilst both Wagner and Meyerbeer had only recently died; there is thus a strong favour shown towards contemporary work – indeed Saint-Saëns' opera *Henri VIII* had been written just five years earlier. Clearly the intention was to broaden the musical knowledge and experience of the students at Kneller Hall, and thus to educate the entirety of the British military music establishment.

This same intention was also evident in the encouragement offered to students to benefit from the wider musical world available in London. The student referred to above, whose memories of 1859-61 are the only real account we

Henry Schallehn (RMSM)

have of the initial establishment, mentions that students were given the opportunity to augment their education with regular trips to the opera at Covent Garden and to concerts at St James's Hall and Crystal Palace. Lieutenant-Colonel MacKenzie Rogan of the Coldstream Guards – the most distinguished military musician of his day – attended Kneller Hall from 1880, and in his memoirs he too talks of this agreeable tradition:

> The students were at this time expected to attend the opera at Covent Garden or Her Majesty's Theatre twice a week, and most of us took advantage of this privilege as the Government grant to the institution included an allowance towards our expenses. I think it was the best form of musical education a student could have. We also had complimentary tickets for the Monday 'Pops' at St James's Hall.

Regrettably but inevitably these entitlements have long since been discontinued; students now wishing to see a production at Covent Garden have to pay their own way. (What has not changed is the inability of public transport to provide an adequate late-evening service. Lt-Col Rogan recalled attending a performance of *Carmen* so riotously successful that it provoked repeated demands for encores; as a result a party of half a dozen students missed the last train from Waterloo and had to walk back to Kneller Hall, arriving at four in the morning.)

The connexions with the London music scene were not entirely one-way, for Kneller Hall students were encouraged to write their own music for public consumption. Walter G Buck, for example, a veteran of the Crimea and subsequently Bandmaster of the 73rd Foot (later the 2nd Bn, The Black Watch), had a cornet polka performed at the Alhambra and a mazurka at the Argyle Rooms whilst he was a student in the late '60s.

Another tradition from the latter part of the century was of an annual outing for the entire School. When this was discontinued is not known, but it was still in existence in 1907, when a trip was made to the Earl's Court Exhibition.

Apart from the regular public concerts, there were also private entertainments known as Pleasant Evenings, at which parlour songs and chamber music were performed by members of the establishment. The programme of one such evening, dating from 8 November 1894, has survived: amongst those performing songs were Student Charles Hackney, later Bandmaster of the 1st Buffs, Student William

Leeson, later Bandmaster of the 1st Battalion, Royal Sussex Regiment, and both Captain Mahoney and his wife – Capt Mahoney had himself been a bandmaster (with the 1st Battalion, York and Lancaster Regiment), but was now the Adjutant of Kneller Hall. Also on the programme was a violin solo by Bandmaster Stretton of the Cheshire Regiment, a man who was soon to play a significant part in the Kneller Hall story.

The Pleasant Evenings were staged partly as a means of passing the time, but more importantly as a preparation for future regimental duties, when such entertainments would be expected; the long years that battalions could spend in India or other outposts of empire demanded some kind of diversion, and the onus often fell on the bandmaster to be the provider. To the same end, the 1890s saw theatrical performances being given once a fortnight in the winter months, under the direction of Mr A Gwylim Crowe. Training was provided too for that other great area of regimental life, church parade, and evidently the Chapel was an important part of the Kneller Hall routine; it is recorded, for example, that on Easter Sunday 1894 Dr A King's 'Mass in Bb' was performed with full orchestral accompaniment conducted by Student Field, organ accompaniment by Student Battishill, and featured soloists including Miss Griffiths (daughter of the Director) and Students Haines, Williams, Laverock and Runciman.

Despite these extra-curricular activities – or conceivably because of the additional work involved – the stress of the course for students was evidently fairly intense, and Lt-Col Rogan tells of a student during his time there who collapsed under the pressure:

> A highly intelligent and well-educated man of middle age, [he] overworked himself in his keenness to master the whole theory of music and broke down under the strain. His mind became a complete blank; he could neither speak himself nor understand what was said to him.

The man was taken to a military hospital in Hounslow where he remained in some sort of nerve-induced coma. Several of the other students took to visiting him a couple of days each week and playing music in the hospital ward. Gradually the man showed signs of recovery, with a major breakthrough coming when the tuba-player in the group started deliberately playing wrong notes. The patient was himself a talented tuba-player and even in his traumatized state could not bear to hear such poor playing; he leapt from his bed and began shaking the student, whilst gesticulating at the sheet of music. 'Within two or three months,' Lt-Col Rogan wrote, 'his brain was restored to its full capacity,' though he does not say whether the man ever returned to the Army.

※

The eighty-five students of the first class were under the direction of six men: the Commandant, the Musical Director and four instrumental professors. Of these six, and despite the original aim to bring army music under more centralized military authority, five were civilians. The exception was the Commandant, Lieutenant-Colonel Henry Sykes Stephens of the 86th Foot, a regiment that now forms part of the Royal Irish Rangers.

Lt-Col Stephens (his rank was actually a Brevet, and he drew only a Captain's pay) had seen little service in the previous decade and a half, having been put on the half-pay list in 1841, and his recall to duty was to be brief; he remained at Kneller Hall until only August of 1857, even though his appointment had been sanctioned directly by the Duke of Cambridge himself. Cambridge had voiced his opinion that 'it was imperative to place an officer of sufficient rank and musical talent in charge of the establishment,' but it is not known what exactly Lt-Col Stephen's musical qualifications were, nor why he was chosen in the first place. Certainly he does not seem to have been intended as anything more than a temporary incumbent: on the very day the Military Music Class opened its doors, the Adjutant-General, G A Wetherall, wrote to Major Whitmore of The Royals, telling him that 'we want an Officer to superintend – and you are the very man.' Just five months later Major Whitmore succeeded Lt-Col Stephens as Commandant.

The first Musical Director was also to enjoy but a short tenure, though in his case it is at least clear why he was appointed. Henry Schallehn, as we have seen, had been active in the campaign to set up Kneller Hall, and it was probably inevitable that his former Commanding Officer would give him the chance to put his passionately argued theories into practice. Unfortunately it appears that Mr Schallehn was not ideally suited to the task. Though he had conducted both the 17th Lancers Band and the 60-piece Crystal Palace Band, he had emerged with no great achievements to his name, save for a reputation for show-manship and self-promotion. Indeed he had lasted just eighteen months at Crystal Palace (his successor, August

Manns, by contrast was to remain for more than 40 years), and a contemporary opinion was that he had 'no exceptional ability', whilst *The Orchestral Times* in 1904 dismissively suggested that he 'was soon found to be as great a failure [at Kneller Hall] as he had been as Musical Director at the Crystal Palace some few years previously'. On 31 December 1858 he too was replaced.

Quite apart from these early changes in personnel, the new school enjoyed a precarious existence. Still semi-official and only installed at Kneller Hall as a temporary measure, it depended for its survival on the goodwill and voluntary financial support of the commanding officers of the various regiments, many of whom had yet to be convinced of the value of the new institution. Even so, an entry in the Duke of Cambridge's diary for 13 August 1857 suggests that day-to-day life settled down soon enough:

Col R T Thompson with family, professors and students, c.1887
(RMSM)

Went with Weatherall by train to Kneller Hall to see the new Musical School I have formed there. It seems admirably established and is working most satisfactorily. Major Whitmore, 1st Foot, superintends and seems to take a great interest in it. A charming locality, and they play and sing wonderfully well.

✳

Much of the credit for the success of the new-born School is attributable to Francis Whitmore. A keen musical enthusiast (an ex-student recalled that 'he was very fond of singing and trained the choir himself'), Whitmore was to remain at Kneller Hall for 23 years and to establish the essential structure that has survived through to the present. In particular he played a key role in striking the necessary balance between musical and military discipline.

This was a highly sensitive issue, and one on which no two authorities seemed to agree. Even as late as 1926, Lt-Col Rogan was still arguing that the Director of Music at Kneller Hall should be a civilian, so that he need not be 'subject to any order which the Commandant might feel inclined to issue.' Nonetheless Lt-Col Rogan, who arrived at Kneller Hall just in time to experience the last months of Major-General Whitmore's era, was unstinting in his praise of the man:

> [He] had to build the institution in the face of strenuous opposition for many years from all kinds and conditions of people, always of course supported by the foreign element which was striving to oust the British military musician from what he considered to be his legitimate position. As with many reforms, vested interests blocked the way, but the Commandant held his ground, and improved it with great ability and loyalty for more than twenty years.

In this struggle to regularize army music, of course, the Commandant had a powerful ally in the form of the Duke of Cambridge. Amongst the battles fought and won in those early days were the standardization of pitch throughout the Army, the excusing of bandsmen from annual drill, and the removal of drums and fifes from band funds.

There was also a clarification of the principal function of Kneller Hall. In December 1859 the Adjutant-General was obliged to write to all regiments on behalf of the Duke of Cambridge pointing out that:

> It is part of the legitimate duties of Regimental Bandmasters to train the lads and boys who are enlisted for employment as musicians, and it is manifestly a perversion of the objects for which the present establishment at Kneller was created when uninstructed children are sent there to learn the rudiments of the profession.

Henceforth, it was decreed, no soldier under the age of 18 or 'who has not acquired some knowledge of music and of playing upon an instrument' should be sent to Kneller Hall. This was to be a place for advanced study, not for novices.

These changes were small, but they all contributed to a gradual shift in attitude, bringing more and more of the Army to a recognition that Kneller Hall could be of some value. In 1865 it became possible to reduce the annual subscription – which had been raised to £10 in 1857 – back to its original level of £8 per regiment. By now there were just 15 regiments left who were not supporting the initiative.

Supporting, that is, financially though not – it must be said – always with enthusiasm. For in some quarters there was still a marked reluctance to accept Kneller Hall as the definitive source of military musicians. In a private letter John Boosey, the leading military band publisher, expressed reservations about the project:

> They are sending a great many Band Sergeants away from Kneller Hall and passing them off as Bandmasters. Now, I do not think that regiments will be long satisfied with the class of men they are sending out, but still they are very cheap and a great many Regiments are trying them.

Mr Boosey had his own agenda for such an argument, for he had mutually beneficial agreements with many civilian bandmasters to supply instruments – a practice that the Duke of Cambridge was attempting to stamp out in his pursuit of economies – but his analysis was not without basis. There were regiments who were contributing to Kneller Hall, accepting a bandmaster from it and then employing a civilian as well, paying him privately in the old way. It is believed, for example, that the 33rd Foot may have engaged in such a practice, though the most famous case was certainly that of the 11th Foot.

The Bandmaster of the 2nd Battalion of the 11th Foot was William Burton, an experienced and capable musician who had spent two decades leading the band of the 59th Foot before moving to the 11th in 1865. Some time around 1872, however, the Colonel of the Regiment decided to augment Mr Burton's services with those of an additional bandmaster, described by Lt-Col Rogan (then a bandsman in the battalion) as 'a very foreign-looking gentleman with very long hair and a rather sallow complexion, who I may remark knew no English.' This Italian musician was given the most prestigious elements of the bandmaster's job, leaving Mr Burton with little to do for twelve months save train the bandboys and conduct at routine military parades.

In a state of some frustration at this curtailment of his role, Mr Burton appealed to Colonel Whitmore at Kneller Hall, asking that the situation be resolved. At this stage the Duke of Cambridge saw an opportunity to further his pet project and intervened personally to broaden the issue under enquiry. All regiments were circulated with a questionnaire to establish the status of their bandmasters, and in 1874 – presumably displeased with the findings – he issued instructions from the War Office that: 'All applications to enlist such men [i.e. civilians] are to be discouraged – more particularly in the case of foreigners.'

Col T B Shaw-Hellier (RMSM)

This was clearly what Cambridge had been aiming at for some time, and Mr Burton's case, by highlighting the absurdities and abuses of the existing system, provided him with a chance to take a major step forward. A circular from Horse Guards dated 20 December 1876 spelt out the progress that had been made towards the goal: 'there are now nearly 120 Military Bandmasters in active employment, all of whom have qualified at Kneller Hall, while there are left only 35 of the old class of civilian Bandmasters.'

The process of centralizing control of military music at Kneller Hall, of course, required more than the support of the Commander-in-Chief; at some point it had to become part of the wider political world and to be given the approval of the Whitehall bureaucracy. A key moment in Kneller Hall's history, therefore, came in 1867 when the government acknowledged the success of the new institution and officially took over the running of it.

The following year saw the epochal general election that brought Gladstone to power and the appointment of Lord Cardwell as Secretary of State for War. Cardwell was to prove an ardent political enemy of the Duke of Cambridge, but ironically it was during his period of office that the government resolved to fund Kneller Hall directly, removing the need for regimental subscriptions. At the same time, grants were for the first time made available to band funds.

Funding, of course, was the most critical issue so far as central government was concerned, then as now. As early as 1857 Cambridge had argued that those who graduated from Kneller Hall as bandmasters should be given the rank of warrant officer and paid five shillings a day, with the same entitlements as schoolmasters within the Army, but – in this if in little else – he was some way ahead of his time. The then Military Secretary responded with a careful calculation that such a move would cost £12,252 8s and 9d per annum and therefore could not be sanctioned; instead the rank of Sergeant Bandmaster was to survive though to 1881.

In that year came perhaps the greatest upheaval that the British Army has ever faced. The return to power of Gladstone the previous year, with Hugh Childers as War Secretary, brought a raft of reforms that swept away the old numbering system and saw most infantry regiments amalgamate under the new territorial system. The Duke of Cambridge, in keeping with his traditionalism, objected strongly to the changes ('anything more distasteful or detrimental to the *esprit de corps*, and therefore the best interests of the service, I cannot imagine', he wrote), but he was fighting for yet another lost cause.

And for bandmasters at least, there was good news in the reforms, with their status once again becoming a matter for debate. The government's initial proposal was that they should be given the rank of staff-sergeant and paid 3s 6d per day, but concerted pressure produced an alternative solution that accorded with the Duke of Cambridge's 1857 suggestion. Lt-Col Rogan had no hesitation in giving credit to the newly appointed Commandant for wringing concessions from Whitehall:

> Colonel Thompson, almost daily for three or four months, spent most of his time at the War Office and other military establishments, explaining what a great injustice would be done to the bandmasters of the Army and, incidentally, what harm would result to the bands and to Army music generally if this suggestion were carried into force.

The result of the protracted negotiations was that bandmasters were for the first time given the rank and pay of warrant officers, a position which remains to this day. Perhaps more than any other move in the first years of Kneller Hall, this established the place of military bandmasters within the Army, providing a status commensurate with their training. There were just 16 civilians left in office (the last such, Randolph Ricketts of the Royal Corps of Signals, was not to retire until 1938), but they were now required to pass Kneller Hall examinations, and the shift had become irreversible.

With the introduction of the new rank, those men serving as sergeant-bandmasters were also called upon to pass the relevant examination in order that they might be promoted. Amongst them were such luminaries as Sgt Dan Godfrey who had led the Band of the Grenadier Guards for a quarter of a century, and who was later to become the first musician to be commissioned, receiving the honorary rank of 2nd Lieutenant on the occasion of the Queen's Jubilee in 1887. Also summoned to Kneller Hall in the wake of the 1881 reforms was Sgt Lawson of the Royal Artillery Mounted Band, who at the age of fifty-five became the oldest man ever to take and to pass the bandmaster's exam.

The transformation of military music was progressing well enough that when the Duke of Cambridge paid another visit on 28 June 1886, he could report in his diary even more positively than before:

The professors, 1859 (RMSM)

Went to Kneller Hall. There met Sir Arthur Sullivan who had come down from London in my wagonette. Heard the band in the Chapel first and then a fine and powerful band, and was very much satisfied with the whole condition of things, as was Sullivan, who said he had no sort of suggestions to offer for improvements.

The visit of Sir Arthur Sullivan was actually something of a return home, for the greatest composer of the Victorian era was the product of a military family. His grandfather, Thomas, had fought in the Peninsular War and for a while guarded Napoleon in exile on St Helena, whilst his father, also named Thomas, had become a bandsman at the Royal Military Academy at the age of fifteen and subsequently – after a period as a civilian – had returned to Sandhurst as Bandmaster in 1845. Arthur was just three years old at this stage, but he soon found the atmosphere of the bandroom stimulating and later wrote that:

> The band my father conducted was small, but very good, for he was an excellent musician. I was intensely interested in all that the band did, and learned to play every wind instrument, with which I formed not merely a passing acquaintance, but a real, life-long, intimate friendship.

Thomas Sullivan left Sandhurst in late 1856, possibly to find more lucrative employment, which it is assumed he found with the opening of Kneller Hall soon afterwards. His reputation as a clarinet teacher and as an experienced soldier enabled him to be appointed as one of the first professors, whilst his musical flexibility ensured that his talents were exploited to the full: he taught also the lower brass instruments and the violin. Even so, however, he still found time to continue his career as a private teacher, spending four evenings a week at Broadwoods School.

At Kneller Hall he built himself an enviable reputation as a source of inspiration for the students, one of whom was later to comment that he 'will always be kindly remembered. He welcomed one with a smile and generally had a little joke to crack or tale to tell, which made the lesson go all the brighter.' His son too, who was by now a chorister at the Chapel Royal, continued his interest in military bands: he is reported to have hand-copied the parts of a march from an oratorio by Sir Frederick Gore Ousley, in which he had sung, for his father's use.

The fact that a man such as Mr Sullivan could be prevailed upon to join the Kneller Hall staff is an indication of the hopes that were pinned on the new institution. The Adjutant-General described the instructors as 'the best professors in England', which may have over-stated the case a little, but it is certainly true that the early years saw the establishment of an impressive faculty.

The Professor of Theory (and soon to be the replacement for Mr Schallehn) was Carl Mandel, who appears to have been highly popular on a personal level and who inspired great affection amongst his students; the anonymous student who has already been quoted above described him as 'a most painstaking and clever teacher, who I am sure will be remembered with pleasure by all who had the good fortune to study under him.' He was also responsible for a work of such exceeding rarity, *Instrumentation for Military Bands*, that not even Kneller Hall possesses a copy; it is said, however, to reveal an overwhelmingly Germanic approach to music, and to have suffered from outdated tuning of instruments. An anonymous correspondent in *The British Musician* in 1894 remembered him as 'a good lovable old man, of great ability, but somewhat narrow views.'

Other professors at Kneller Hall from the outset included Carl Zeiss, formerly professor at the Brussels Conservatoire and first trumpet in the orchestra of Her Majesty's Theatre, who taught cornet and trumpet ('a clever performer and teacher, but rather hard on the boys'), and Mr Sam Hughes who instructed in the ophicleide. More significant yet was the arrival in 1858 of Henry Lazarus to teach the clarinet.

Mr Lazarus epitomized the close ties that had developed between the senior bands of the Army and the mainstream world of civilian music. At the age of fifteen he had been appointed assistant to the Bandmaster of the Royal Military Asylum at Chelsea, but was soon headhunted by the Coldstream Guards, then under the leadership of the elder Charles Godfrey. There he came under the influence and patronage of Thomas Willman, the previous Bandmaster of the Coldstream and the most famous clarinet player of his day.

On Mr Willman's death in 1840, Mr Lazarus effectively stepped into his shoes, becoming principal clarinet at the Opera and later being appointed professor of his instrument at both the Royal Academy of Music and the Royal College of Music as well as at Kneller Hall. (Curiously, like his predecessor, he adopted an unusual playing technique – where Mr Willman played with the reed against his upper lip, Mr Lazarus always insisted that both lips should cover the teeth in order to get the best sound.)

In his long career playing for all the leading operatic and theatrical companies in London, Mr Lazarus could count many notable achievements, and innumerable alliances with the finest musicians of the time. He always said that he learnt the most from Sir Michael Costa, but perhaps the most memorable of all his performances were in the British premieres of Mendelssohn's oratorios, *Lobgesang* and *Elijah*, under the conducting of the composer, the latter shortly before the great man's death in 1847.

Although the prejudice that the continentals produced better brass-players still existed in the late 19th century, the reverse was believed to be true of clarinettists; when asked in 1894 – shortly before his own death – what is what that made British players superior to their European counterparts, Mr Lazarus replied that 'perhaps it is the roast beef and solid diet of our country.'

Ten years after his death *The Orchestral Times* called him 'the greatest clarinet player of the 19th century', rating him even above Thomas Willman himself.

Kneller Hall c.1894 (RMSM)

Another veteran of Charles Godfrey's band – and, incidentally, of the Crystal Palace – was Bandsman Phasey, who almost single-handedly brought the euphonium to a popular audience in Britain. He also made some significant contributions to the technical evolution of the early incarnation of the instrument, particularly with his enlargement of the bore, and was so influential that he was at one point asked if his name could be used to endorse the instrument; he politely declined the opportunity to become immortalized as the father of the Phaseyphone, and recommended the name euphonium instead. In 1859 he too was appointed to the staff at Kneller Hall.

Amongst the other instructors in the first years were Thomas E Mann who taught the French horn from the '50s until his death in 1897, Mr Hawkes of the Royal Italian Opera who taught the trombone, and Albert Hartmann, a brilliant German flautist who had come over to Britain to join Mr Schallehn at Crystal Palace and who went on to become Bandmaster of the 17th Lancers (Mr Schallehn's old band) and to be awarded a Doctorate of Music at Oxford. There was also a Mr Cioffi, whom one student enigmatically remembered as being:

> a marvellous performer on the slide trombone. His silk hat was lined with newspaper cuttings relating to his performances. He was always careful to enquire of a new pupil if he could eat his loaf because if he could not eat a loaf of bread it was no use trying to learn the trombone.

This establishment was headed, of course, by the Director of Music. On his death in 1874, Carl Mandel was succeeded in the appointment by Charles Cousins, who had previously been a musician in the 1st Life Guards and civilian Bandmaster of the 2nd Dragoon Guards (Queen's Bays). Unusually for a civilian, he had been prepared to serve overseas; indeed he had travelled to India to join the Bays, and whilst there had added a knowledge of Hindi to his multilingual abilities (he already spoke French, German and Italian). His obituary in *The British Bandsman* remarked that this was to stand him in good stead at Kneller Hall 'for there not only British lads are taught, but natives of our colonies and dependencies, irrespective of race or creed.' This is the first mention of overseas students at the School.

It was during Mr Cousins' time that Kneller Hall received its final stamp of official approval, with General Order 141 dated August 1887:

> Her Majesty the Queen has been graciously pleased to approve of the School of Music, Kneller Hall, being in future styled, 'The Royal Military School of Music'.

Victoria's direct involvement in the advancement of the status of military music was emphasised still further the following year, when her private secretary, Sir Arthur Bigge, wrote to the Secretary of State for War. He expressed the Queen's concern that Bandmasters lacked the opportunity for advancement, given the fact that 'a good Band helps to make a good Regiment and thus may fairly be reckoned as a necessary factor in the efficiency of the Army.' She therefore proposed that Charles Godfrey (the younger) of The Blues, Ladislao Zaverthal of the Royal Artillery and George Miller of the Royal Marines should be commissioned, to join Charles' brother, Dan, who had been so honoured the previous year. These proposals, Sir Arthur Bigge added, were 'only suggestions', though they were of course immediately acted upon.

Being a civilian, Mr Cousins was unaffected by this step forward. Despite his status, however, he was by every account held in very high regard by the military establishment, particularly by the three Commandants under whom he served, and by the wider musical world. His death on 28 May 1890 from pneumonia was noted in Institution Orders with words of unqualified praise, whilst the *Daily News* reported:

> Most of the bandmasters, and a large number of the best bandsmen in the British army have been trained in their duties under his supervision. He was an enthusiast as to military music, upon which subject he was an admitted authority; and it is no exaggeration to say that the vast improvement which, during the last decade, has been effected in regimental bands, must, in great part, be attributed to his influence, precept, and example.

So great was the respect in which he was held that a collection was taken amongst his colleagues and friends and in 1894 the Cousins Memorial Prize Medals were created. These medals, one silver and one bronze, are competed for each year by the pupils at Kneller Hall and awarded 'for

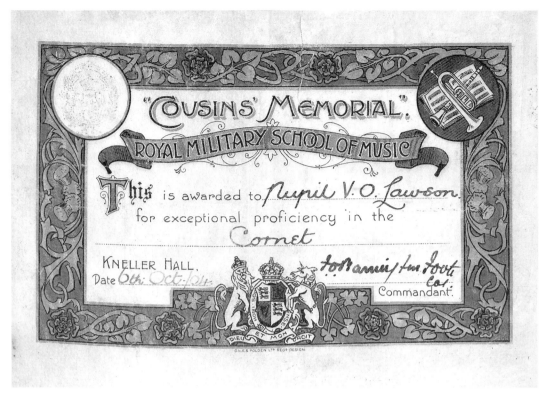

Cousins Memorial Parchment, 1904 (B HOUSEMAN)

proficiency in music coupled with exemplary conduct'. The tradition continues to this day, preserving the name and memory of the School's first great Director of Music.

Mr Cousins' final engagement had been a concert on the opening evening of the Royal Military Exhibition on 7 May 1890. As part of the Exhibition celebrations, a competition had been launched for original compositions in four separate categories: a march, a piece of sacred music, a fantasia and another selection. Bandmaster Frayling of the Honourable Artillery Company won first prize for his march, but the remaining three categories were all taken by the senior student at Kneller Hall, Joseph Manuel Bilton, beating entries from bandmasters and musicians far more experienced than he. The journal *Musical World* marvelled: 'The results are certainly remarkable, if not unprecedented, and augur well for Mr Bilton's future.'

Mr Bilton's future was indeed to be bright, culminating in an appointment as Director of Music of The Blues, but the recognition of his talent was to come even more quickly than he might have anticipated, for he was called upon to step in as temporary replacement whilst a successor to Mr Cousins was found. *The Orchestral Times and Bandsman* of the time commended the choice, saying that Mr Bilton was 'not only an able conductor, but a good all-round musician of an advanced type.' It was he who conducted the Kneller Hall band for the closing ceremony of the Military Exhibition on 1 November 1890.

The death of Mr Cousins provided the opportunity to realize one of the original intentions of Kneller Hall: the recognition of serving musicians. It was decided that in future the position of Director of Music at the School would carry the rank of Honorary Lieutenant, and that it would only be open to enlisted bandmasters. Who that man should be was uncertain; there is an uncorroborated story in the *Portsmouth Mail* of the era that Bandmaster George Miller of the Royal Marine Light Infantry (Portsmouth Division) was offered the post but turned it down. If such an approach was made, it would explain the delay in appointing a new Director, for it was not until November 1890 that the following notice appeared in *The Orchestral Times*: 'A competitive examination is to be held in London on 3rd November, of the candidates for the present vacancy.'

This was the first time that such an exam was held, and it is believed that seven bandmasters submitted themselves for the competition, with three candidates proving successful, including Albert Williams of the 10th Hussars (later Dr Williams of the Grenadier Guards). The choice, however, went to the senior of the three who had passed, and on 24 December 1890 Bandmaster Samuel Griffiths was promoted to 2nd Lieutenant and appointed Director of Music of the School, the first serving soldier to hold the post.

Mr Griffiths had enlisted into the Band of the 2nd Battalion, 1st Foot as a fourteen-year-old bandboy in 1862 and, having passed through the bandmaster course at Kneller Hall, had returned to his Battalion as a Bandmaster Sergeant in 1874, being promoted to Warrant Officer with the 1881 reforms. He was appointed to the Royal Military College in May 1890, but the vacancy at Kneller Hall meant that he spent just a few months at Sandhurst before moving on.

During his time at Kneller Hall, Samuel Griffiths wrote the first significant text-book on band arranging, entitled *The Military Band*, published by Rudall Carte, and a further short work, *Hints on the Management of Army Bands*. Both were to remain in use for many years, with the former becoming the standard work on arrangement and conducting. He also had a reputation as a composer, producing an overture 'Hermolin' and a memorable motet 'God be Merciful unto Us'. Less well known is a 1892 publication entitled the *Kneller Hall March Journal* that included his arrangement of 'Christmas Carols'; the remainder of the journal comprised quick marches written by students and others – 'Midlothian' by W F Cooper, 'The Students' by J M Coward, 'Lynwood' by J Ord Hume, 'Fuzzy Wuzzy' by A Stretton and 'Route Marching' by W J Bentley, the latter two inspired by the poems of Rudyard Kipling.

Mr Griffiths' incumbency, however, was to be all too brief, for like his two predecessors he died whilst still serving. An account of his death was given many years later by Arthur Hinds, who had been a student in the mid-1890s: on 31 October 1895, he recalled, the orderly student was taking the outgoing mail to the Post Office on the corner of Whitton Dene, when he saw Mr Griffiths come out of the office and immediately collapse. By the time the student reached him, he was already dead. The students were particularly impressed by the fact that Mr Griffiths' wig came loose as he fell – no one had previously known that he wore a hair-piece.

If there was some lack of dignity in such a story, the funeral was to leave no doubt of the esteem in which Mr Griffiths was held. The coffin was carried on a gun carriage drawn by two black horses and preceded not only by the Kneller Hall band but by those of the 4th Hussars and of the Royal Scots, the latter complete with pipes. The service was led by the Rev R T A Hourdin, the School's Chaplain, and included the Kneller Hall choir singing Sir John Goss' anthem 'O Saviour of the World' (which had also been sung at Mr Cousins' funeral), while the burial itself – at Twickenham Cemetary – was accompanied by three volleys of musket-fire and the pipes playing 'The Death of a Chief'. The staff and students of the School sent a wreath of orchids in the shape of a five-string lyre, with one string broken.

A memorial fund was set up and raised £298 5s 11d, from which a memorial brass was purchased for the Chapel, and a marble cross for the grave; the remainder was given to Mr Griffiths' widow. But perhaps the most significant tribute (albeit unintentional) to the work of both Mr Cousins and Mr Griffiths came in an anonymous contribution to *The British Musician* in 1894. As a veteran of 40 years standing in military music, the correspondent complained that in the modern era 'every band and every bandmaster seem built on the same models, the same style of playing, the same works.' This regularization of Army bands was, of course, exactly what Kneller Hall had been set up to create.

CHAPTER 4
THE STRETTON ERA

CAPT F H MAHONY, COL F GLENNIE, MR A J STREETON (HON LT), 1896
(RMSM)

The death of Samuel Griffiths in 1895 was wholly unanticipated and caused some concern at Kneller Hall; it had been expected that Mr Griffiths would remain in his post until at least his 55th birthday in 1902, possibly even through to his 60th in 1907, and no thought had therefore been given to the question of his successor. As a stop-gap measure the Commandant, Colonel Farquar Glennie, who had himself been in his post for barely a year, swiftly appointed Student W H Moss as Acting Director of Music, to be replaced later in the year by Student P F Battishill when Mr Moss departed to take up a position with the 2nd Battalion, The King's Shropshire Light Infantry.

Meanwhile the various options for a more permanent appointment were considered. Again, according to the Portsmouth Mail, an approach was made to Bandmaster George Miller, and again he declined the offer. (Coincidentally, Mr Miller's son, also called George Miller, was a student at Kneller Hall at the time, and was largely responsible for organizing the orchestra.) In his place the front-runner was widely considered to be Peter O'Donnell, who at the age of 41 had been Bandmaster of the 2nd Battalion, The South Wales Borderers for ten years, and had consistently received very favourable confidential reports from his commanding officer.

Undoubtedly Mr O'Donnell was an excellent musician and an inspiration to others, this latter evidenced by the fact that all three of his sons followed him into the Army – all later served as Directors of Music in the Royal Marines before moving on to other posts with the Royal Air Force and the BBC. Despite his qualifications, however, Mr O'Donnell was passed over for the position at Kneller Hall. An item from the *British Musician* of the time suggests that an examination was again held, though no further details appear to exist; if there was such a competition, it is possible that Mr O'Donnell participated and lost. An alternative explanation for his failure to progress is that during his time as a student at the School, though he had shown great promise, he had come into conflict with the Commandant, and that his final report was sufficiently damaging that it cast a shadow over his future promotion prospects.

If Kneller Hall did thus miss out on a potentially valuable director, the institution was ultimately to have no cause for complaint with the candidate who was selected, even though some eyebrows were raised at his lack of experience. Arthur Stretton was just thirty-two when he was promoted to Lieutenant and given the position of Director of Music, Kneller Hall; he had furthermore been Bandmaster of the 2nd Battalion, The Cheshire Regiment for less than two and a half years. Nonetheless he was to remain at the School for a quarter of a century – the longest period anyone has ever held, or indeed is ever likely to hold, the post – and any initial misgivings over his appointment were soon dispelled by his conduct.

One immediate benefit that came with the arrival of Mr Stretton was the strengthening of the role of the string orchestra, thus helping resolve a major debate that had been raging within military music circles for many years. Most regiments of the time favoured the playing of string instruments by their bandsmen, recognising the valuable social and public roles that string bands could fulfil, but there were those in the army hierarchy who regarded such activity as a frivolous diversion from the true function of soldier-musicians. Typical of many was the Duke of Cambridge who in 1874 had criticized 'the use of String instruments by the Band, a proceeding at once expensive and inconsistent with the object for which Bands are maintained in all Armies, i.e. the performance of martial rather than operatic music.' Similar sentiments had been displayed as recently as 1889, when the Kneller Hall Diary had reported:

> Under WO/103/KH/385/21-1-89 an application for Grant of £40 per annum for instruction in stringed instruments is refused, as a knowledge of this branch of music is held to be outside the military requirements of a Band.

This did not necessarily imply any criticism of the small string bands that had long been regular fixtures at Mess dinners and the like, but was clearly an attempt to limit the growth of full-scale orchestras within the Army.

But in 1891 the new timetable came into effect – 'approved by His Royal Highness, the Commander-in-Chief', as the Kneller Hall Diary notes, suggesting that the Duke of Cambridge had over the years become convinced that the bandsman's role need not be entirely restricted to 'martial music'. Under the provisions of the timetable, two hours were set aside on four evenings a week for string band practice by the pupils, and an hour on Wednesday morning for string band rehearsal by students and pupils. Furthermore a report by the Commandant the following year stated that the first objective of the students' course was to provide 'a thorough training on all instruments constituting a

Time Table of the Classes for Musica

TIME Hour	Minutes	MONDAY Musical STUDENTS	Senior	Junior	General STUDENTS	Senior	Junior	TUESDAY Musical STUDENTS	Senior	Junior	General STUDENTS	Senior	Junior	WEDNESDA Musical STUDENTS	Senior	Junior
9	0	Theoretical Instruction	Instrumental Instruction			School for Candidates for 1st Class Certificates		Theoretical Instruction	Instrumental Instruction			School for Candidates for 1st Class Certificates		Rehearsal for Full Band		Instrumental Instruction
,,	15															
,,	30															
,,	45															
10	0															
,,	15															
,,	30															

HALF-AN-HO...

TIME Hour	Minutes	MONDAY Musical STUDENTS	Senior	Junior	General STUDENTS	Senior	Junior	TUESDAY Musical STUDENTS	Senior	Junior	General STUDENTS	Senior	Junior	WEDNESDA Musical STUDENTS	Senior	Junior
11	0	Theoretical Instruction	Instrumental Instruction / Elementary Theory			Special Class for 1st Class Certificates	Special Class for 1st Class Certificates	Theoretical Instruction	Instrumental Instruction / Elementary Theory	Instrumental Instruction and Singing Practice					Rehearsal for String Band	
,,	15															
,,	30															
,,	45															
12	0															

TWO HOURS FOR D...

TIME Hour	Minutes	MONDAY Musical STUDENTS	Senior	Junior	General STUDENTS	Senior	Junior	TUESDAY Musical STUDENTS	Senior	Junior	General STUDENTS	Senior	Junior	WEDNESDA Musical STUDENTS	Senior	Junior
2	0	Rehearsal for 1st Half Band / Instrl. Instn.	Rehearsal for 1st Half Band / Instrumental Instruction	Instrl. Instn. / Black Board Notn. / Instrumental Instruction	School	School for those not in possession of 2nd Class Certificates		Rehearsal for 2nd Half Band / Instrl. Instn.	Rehearsal for 2nd Half Band / Instrumental Instruction	Instrl. Instn. / Black Board Notn. / Instrumental Instruction	School	School for those not in possession of 2nd Class Certificates		Inspection of Instruments and Playing in Public by the Full Band, about 120 in number		
,,	15															
,,	30															
,,	45															
3	0															
,,	15															
,,	30															
,,	45															
4	0															
,,	15															
,,	30															

HALF-AN-H...

TIME Hour	Minutes	MONDAY Musical STUDENTS	Senior	Junior	General			TUESDAY Musical STUDENTS	Senior	Junior	General			WEDNESDA
5	0	Rehearsal by Full Band	Rehearsal by Full Band	Elemntry. Instrctn.				Rehearsal by Full Band	Rehearsal by Full Band	Elemntry. Instrctn.				
,,	15													
,,	30													
6	0													

THREE-QUARTERS-OF-...

TIME Hour	Minutes	MONDAY Musical STUDENTS	Senior	Junior	General STUDENTS			TUESDAY Musical STUDENTS	Senior	Junior	General STUDENTS			WEDNESDA
6	45	Volntry. Independent Study	String Band Practice	String Band Practice	School for Candidates for 1st Class Certificates			Volntry. Independent Study	String Band Practice	String Band Practice	School for Candidates for 1st Class Certificates			
7	0													
,,	15													
,,	30													
,,	45													
8	0													

Kneller Hall,

Hounslow,

APRIL 1st, 1891.

Divine Service (Choral) in the Chapel, at 11 a.m

MEMO.—Spring Drills, Bathing Parades, Marching out, Running Drill and K...
Medical Inspection is held on Monday at noon. There is also a Parade daily (Sundays except...

̶HOOL OF MUSIC,

̶for General Education at Kneller Hall.

THURSDAY					FRIDAY						SATURDAY				TIME	
Musical		General				Musical		General				Musical		Genl.		
PUPILS		STUDENTS	PUPILS		STUDENTS	PUPILS		STUDENTS	PUPILS		STUDENTS	PUPILS		Junr. PUPILS		
Senior	Junior		Senior	Junior		Senior	Junior		Senior	Junior		Senior	Junior		Hour	Minutes
Instrumental Instruction			School for Candidates for 1st Class Certificates		Theoretical Instruction	Instrumental Instruction			School for Candidates for 1st Class Certificates		Rehearsal by Full Band			Instrumental Instruction / School		9	0
															,,	15
															,,	30
															,,	45
															10	0
															,,	15
															,,	30
RECREATION.																
			Special Class for 1st Class Certificates	Special Class for 1st Class Certificates		Singing Practice						Practice in the Chapel by the Choir			11	0
															,,	15
															,,	30
															,,	45
															12	0
̶ND RECREATION.																
	Rehearsal for Full Band, Pupils only	School	School for those not in possession of 2nd Class Certificates		Theoretical Study	Instrumental Instruction	Rehearsal for Full Band, Pupils, only	School	School for those not in possession of 2nd Class Certificates			Half-Holiday			2	0
															,,	15
															,,	30
															,,	45
															3	0
															,,	15
															,,	30
	Instrumental Instruction					Singing Practice & Instl. Instn.									4	0
															,,	15
															,,	30
RECREATION.																
Practice	Elemntry. Theory	Singing Practice & Instrumental Instn.			Theoretical Study	Elemntry. Theory	Singing Practice & Instrumental Instn.								5	0
															,,	15
															,,	30
															6	0
̶ FOR EVENING MEAL.																
̶pendent Study	String Band Practice	String Band Practice	School for Candidates for 1st Class Certificates		V̶olntry. Independent Study	String Band Practice	String Band Practice	School for Candidates for 1st Class Certificates							6	45
															7	0
															,,	15
															,,	30
															,,	45
															8	0

̶ndays, with Organ and Orchestral Accompaniment.

̶take place at fixed hours between Reveille and 8 a.m., according to time of year.
̶.m., from which, after Inspection, the Students and Pupils march off to their several studies, &c.

T. B. SHAW-HELLIER, Colonel,
Commandant
Royal Military School of Music.

military and string band.' Undoubtedly there was a significant struggle over the extent of instrumentation within the Army lying behind the recording of these bare facts.

String Orchestra, pictured on the retirement in 1900 of Mr F W Barnard; in centre Col Farquar Glennie with his Stradivarius (RMSM)

Mr Stretton's contribution to this change of attitude stemmed from his early training. His career had started with the Royal Artillery, a band which had from its inception been double-handed – that is, with bandsmen playing both wind and string instruments – and which lays claim to have the oldest British orchestra in continuous existence. By the 1880s, the Gunners' orchestra was even more successful than the band itself, largely thanks to the leadership of Ladislao Zavertal, a classically-trained musician who in his youth had written an opera with his father and who numbered amongst his friends Antonin Dvorak. His uncle, Joseph Sawerthall, had previously been appointed Director of Music of the Royal Engineers specifically to form an orchestra to rival that of the RA.

With this experience behind him, Mr Stretton laid new emphasis on the Kneller Hall string band. The success of his endeavours to improve its standing was such that on 22 June 1897, the orchestra played by special invitation at St Paul's Cathedral as part of the celebrations for Queen Victoria's Diamond Jubilee. Just four short years later, the orchestra returned to St Paul's under more sombre circumstances to play at the funeral service for the Queen. The death of Victoria had resulted in the issuing on 23 January 1901 of an Army Order that:

In consequence of the death of Her Most Gracious Majesty, the Queen, all Trumpet and Bugle sounds, and blowing and playing of musical instruments will be suspended until further orders.

Other royal engagements were also undertaken by the students and pupils around the turn of the century. Even though the Duke of Cambridge had been forced to resign from his position as Commander-in-Chief in 1895 (he recorded sorrowfully that 'I still feel equal to the performance of my duties, but I must submit as best as I can'), he was still a regular visitor to the institution that was perhaps his finest achievement. He often brought with him various other distinguished visitors; on 14 May 1901, for example, he was accompanied by the Duchess of Mecklenburgh-Strelitz, together with her daughter Princess Marie, and the Duke and Duchess of Teck, whilst the following year saw a visit from Princess Christian and Princess Louise of Schleswig-Holstein, in the company of the Rajah of Bikaner.

These royal duties reached their culmination on 9 August 1902, when eight State Trumpeters under the direction of Professor W O'Keefe played in Westminster Abbey for the Coronation of Edward VII, whilst the Band played outside in Parliament Square. On 25 October that year the Band returned to Parliament Square for the Royal Progress through London. In recognition of services rendered during the Coronation, Colonel Barrington Foote was awarded the Coronation Medal in silver, with bronze medals going to Student Hinton – the Acting Sergeant Major – to Prof O'Keefe and to the trumpeters: Students Adams, Banbury, Featherstone, Fowles, Murray, Saunders and Sylvester. Why the names of only seven trumpeters are recorded, when we know that eight were present at the Coronation, is unclear.

A more significant name missing from this list of awards was that of Mr Stretton. Presumably no slight was intended, for the *London Gazette* of 30 June 1903 recorded:

The King has been graciously pleased to make the following appointment to the Royal Victorian Order – To be a Member of the 5th Class: Lieutenant A J Stretton, Director of Music at the Royal Military School of Music.

❋

This period was also, of course, one in which many bandsmen were called upon yet again to lay down their instruments and serve in the ranks, with the intensification of the

Boer War. Kneller Hall was not directly affected, which it was to be in the two great conflicts of the 20th century, but there were commitments to be met at home, including a Grand Military Concert at the Royal Albert Hall in 1897 in aid of the War Fund for the 'widows and orphans, and sick and wounded in South Africa'. On the conclusion of hostilities there were further duties: a Thanksgiving Service at St Paul's Cathedral on the return home of the City Imperial Volunteers and, on 13 November 1902, a Requiem Service at Brompton Oratory in memory of the Roman Catholic soldiers who had fallen in the war.

Pupils c.1904 (RMSM)

A more tangible commemoration of the conflict for Kneller Hall came in 1906 with the presentation, by authority of the Secretary of State for War, of two Maxim Guns mounted on tripods that had been captured from the Boers. These were placed outside the Hall but were, it should be noted, for decorative purposes only.

Further royal engagements were also undertaken in the new reign. In May 1903 the Band played at the opening of Kew Bridge by the King, whilst the School was visited by Princess Victoria of Schleswig-Holstein the same month. A year later, on 27 May 1904, Edward VII, together with the Queen and the Prince and Princess of Wales, went to Kneller Hall – the first time it had been so honoured by a reigning monarch. Following their departure, an Institution Order was issued:

> It gives the Commandant the greatest pleasure to convey to the Staff, Students and Pupils His Majesty's expression of satisfaction at everything he saw and heard. His Majesty was graciously pleased to say that 'nothing could be more satisfactory'.

Such compliments, combined with the increasing number of prestigious bookings for both orchestra and band, was most gratifying, but it is said that imitation is the highest form of praise, and in this context perhaps the greatest compliment to Kneller Hall came with the decision in 1903 to open a Royal Navy School of Music at Eastney. The establishment of this new institution, it was announced, was to include a 'Musical Director – to receive a salary of £250 per annum and rank as a Warrant Officer'.

This being a bandmaster appointment, the advice of the Commandant at Kneller Hall was sought on the question of who was to fill the role of Musical Director. It can only be seen as a tribute to Mr Stretton that his younger brother, Edward Charles Stretton, was chosen. Having joined the Royal Artillery at the age of 12, Charles Stretton had become Bandmaster of the 1st Battalion, The York and Lancaster Regiment in 1900 and was serving with that regiment in India when he was recalled for his new post.

For three years the two Stretton brothers were responsible for the musical training of the Army and the Navy. Then in 1906 Ladislao Zaverthal finally retired from his post at the helm of the Royal Artillery Band, and Charles was chosen to replace him, despite competition from a huge field that included such titans as Dan Godfrey of the Bournemouth Municipal Orchestra and Alick Maclean, son of the distinguished Musical Director of Eton. The latter had indeed already been chosen for the job by the Regiment, before Edward VII stepped in to recommend Mr Stretton, who had fortuitously just returned from a royal visit to India and Burma on board HMS *Renown*. Charles was to remain with the Gunners for 29 years, retiring in the rank of Major.

A few months before his younger brother took this step forward with his career, Arthur Stretton too broke new ground, as the *London Gazette* noted:

> Quartermaster and Hon Lieut. Arthur J Stretton MVO, Royal School of Music, is granted the honorary rank of Captain. Dated 25th March 1906.

This was the highest rank that a Director of Music of Kneller Hall had yet achieved.

❋

1907 was a big year for the School, being the 50th anniversary of its foundation. A commemorative luncheon was given on 30 August by the Commandant, Col Balfour, and his wife, with the following in attendance: Captain J M Brett (the adjutant), Captain Stretton, the Rev T P Moreton (chaplain), Sergeant Major H J Lacey and Professors J H Colton, J H Geary, W H Hayward, A E Ingham, F W Julien, A Matt, W O'Keefe, R G Owen, C Parker, W Wallis, J Ward and J Wilcocke. The only member of staff unable to attend was one of the flute tutors, Mr G Clinton.

The evening of 25 September saw further celebrations with a Jubilee Concert attended by over 8000 people. All items on the programme were conducted by students:

Fest March	Tannhäuser (Wagner)	Student J Goodered
Overture	William Tell (Rossini)	Student C Hindmarsh
Suite	Scénes Alsaciennes (Massenet)	Student G O Walker
Idyll	The Forge in the Forest (Michaelis)	Student F J Ricketts
Cornet Solo	Mia (Hartmann)	Student E Adams
American Sketch	Down South (Myddleton)	Student A E Noble
Idyll	Bells on the Water (Watson)	Student A L Wallace
Song	The Rosary (Nevin)	Student A L Wallace
Selection	The Merry Widow (Lehar)	Student H B Lovell
Whistling Valse	Wiener Mad'ln (Ziehrer)	Student H Stockey
Grand Fantasia	The Battle of Waterloo (Eckersberg)	Student H Dudley
	God Save The King	
	The Last Post	

The *Richmond and Twickenham Times* reporting on the concert was particularly impressed by the finale:

> 'The Battle of Waterloo' was an almost desperately realistic affair. With the free use of bombs and rifles, star shells and coloured fire, and the marching of detachments of the band from various parts of the park towards the central bandstand, the whole business was most exciting. The noise and glare of it woke up the country for a long way round.

But the most important development of the Jubilee – at least for historians – was a decision that, with Kneller Hall now clearly here to stay, it would be of value to keep a diary for the institution. Students were given the task of scouring what records existed to produce some sort of history of the first fifty years, and a resolution was made to keep a better account in the future; it is thanks to the endeavours of these unknown students that we know as much as we do of the early years of the School.

Albert Matt, Professor of Trombone 1900-14 with his pupils (MATT)

It was in the Jubilee year also that a new forage cap, complete with peak, was adopted. The students' cap badge – a lyre, similar to that worn by serving bandsmen – was found to be too large for use and was replaced by a newly designed metal badge, using the monogram 'RMSM', surmounted by a Tudor Crown. It was not, however, until 1909 that official authorization for the change was received from the Director of Equipment and Ordnance Stores. A further change came the following year when the embroidered badge on the shoulder straps of the students' frock coats was replaced by a 'badge, band' in gilding metal.

Refinements were also being made in this period to the buildings, and particularly to the Chapel. In 1906, we are told, 'a five light Corona was fixed in substitution of the ineffective standard lights hitherto in use', whilst the ornamental painted windows were moved down from the gallery, where only the band and choir could see them, to the lower level where they might be appreciated by the general congregation. Two years later the fixtures were cleaned and redecorated, and in 1909 two new windows were installed, one bearing the names of the Commandants, the other the names of the Adjutants of the School. 1911 saw the addition of the portable stone font and brass font ewer.

The necessity for a more substantial change, in terms of the everyday life of the students, was indicated in December 1906 when the School was inspected by General Lord Methuen, Commander-in-Chief of Eastern Command. He paid tribute to the students, whose 'conduct, tone, keenness and love for music makes, and will always make, not only their lives, but the lives of many others very happy', but added that 'my only regret is that there is not a separate, and better adapted, room for the practice of the Band.' At the time a large room in the main building was doubling up as practice room and dining hall. Eighteen months later building on an outside practice room was completed, and on 22 January 1909 the official Diary records that:

> The room which was hitherto used as a practice and Dining Room, having been re-appropriated as a Dining Hall was this day opened as such. The total cost of equipment, cutlery, delf, linen &c. amounting to £83 5s 10´d was borne entirely by Institution funds.

The years immediately preceding the outbreak of the Great War were deceptively tranquil ones. The Kneller Hall band found itself regularly called upon for public engagements, including the Nelson Centenary Celebrations in 1905, the opening of the Union Jack Club in 1907, and a Memorial Service at St Paul's for the victims of the *Titanic* disaster in 1912.

On 20 May 1910 the orchestra played at St Paul's for the funeral of Edward VII, just as it had for that of his mother. And the Coronation of the new King in 1911 was again celebrated by the Band with a performance in Parliament Square, and a major role in the Royal Progress through London. Coronation medals were presented to Colonel Somerville, Major Brett, Major Stretton and Sergeant Major Lacey.

For Colonel Somerville and Major Stretton, an even greater honour was the invitation later that year to travel to India to make arrangements for the Delhi Durbar, one of the greatest ceremonial occasions in the history of the British Empire. (During their absence Bandmaster Richardson of the 2nd Battalion of The King's Own Royal Regiment was appointed temporary Director of Music; coincidentally the King's Own was Col Somerville's regiment.) In recognition of their service, both Commandant and Director were made Members of the Fourth Class of the Royal Victorian Order. The following year George V made a more unusual contribution to the School, with the presentation of a pair of swans to replace two that had died.

But perhaps the most significant development in these years was the building of a close association between Kneller Hall and the Worshipful Company of Musicians. The Clerk of the Company wrote to the Commandant, Colonel Balfour, on 15 July 1908:

> I have much pleasure in formally informing you that at the Meeting of the Court of the Company yesterday it was on the proposition of Colonel T B Shaw Hellier [the former Commandant] unanimously resolved to present the Company's Silver Medal annually to the Royal Military School of Music for the most talented Student of the year.

The first student to receive this coveted medal was Student Bandmaster Henry Finucane.

The fact that this ancient institution – which had been granted a Royal Charter by James I – took an interest in the School was truly a mark of the growing status of military music. This was further confirmed in 1909 when the Commandant hosted a garden party at Kneller Hall for guests including the Lord Mayor of London, the senior officers of the Worshipful Company of Musicians, the composer Sir Alexander Mackenzie (Principal of the Royal Academy of Music) and Sir George Martin, the organist of St Paul's. A band of 180 played the following programme:

1	Grand March: 'Coronation'	Godfrey
2	Overture: 'The Land of the Mountain and the Flood'	McCunn
3	'Gipsy Suite'	German
4	Prelude to 'Colomba'	Mackenzie
5	Song: 'The Better Land'	Cowen
6	Selection from the works of Edward Elgar	arr. Stretton

Summer concert, pre-World War I (RMSM)

7	Glees:	(a) 'Image of the Rose'	Reichardt
		(b) 'Hail, Smiling Morn'	Spofforth
		played by 30 trombones	
8	Marching Song: 'Follow the Colours'		Elgar
9	Symphony in B minor: 'The Unfinished'		Schubert
10	'Two Characteristic Dances'		Coleridge-Taylor
11	Selection: 'Ivanhoe'		Sullivan

The inclusion of a specially arranged selection by Captain Stretton of Elgar's music was in honour of the attendance of Sir Edward, then at the height of his fame and success. His compliments to the Director of Music and the Band naturally brought great satisfaction.

The peace and stability of Edwardian England being enjoyed at Kneller Hall was to be rudely disturbed, as the official Diary for 1914 records:

> At 10.20pm on this date [4 August] the Order to Mobilise was received and arrangements were at once made to carry out the Mobilisation Regulations.
>
> All students (except three who belong to the Royal Artillery and Guards) and pupils over 18 years were returned to their units, under War Office authority.

The Great War has passed into history as the most severe trial the British Army has ever faced, and the bands were not to be immune to its effects, as the War Office order indicates.

Bands were disbanded and the musicians returned to the ranks to serve as stretcher-bearers, medical orderlies and combatants, with heroic and vital service being rendered by many; in particular, the contribution of Thomas Edward Rendle of the 1st Duke of Cornwall's Light Infantry is remembered – the only bandsman to be awarded the Victoria Cross during the conflict.

Despite the disruptions to military music, Kneller Hall could at least count itself fortunate that it was in safe hands. Arthur Stretton had by now been in his position for the better part of two decades, whilst the Commandant of the day was one of the School's greatest-ever servants, Col T C F Somerville. This former commanding officer of the 1st Battalion of the King's Own Royal Regiment had been appointed in 1910 and was actually due to be replaced towards the end of 1914. With the outbreak of hostilities, however, the War Office decided that he was to remain in his post until further orders, whilst the Commandant-designate, Col B E Ward of the 1st Middlesex Regiment, was sent to France. In October it was reported that Col Ward had died of wounds whilst serving with the Expeditionary Force, and Col Somerville was destined to stay at Kneller Hall until his retirement in 1919.

The character of this most influential of Commandants was summed up in the obituary that appeared on his death in 1942 in *The Lion and the Rose*, journal of the King's Own Royal Regiment:

Col Cameron Sommerville
(RMSM)

> [He was] in many ways the antithesis of the traditional Army officer: totally indifferent to everything connected with horses and without any aptitude for, or interest in, sport and games. Widely read and possessed of considerable powers of appreciation of literature and painting, it was in music that his nature found its true outlet.

Such a man was invaluable at a time of uncertainty, and his reminiscences of the period – published after the war in *The Leading Note* – are the best account we have.

The disappearance of the students and older pupils was soon compensated for by the arrival of thirteen of the most recently-created bandmasters, together with their band-boys. (Bandmasters were exempted from the move into the ranks, though there was the occasional exception, such as William 'Paddy' Dunn of the 2nd Battalion, 60th Rifles who secretly enlisted as a rifleman and later won the Military Cross.) There was some disquiet amongst those who had only just left Kneller Hall to take up their positions when obliged to return, but their presence did at least ensure some continuity – the Wednesday after they appeared, the weekly concert made a welcome return to the schedule of activities and was to continue throughout the War.

The closing down of the regimental bands was a typically obtuse decision by the War Office, and one that was inevitably to be repeated with the same consequences in the Second World War since bureaucrats have seldom been noted for the readiness with which they learn from their mistakes. Early in 1915 Sir John French wrote from France insisting that the Expeditionary Force desperately needed bands, if morale in the ranks was to be maintained; simultaneously it became clear to those with eyes to see that bands could play a useful role in aiding recruitment (conscription was yet to come).

A new programme was therefore undertaken on two fronts: instruments and music were despatched to France for use by the bandsmen already there, whilst young bands were formed at home. The former necessitated the collection of materials from the regiments by Kneller Hall to be sent overseas. Colonel Somerville noted that some initially saw this as an opportunity to off-load the more antique and useless items from their stocks, but such pieces were returned with a request for a better effort, and eventually the standard was raised. Nonetheless, he pointed out, 'it wasn't any use sending out first-class new instruments under the circumstances obtaining in that first bad winter.' And those circumstances ('the enemy's shells, the mud, the rain and wind') meant that the operation to keep the frontline bands fully supplied was a continuing problem right through the hostilities.

Back at home there was a different problem. Boys could be used as musicians, but as soon as they reached 17½ years of age they became eligible for active service and had to be transferred into the ranks. An eager search was consequently undertaken by Bandmasters through school rolls in an attempt to find suitable candidates for the new bands: 'At first boys of 15 and 16 were eagerly taken, but when it was realized how soon these lads would have to leave the band, the struggle began to get those whose fourteenth birthday had only just passed.' It was discovered that most boys could, with an intensive programme of instruction, be playing in public 18 months after they had first taken up their instruments.

One unexpected by-product of this emergency period was the inauguration of Kneller Hall inspections. With the young bands being both inexperienced and lacking in the support they would normally receive from their regiments, it was decided that Colonel Somerville and Major Stretton would undertake an annual inspection of every band in the country. 'Not unnaturally we were not received with open arms on our first tour of inspection,' recorded Colonel Somerville, but gradually things improved, and 'this attitude changed to one of pleasure when Bandmasters found their efforts to keep their bands up to the mark appreciated.'

This was a new development and a new role for Kneller Hall. Previously it had exercised its influence over Army music solely by its training of future bandmasters; now the possibility of a more direct intervention offered itself, and Colonel Somerville for one was enthusiastic about the possibilities, commenting later that 'I consider it a great misfortune that the need for retrenchment in expenditure on the Army should have put an end to these most valuable inspections.' Other were not so keen on this interference from the centre; writing in 1926, when a regular system of periodic inspections had been instituted, Lt-Col Mackenzie-Rogan recalled happier days before the War:

> Most bands did well at that time. It was not considered necessary for a Commandant of Kneller Hall, accompanied by the Director of Music, to tour the country on inspection duty, visiting military bands and criticizing the work of accomplished and energetic bandmasters.

Just before the War, in June 1914, it was announced that henceforth Directors of Music would be given the honorary rank of Lieutenant, though it was not until peace was restored that the decision was to be implemented fully; in 1919 it was specified that the leaders of the bands of the Household Division, Royal Artillery, Royal Engineers and Royal Marine Light Infantry would be directors of music, with the appropriate rank. The following decade the rank ceased to be merely honorary. Meanwhile Arthur Stretton – already the first Kneller Hall Director to make Captain, and then Major – took a step further, being promoted to Lieutenant-Colonel on 3 June 1918, the first musician in the Army ever to reach this eminence.

Peace brought a return to more normal musical activity, of course, but it also saw the retirement of Col Somerville in May 1919 after a distinguished period of service. He left behind the Somerville Prize, which continues to be awarded; later

The School Band, 1911. Note Std Adkins fifth from left, back row (RMSM)

he also presented an oak altar reading-desk for the Chapel. It was perhaps not much compensation for his departure, but the same month that he left the Trophies Committee sent Kneller Hall two 150mm howitzers, two 77mm field guns and two 105mm long howitzers – all captured from the Germans – for display purposes.

An even greater loss was soon to come with the retirement of Arthur Stretton, but there were still some important changes to be made in those last couple of years. In 1921 the examination of students was re-organized with the creation of an examination board comprising a representative from the Royal Academy of Music and one from the Royal College of Music, together with a nominee of the War Office; those who wished to become bandmasters were now required to obtain half-marks in each of their final harmony, counterpoint and instrumentation papers, with an aggregate minimum of 160 marks out of the possible 300. Later in the year instruction in the training of male voice choirs was introduced, with a professor appointed for this purpose.

This period too saw the building of a new bandstand by the Royal Engineers, and the return to the routine of receiving distinguished visitors to the School: the most notable in 1920 was Dr Albert Mitchell, MusDoc (Oxon) of the United States Army, whilst 1921 brought the Crown Prince of Japan, in whose honour the Band played a selection of Japanese airs.

On 22 September 1921 Lieutenant-Colonel A J Stretton MVO finally retired. None could have predicted it at the time, but the next period of incumbency was to be even more important and eventful.

CHAPTER 5

THE AGE
OF ADKO

THE SCHOOL BAND ON THE WOODEN BANDSTAND,
CONDUCTED BY LT ADKINS, 1924 (RMSM)

There is no doubt that the Directors of Music at Kneller Hall had thus far proved a distinguished and accomplished line of musicians. If some critics had reservations about the suitability of Herr Schallehn for the job, they would at least have admitted that his contribution as propagandist was immensely valuable, and in any event no such questions hovered over Mr Mandel, Mr Cousins, Lt Griffiths or Lt-Col Stretton – these were all honourable and fine servants of army music. None of them, however, could truly be said to have been plucked from the highest echelons of the military establishment: neither of the serving Directors had been of commissioned rank prior to their appointment, and none had come to the School from any of the senior bands – the Guards, the Artillery or the Engineers.

This fact is in such stark contrast to the present system – under which eight of the last eleven Directors have come from the Guards, two from the Gunners and one from the Engineers – that it requires some explanation. The truth is that, notwithstanding the endeavours of the early incumbents, the post at Kneller Hall was not seen as holding the same prestige as the major appointments in London. The importance of the School as a training ground was no longer doubted, with virtually all the civilian musicians having long since departed the service, and the status of the band and orchestra had been confirmed by Victoria's endorsement and by the favour shown to Arthur Stretton by both her and her successor, but it was still somehow lacking in the glamour attached to the older bands. It is almost as though the Director of Music of the School was seen more as an administrator than as a rival to the great showmen of the times.

There was some justification for such a feeling. Unlike other directors of music, the Director at Kneller Hall had his musicians for only a brief period of time, and was thus unable to stamp his personality so completely on his band; he was, furthermore, not offered the chance of the major overseas concert tours that were becoming standard with other bands. Admittedly there were prestigious state occasions and royal visits, but so too were there for others, as military music continued its ascent to establishment respectability. And the summer concert series, though popular, did not attract the fashionable London audiences nor enjoy the same earning power that the Gunners or the Guards could boast.

When, therefore, the retirement of Lt-Col Stretton left a vacancy at Kneller Hall, there was no jostling for position amongst the senior musicians of the Army, seeking to take over. Coincidentally the posts at the Grenadier Guards and the Coldstream had also come vacant in the previous eighteen months, thus absorbing the most senior of those seeking promotion, whilst the other great regiments had long-standing directors with no desire to move: these included such illustrious names as Charles Stretton of the Artillery, Neville Flux of the Engineers, and Manuel Bilton of The Blues. Even had there been a wish to appoint an established figure, the opportunity to do so simply did not exist. What no one expected was that the choice would fall on a man who would come to eclipse even these giants of military music, and in the process establish Kneller Hall as the key position of authority and power.

Hector Adkins was at the time Bandmaster of the 2nd Battalion, The Suffolk Regiment, where he was already winning himself a reputation for single-mindedness, even perhaps of fanaticism, in imposing his will upon his men. One of those who was to come into contact with him repeatedly during his tenure at the School was Charles Nalden, who served under him as pupil, student and later professor, before emigrating to New Zealand where he was appointed to the chair in music at the University of Auckland. In his autobiography *Half and Half*, probably the finest set of memoirs written by a former military musician, Mr Nalden describes his first encounter with Mr Adkins in 1923:

Hector Adkins (RMSM)

> 'Adko' was indeed a fierce-looking man. Already in the process of developing a Kiwi dark-tan complexion, he sported a ginger moustache, which was waxed at both ends. This in turn was set over a pair of thin, tightly-drawn lips which when parted revealed an array of fang-like teeth … His hair, like his moustache, was ginger. But the most frightening aspect of his make-up was his pince-nez style eyeglasses, which appeared to exaggerate the Reynard-orientated inwards slant of his eyes.

Despite this frightening appearance, Mr Adkins was also an accomplished musician, with a Bachelor of Music degree and LRAM and ARCM diplomas to his credit even before succeeding Lt-Col Stretton. Promoted to Lieutenant and appointed to Kneller Hall, he was to bring both his authority and his ability to bear in his new job.

One of the key features of his period at the School was the emphasis placed upon building bridges to the mainstream of British music. The appearance of Sir Edward Elgar in an audience at a 1909 concert had already given a stamp of approval to Kneller Hall, and Lt-Col Stretton had made sure to leave a rich legacy for the new man to develop. An entry in the Diary just a week after Mr Adkins' arrival reads:

> A recapitulatory concert of new works for the military band, originals and arrangements of orchestral pieces, sent in response to a public offer by the commandant to perform such, was held on 29th September. It was attended by Sir Charles Stanford, Sir Hugh Allen, Dr Vaughan Williams, Mr Adrian Boult and other professional musicians; also by several musical critics and representatives of musical publishing firms.

Sir Hugh Allen was then a professor of music at Oxford University, whilst Sir Charles Stanford was not only a composer in his own right, but also a professor of music at Cambridge University and professor of composition at the Royal College of Music, in which latter capacity he had taught Ralph Vaughan-Williams. Adrian Boult, of course, was the greatest British conductor of his generation.

It is unfortunate that no programme has survived of such an illustrious concert, so that we do not know what works these great names had contributed to the occasion. The following year, however, on 30 June 1922 a concert was given at the Royal Albert Hall in the presence of the King, at which Dame Ethyl Smyth conducted the overture to her opera *The Wreckers*, and for which Gustav Holst specially revised his 'Suite in F', with the addition of 'Song of the Blacksmith'. At the same concert Lieutenant Walton O'Donnell of the Royal Marines, and later of the BBC's Wireless Military Band, premiered his 'Three Humoreskes'.

The desire to build a new repertoire for military band was further evident in a concert on 3 October 1923, with the following programme:

1 Overture: Othello   H A Keyser
         conductor – Student L Pay LRAM ARCM
2 Russian Dance: Gopak   J Verney
         conductor – Student W Fitz-Earle
3 Three Roundels: Herbert Bedford
              a)   The King of Spades
              b)   The Queen of Hearts
              c)   The Knave of Diamonds
              conductor – Student R Marshall
4 Toccata and Fugue in C Major   Bach
         arranged by Student D Plater LRAM ARCM
              conducted by the arranger

5 Suite: The Planets   Holst
- a) Mars
- b) Mercury
- c) Jupiter

       arranged by Students L Pay LRAM ARCM and G Smith
              conducted by the Director of Music

6 Variations on Two Short Themes   J Verney
            conductor – Student B Grumbley

7 Folk Song Suite: Vaughan Williams
- a) Seventeen Come Sunday
- b) Sea Songs
- c) My Bonnie Boy
- d) Folk Songs From Somerset

       The composer's first work for military band
         conductor – Student S W Webber ARCM

8 Prelude: Beatrice   Percy Harrison
         conductor – Student W C Windrum

Items 1, 2 and 8 had all been sent in response to a request for original compositions, but the real coup was to secure Dr Vaughan Williams' first piece for military band. (Curiously the printed version of the 'Folk Song Suite' does not include the second movement, 'Sea Songs', though it does survive as a separate march.)

This attempt to take military bands towards more serious concert material was possible to some extent only because Mr Adkins was himself a talented and educated musician, as evidenced by the demand for his lectures beyond Kneller Hall; a typical such engagement was at the Royal College of Music in July 1923, where he lectured on 'The musical potentialities of the military band', with the assistance of a band of 46 musicians.

He was greatly encouraged in these pursuits by the then Commandant, Colonel J C Somerville, who – like his predecessor and namesake – was evidently a keen amateur lover of music. (It should also be recorded that this had been true too of other Commandants: Colonel Farquar Glennie, for example, in the late 1890s had been renowned as a fine violinist, who numbered amongst his most treasured possessions a Stradivarius.)

Col Somerville was also an advocate of better music, and in an article in *The Army Quarterly*, he was fiercely critical of the low standards being set by regimental bandmasters with the encouragement of their officers. The civilian taste in music, he pointed out, had improved in Britain, thanks in large part to the efforts of Sir Henry Wood (who visited Kneller Hall

Col J C Somerville (RMSM)

in 1923 with Eugene Goosens and Ethel Smyth, and who later was invited to adjudicate the conducting competition), but this progress had not been matched by that of the military:

> We in the Army have been content to continue in the old rut, croaking to one another like frogs in a pond – damned impenetrably from the main stream of progress – and continuing to regard the overture to 'William Tell', 'Zampa' and other such rococo claptrap as the summit of ambition for the band to play or the soldier to appreciate.

It need not be thus, he argued, and he called instead for a more adventurous choice of programming to emphasize the likes of Bach, Handel, Mozart, Beethoven and Wagner.

Col Somerville's thesis was not without its flaws. The claim that these named composers were worthy of attention because they had stood 'the test of time' implied a somewhat limited scope for bands, suggesting that they should follow rather than lead musical opinion. (It also, incidentally, failed to recognize the durability of Rossini.) More importantly, it did not do full justice to the strides that military bands had already made.

Wagner had long been a much favoured composer in military circles, and a 1902 concert by the Royal Artillery included orchestral works by Elgar and Dvorak, together with pieces by Wagner and Mendelssohn arranged for band, in addition to the ubiquitous 'William Tell', and an original selection from his own opera *Una Notte a Firenze* by the Bandmaster, Ladislao Zaverthal. Though the Gunners were undoubtedly the leading band of the time, others too ventured beyond what Col Somerville refers to as 'shoddy, unoriginal stuff'. The 7th Dragoon Guards included pieces by German, Beethoven, Liszt and Grieg in a concert series in 1907, and a programme survives of a concert given by the Band of the 48th Foot under Signore Tamplini as far back as 1853: it comprised two works by Donizetti, another by Meyerbeer, and two premieres, one by Manzaroeli and one by Tamplini himself. Donizetti and Meyerbeer may not have been the artistic equals of Beethoven, but it is difficult to believe that many soldiers would have heard such music at all if their band had not been playing it.

Kneller Hall too had not been reluctant to tackle the classics: the 1893 concert season had featured symphonic works by Beethoven, Mendelssohn, Schubert, Massenet, Haydn and Mozart, whilst one of the Pleasant Evenings of that year had been exclusively devoted to the music of Mendelssohn.

(Indeed such predilections occasionally brought problems for the School. The late Henry Pipe, a student in the '20s and subsequently Professor of Clarinet, used to tell of a visit by George V to Kneller Hall. The King was being entertained with a programme of Tchaikovsky and similar composers when his attention was seen to wander; he began singing aloud and stamping his foot, to the consternation of both the Director and the royal entourage, until a young clarinettist, casting protocol aside, called out, 'He wants to hear "Colonel Bogey", sir.' The march was sent for and played, apparently bringing more satisfaction than the more elevated classical repertoire had managed to do.)

Even with these reservations, Col Somerville's intervention was undoubtedly positive. The 1923 programme quoted above was notable for its preponderance of new works (even Holst's 'Planets' suite was contemporary, having received its first orchestral performance just four years earlier), and the desire to stay in touch with 'the main stream of progress' was evident in Kneller Hall concerts throughout the period.

It should be stressed, however, that Col Somerville was far from being an elitist when it came to music. Indeed his entire argument was based on a belief that all that was keeping soldiers from the great works of past and present was lack of familiarity. Only play the stuff, he suggested, and it will soon enough become accessible to all. The fact that he was right was attested to by the experience of many bands in the '20s as levels of sophistication rose generally.

Mr Austing, Bandmaster of the 2nd Battalion, The Black Watch, for example, earned himself a reputation within the regiment as something of a musical purist and initially received complaints that he was playing too much unfamiliar music. The endeavour could be seen to have paid off, however, when he began Sunday evening request concerts; the regimental journal, *The Red Hackle*, reported: 'The pieces asked for have shewn a surprisingly high level of musical appreciation: Beethoven's "Leonora" overture, the 5th Symphony, Schubert's "Unfinished Symphony", Wagner's "Flying Dutchman" overture and "Lohengrin".' Mr Austing had been at Kneller Hall under Samuel Griffiths, but with Hector Adkins and Col Somerville in command, the musical education provided for future bandmasters was to rise still higher.

The most concrete symbol of Kneller Hall's growing involvement with the mainstream comes in a famous photograph taken at Wembley on 23 April 1924 at the grand opening of the British Empire Exhibition. It was an event at which massed choirs were accompanied by the Kneller Hall Band, and the photograph shows the conductor's rostrum occupied by both Mr Adkins, in full dress uniform, and Sir Edward Elgar, who that year became the Master of the King's Music. Sir Percival Phillips described the scene in the *Daily Mail*:

> Far away in the distance was a tall crimson pulpit set close against the opposite end of the arena where Sir Edward Elgar directed the massed choirs. They towered above him in the form of a gigantic white 'T', with the band of the Royal Military School of Music a mere splash of scarlet in the centre.

Music performed included Vaughan Williams' newly composed 'Toccata Marziale', Gordon Jacob's military band arrangement of 'A William Byrd Suite', Dame Ethyl Smyth's 'The Wreckers' overture, Holst's 'The Planets' and, inevitably, 'Land of Hope and Glory' – the last three benefiting from the presence of their composers at rehearsals.

Both Mr Adkins and the Band were to return to Wembley a month later, as recorded in the Kneller Hall Diary:

Lt Adkins and Sir Edward Elgar at Wembley, 1924
(RADIO TIMES)

> Under instructions from the War Office the organization of a massed band to perform at the Empire Day ceremonies, the Thanksgiving Service on Sunday the 25th May and in a series of concerts throughout the following week was undertaken by the authorities of the Institution.
>
> Five bandsmen on an average were selected from every unit on home service and with the entire personnel of Kneller Hall rehearsed at Hounslow Heath Aerodrome from 5th – 22nd May, when all moved into camp at Wembley. Corps of 300 drums and fifes, and 100 pipers were organized at the same time to play in the introductory part of each programme.

This series of eight days of concerts was probably the biggest ever staged by British massed bands up to that point: it involved more than a thousand performers including six hundred bandsmen, it required the services of eight bandmasters to assist Mr Adkins in training the bands, and it featured each of the Directors of Music then serving in the Army conducting one item apiece. In addition, Mr Walton O'Donnell of the Royal Marines was invited to conduct three of his own compositions, again demonstrating Kneller Hall's commitment to new works.

The Empire Exhibition was such a success that it was repeated the following year; again Lt Adkins conducted the Kneller Hall Band as it accompanied the massed choirs of the Chapel Royal St James, St George's Chapel Windsor, St

Paul's Cathedral, the London Church Choirs Association and other London churches under Dr Charles Macpherson. And the associations with the classical music world were renewed in 1932 at a World Celebrity Concert at the Albert Hall, with the trumpeters joining the BBC Symphony orchestra and the Royal Philharmonic Orchestra; conductors included Dr Adrian Boult, Sir Edward Elgar, Sir Landon Ronald, Sir Henry Wood and Capt Adkins.

＊

In Col Somervile's article in *The Army Quarterly*, he had set out various proposals that he felt would improve the standing and performance of military musicians. Some were doomed to failure – such as his call for bandmasters to be given the opportunity to be commissioned after a probationary period with their regiments – but others were to be implemented during or soon after his time.

Amongst them was his proselytising in favour of male voice choirs, stemming from his 'belief that through concerted vocal music lies the road to musical salvation, not only of the Army but of the nation.' He may have been a little optimistic in this latter, but as we have seen the choir had been a feature at Kneller Hall life from the outset (particularly promoted by Francis Whitmore in the early days) and a course of male voice choir teaching had been instituted in 1921. At the Albert Hall concert of 30 June 1922 referred to above, the Kneller Hall choir sang two of Gustav Holst's songs, in what was probably their first public appearance outside the School. The effects were soon felt throughout the Army, however far-flung the postings: Bertie Gubbins, for example, left Kneller Hall to become Bandmaster of the 1st Suffolks in 1924, whilst that battalion was stationed in India; within a couple of years he was conducting a choir from his band in its debut concert, performing his own arrangement of Beethoven's 'Creation' anthem.

Col Somerville also suggested an annual conference to be held at Kneller Hall and attended by all directors of music and 'representative bandmasters from each Command, elected by the bandmasters of the units comprised in it.' The purpose of this conference – what might be seen as a kind of musical synod – would be 'the interchange of ideas and the ventilation of grievances'. In particular, one of Col Somerville's most pressing queries could be addressed: the determination of the minimum size of a band and its instrumentation. This too would be dealt with in 1921, with the Kneller Diary recording on 7 December that:

> A Conference attended by the Directors of Music and representatives of the Royal Navy, Royal Marines, Royal Air Force, bandmasters of the Army and music publishers was held at Kneller Hall to deliberate the numbers and instrumentation of the minimum Military Band, and other questions of importance therewith.

Though this was a one-off event, a subsequent conference the next month at the Royal College of Music saw the Kneller Hall curriculum discussed in detail, with the result that the teaching of strict counterpoint was discontinued in favour of aural training.

A more regular institution came into being in 1923 when the first Annual Conference and Dinner was held of the Kneller Hall Club. This was an initiative of Mr Adkins, and it included all graduates of Kneller Hall, rather than just the elected representatives suggested by Col Somerville. The 1923 Conference was held at the School on 15 December, followed by a dinner at the Café Monaco in London; 7 directors of music and 51 bandmasters attended, and though these numbers were down the next year, the tradition was firmly established. A Club Tie was also introduced.

Even more significant was the argument put forward by Col Somerville in favour of band inspections. These, as we have seen, had been initiated during the Great War but subsequently discontinued when the Army budget was cut. Col Somerville recommended the appointment of two travelling Inspectors from amongst the directors of music – one for the UK, Channel Islands and Mediterranean, the other for India and the Far East – in order that some kind of external expert authority be available to judge the competence or otherwise of serving bandmasters.

In the event this Inspectorate was not created, but in May 1926 War Office authority was given for ten bandmasters each year to return to Kneller Hall for testing, so that future promotions to directors of music might be based on direct knowledge and not simply the sometimes ill-informed opinion of commanding officers.

At the same time it was decreed that the Commandant and Director of Music should visit and test as many bands as possible. Initially a voluntary scheme, this became an official requirement for bands from 1931, with twenty bands to be inspected every year. As the programme of inspections got into its stride, it provided new evidence for the general improvement of musical standards in the bands – the 2nd Royal Warwickshire Fusiliers were visited in 1929, for example, and chose as their inspection pieces Drysdale's overture 'Tam O'Shanter' and a selection from Wagner's *Rienzi*.

Even so the system of deciding which bandmasters were suitable for promotion to director of music was not yet satisfactory, and eventually Mr Adkins put forward the idea that an advanced examination in music should be created. The result was an Army Council Instruction dated 21 August 1929 which brought into existence the qualification 'psm' (passed school of music), which would in future be the requirement for commissioned musicians.

Eighteen serving directors of music were immediately awarded the new qualification without examination. Captain George Miller of the Grenadier Guards received certificate number one, whilst others now entitled to use the initials psm included: Capt Andrew Harris (Welsh Guards), Capt Chares Stretton (Royal Artillery), Capt Neville Flux (Royal Engineers), Capt Robert Evans (Coldstream Guards), Capt Percy O'Donnell (Royal Marines), Capt Rudolph O'Donnell (Royal Marines), Capt Hector Adkins (RMSM), Lt William Gibson (Life Guards), Lt F J Ricketts (Royal Marines), Lt James Hurd (Irish Guards), Lt William Dunn (Royal Horse Guards) and Flight Lieutenant John Amers (Royal Air Force). The certificates for these were written and signed by the Commandant and Director of Music but for some reason never issued; number one is on display in the Kneller Hall museum, whilst numbers 2–18 still languish in the School's archives.

In September of the same year the first psm examination was held, though the Diary records that neither of the two candidates was successful in getting marks of 75% and they were therefore failed; it adds, 'the examination was not unfair and the results were disappointing.' On 17 December there was a second attempt at the exam, this time with six candidates sitting: Bandmaster Sam Rhodes of the 1st Battalion, The Royal Scots passed and thus became the first man to qualify for commission under the new system – eight years later he became Director of Music of the Scots Guards, eventually retiring in the rank of Lieutenant-Colonel.

When the psm was held the next year, on 4 September 1930, there was only one candidate, Arthur Hibbert. He had completed the course at Kneller Hall and been selected as Bandmaster of the King's Royal Rifle Corps, but had not yet joined his unit and was therefore still classified as a student.

Even so, he argued that he was technically a bandmaster and so was entitled to sit the exam. He passed, becoming the first and only student to do so, and went on to enjoy a brilliant but tragically brief career. A gifted academic and portraitist as well as musician – his arrangement of 'Orpheus in the Underworld' is still played – he was the first official Bandmaster of the Royal Corps of Signals, following on from Mr Randolph Ricketts (better known as Leo Stanley). He died in service at the age of 41.

Finally Col Somerville had argued in his article that of all the factors responsible for the inability of military bands to keep pace with developments in civilian music 'one of the chiefest has been, and must continue to be, adherence to the old high pitch.' Consistent tuning throughout the Army had been one of the Duke of Cambridge's great battles but it was one he had lost, and regrettably in the '20s the military standard was still not in accordance with the accepted norm. Col Somerville noted that:

> When the Philharmonic in 1885 adopted the International, or Continental pitch, with the laudable intention of helping to standardize it throughout the civilized world, an effort was made by Kneller Hall to bring the Army into line at the same time. The Powers that Were at the War Office had no objection to the change in principle: all they stipulated was that it should be carried out 'without expense to the public'. The result was a foregone conclusion.

Indeed it was. A cost of £20,000 was estimated and the proposal disappeared without trace. By 1928, however, the discrepancy had become intolerable and an order was issued that all bands should convert to the continental pitch, the process to be completed by mid-1930. It was now even more expensive and several regiments were unable to find the money to buy new equipment; in a great many cases brass instruments were instead converted by the addition of extra tubing on the slides – such converted pieces could still be found in use as late as the 1950s.

Whilst these amendments were made to the structure of military music, the physical establishment at Kneller Hall was not neglected. In April 1923 a new Students Mess was opened, following the conversion of the Commandant's stables, with the old mess becoming the guard room. One of Mr Adkins' first requests on taking over the reins had been for the construction of sound-proof rooms for the use of professors giving lectures, and the beginning of the spring term in 1924 saw the first eight of these come into operation, with another twelve being opened in 1929. Further structural modifications were undertaken in late 1924, though the most profound development came on 22 May 1925 with the installation of electric lights throughout the School. (It should also be noted that Kneller Hall had entered the world of modern communications some time earlier, when the first telephone was installed in the Commandant's office back in October 1906.)

Outside too, changes were being made, with the creation of a nine-hole golf course in 1927, and the building in 1932 of a squash court; the marking stone of the latter (still visible today) was laid by Pupil R Hilling, 2nd Battalion, King's Royal Rifle Corps. The same year the Diary records that:

> The old wooden Bandstand was condemned as unsafe and out of date; a new Bandstand was sanctioned by the War Office, commenced in February and completed by the end of April. It is semi-circular in shape and constructed of reinforced concrete. It accommodates 160 players with comfort and possesses excellent acoustic properties. It was used for the first time at a concert on May 18th.

The old wooden bandstand had been erected only in 1921 by the Royal Engineers on the site of the original structure, but its safety had not been enhanced by the disappearance of various bits of wood for use as kindling in barrack-room fires. In any event, the Director of Music disliked the shape and had long wished to be rid of it. The new bandstand, popularly known as The Rock, is believed to have been designed by Arthur Hibbert whilst still a student; it fared somewhat better than its predecessor, lasting through until 1995.

Mr Adkins' firmly stated views on the construction of the bandstand were typical of the man. He was at times fiercely opinionated and always determined that he would go his own way, regardless of the consequences. Typical was his acceptance in 1926 of a two-week engagement for two concerts daily at the London Coliseum. Notices were highly complimentary and the publicity gained was enormous, but such an intrusion into the territory of the major London bands hardly went unnoticed. Questions were asked in Parliament and the national press entered the debate, with the result that a new order obliged the Commandant to obtain the approval of both the DPS and HQ Eastern

Command before accepting such bookings in the future.

The band ended that year with a gross income of over £6600, of which less than £800 came from performances at Kneller Hall itself, and of which £2000 was paid into the School funds, so clearly Adko (as Mr Adkins was by then known throughout the service) was doing something right. He was, however, attracting what was seen as undue publicity, and making himself some enemies in the process. Similar problems were to recur in 1937 when the Commanding Officer of the Royal Army Service Corps at Hounslow queried whether it was appropriate for School funds to benefit from the public concerts, when War Office buildings were being used for free; despite opposition from Kneller Hall, it was decreed that in future a rent of 5/- per concert would be levied.

In 1927 the Director was involved in a car accident, resulting in a minor fracture of the ankle and injuries to the chest. The War Office was informed that he was unable to carry out his duties for a while, which left him plenty of time to write music and to book further engagements, including a two-week stint in Edinburgh in December that year, a commitment that necessitated the re-organization of the annual school leave.

According to one ex-bandmaster, Adko had a box made to carry the drum kit on these engagements, approximately 6ft by 3ft, which was placed in the front of the band coach, the first seats having been removed. At the concerts an extremely large Union Jack was hung at the back of the stage, and on the return home the flag was carefully folded and placed on the reversed side of the lid of the box to form a bed for Mr Adkins.

Another of his innovations was the application of splints to the students' arms, so that they could not bend their elbows when conducting and instead had to use their wrists; this, he insisted, was the only correct technique. It was a rather primitive method of making his point, but it did produce some fine conductors, and as one of his students, Major Alf Young, later Director of Music of the Royal Engineers and Professor of Instrumentation at Kneller Hall, commented in retrospect:

> Maybe Adko was a bit brutal but those who made it to the top owe him much. He also looked after his 'boys' no matter whether you were the youngest pupil at Kneller Hall or a seasoned director of music. He was also a first-class musician, both in the practical and academic sense.

A similar assessment was made of the great man by Gilbert Vintner, who was one of the outstanding pupils of the '20s, being awarded a one-year scholarship to study the bassoon at the Royal Academy of Music. Having served as an RAF bandmaster during the War, Mr Vinter became conductor of the BBC Midland Light Orchestra in Birmingham. Asked about Mr Adkins by one of the present writers in 1947, he commented that Adko's larger-than-life character often obscured for many people the very real musical talent that he possessed.

That talent continues to make its effects felt today. One of Adko's legacies, for example, was the famous Kneller Hall Fanfare Trumpet. Having established that the old Aida-type trumpet was unbalanced when a banner was attached to it, he designed a new model, made by Boosey & Hawkes, which has survived.

In 1932 the BBC suggested that a uniform method of playing the National Anthem should be agreed, and consulted Sir Edward Elgar, Dr Adrian Boult (musical director of the BBC) and Captain Adkins. Two versions were produced for military band by the Director of Music – one in the key of F

Adjudicators at the first Henry Hall Dance Competition c.1938 (Mr Henry Hall seated third from left). The winner of the competition was Std Fred Holyoake with his composition 'Midnight Oil'; runner-up was Std Vic Webster with 'Lost in The Mist Waltz' (V WEBSTER).

*Mr Louis Armstrong with
Kneller Hall fanfare trumpeters*
(RMSM)

major for use when audiences were expected to sing, and one in B flat major for use as a salute – and both having been approved by the King, were authorized in King's Regulations. They remained the standard versions until 1966, when a single version in G major was arranged by Colonel Basil Brown, Mr Adkins' nephew who was then Director of Music at Kneller Hall.

Perhaps the most significant contribution Adko made to Army music during this period was his *Treatise on the Military Band*, published in 1931 by Boosey & Hawkes. Though some elements of this book are now a little out of date, the essential principles are still valid, particularly in the section on arranging. For over sixty years it has played a central role in the teaching of military music, and it was partly in recognition of this influence that Major Adkins (as he then was) was awarded the degree of Doctor of Music by Edinburgh University in 1939.

These achievements, however, as Alf Young and Gilbert Vintner suggested, were often outweighed in people's perceptions by the idiosyncrasies of the man's behaviour.

Typical are the many stories told of his exploits on the golf-course (the Kneller Hall course was enlarged from nine to twelve holes in 1933). One former director of music recalled how on one occasion Adko had put the percussion section on extra practice for not paying attention in full band rehearsal. The musicians were told to report outside the officers' entrance with marching band drums, where they discovered that their extra practice took the form of marching in front of the Director as he made his way around the golf course. On another occasion, a cymbal player was ordered to parade in front, playing the cymbal part of a march; he did so only to find himself receiving more 'extras' for being out of tune in his humming of the melody, and for being out of step – given that he was the only man on parade, this latter judgement seems a little harsh.

Std Vic Webster practising clarinet whilst duty sergeant, 1934 (V WEBSTER)

Adko's playing of the game was reputedly even more unorthodox. Mr Nalden remembers him in one tournament becoming frustrated on the green and, peremptorily announcing that 'nowhere in the rules of golf did it state that the putter could not be used after the manner of a billiards cue', proceeding to do just that.

❄

The normal musical activities of the Band, of course, continued throughout this period, as did more prestigious engagements. Easter 1929 found it playing by special invitation for the King and Queen at Bognor, where George V was recuperating from an illness (though, remembering his earlier visit, the King made sure to choose the material himself), whilst Armistice Day that year saw the full Band of 150 musicians accompanying the service at St Paul's Cathedral; the following year came the first performance at a Buckingham Palace garden party.

Another first came soon after, in August 1930, when the Commandant, Director of Music and 60 musicians visited Belgium to participate in the celebrations of the centenary of Belgian independence, this being the first overseas trip of the Kneller Hall Band. In addition to two public concerts in Brussels and Ostend – with civic welcomes in both towns – it also played for a reception at the British Embassy and mar-ched to the Cenotaph, where the Commandant laid a wreath on the Grave of the Unknown Warrior. The response was overwhelming, with the newspaper *Le Peuple* enthusing:

It was a revelation! Never before have we heard such an original combination. It is a band which had no instruments of wood – clarinets and oboes are of nickel. As in French bands, saxophones are strongly represented, trumpets are replaced with cornets, and for special effects they employ 'Theban' trumpets, as for example in *Lohengrin*.

At a given moment the musicians put down their instruments, moved like clockwork, and became a humorous choir. And this is not all. They changed instruments and taking violins, banjos, guitars and a couple of pianos, starting away on jazz in a wickedly 'light hearted' manner.

All these young 'gay dogs' abandoned the rigidity of dummy dolls and seemed to dance in their seats like the Jack Hylton boys! Extraordinary!!

In November 1933 Captain Adkins travelled even further afield, having been given leave of absence that he might take up the Australian government's invitation to visit the Dominion. The purpose of the three-month trip was to train the newly formed Australian Broadcasting Commission National Military Band and so much interest was aroused by his coming that the studio was packed with spectators, officials and journalists for the first rehearsal. Adko, how-

The School Band at the Canadian National Exhibition, 1934 (PUBLIC ARCHIVES, CANADA)

ever, was not a man to let a little media interest interrupt his style and he began the session with a characteristically stern warning:

'Now I want from the band a good tone, to be well in tune and to pay strict attention to everything I ask for. If any of you make a wrong note you may expect to get it in the neck from me.'

A highly successful tour, beginning in Sydney and ending in Perth, ensued before Captain Adkins handed over the baton to Mr Stephen Yorke DCM, formerly Bandmaster of The Gloucestershire Regiment, who was to remain as conductor of the Band right through until its disbandment in 1951.

The tour finished in April 1934; two months later the *London Gazette* reported that Captain Adkins had been promoted to Brevet Major.

A further tour was undertaken that year when a 50-piece Band spent a fortnight playing at the Toronto Exhibition to great acclaim. Amongst those who heard them was the famous Canadian composer, Robert Farnon, who later wrote of his student days in Toronto:

A highlight for me was the appearance of the Kneller Hall Band in 1934 when, as a budding composer, I was overwhelmed by the wealth of orchestral sounds the players produced. Never before had I heard such a high standard of playing by bandsmen, and the special arrangements of classical and popular works were indeed an influence on my writing in the years to come.

The visit was so successful that it was repeated in 1935.

Ceremonial duties were also undertaken with an involvement in the Jubilee Celebrations of George V in 1935 and, two years later, yet another performance in Parliament Square for a coronation. Unlike the previous two coronations, however, that of George VI saw a complement of sixteen trumpeters and six drummers playing inside the Abbey, under the baton of the Director of Music. The Band outside played fanfares specially written for the occasion by Major Adkins as the various members of the royal family arrived. Coronation medals were awarded to the Commandant, Adjutant, Director of Music and the RSM as well as to those inside the Abbey and six other members of the Band.

The connexion with the new sovereign was due to be sealed in June 1938, with a royal visit to Paris. In the event, however, the King was obliged to postpone his trip, though the Band fulfilled its booking. It was to be the last overseas tour before the outbreak of war.

CHAPTER 6

CHURCHILL
HOUSE

CHURCHILL HOUSE, ALDERSHOT, FORMERLY HOME OF VISCOUNT ARCHIBALD
WAVELL. THE GROUP PICTURED ARE NOT FROM THE SCHOOL. (RMSM)

The Second World War brought far greater disruption to Kneller Hall than the Great War had. On 2 September 1939, the day before Neville Chamberlain's famous wireless broadcast, the Commandant was ordered to implement the previously prepared mobilization plan. All pupils returned to their units and all but eight students went back to their depots, Colonel J Griffin (the Commandant) was placed on the General List to be sent on 20 October to join the British Expeditionary Force in France, whilst the building itself was commandeered by the staff of General Headquarters Home Forces, with the Adjutant, Brevet Lieutenant-Colonel R C Jones, being appointed Camp Commandant.

In these circumstances, it was feared and expected that the training function of the School would be suspended – at least until those in authority were obliged yet again to recognize the value of music in wartime. Thankfully, however, the War Office opted instead to find new premises for a modified school of music, and on 5 December Major Adkins and thirty students were taken in a convoy of lorries to the appropriately named Churchill House in Aldershot.

Despite the reprieve, there might still have been those who felt that some cause for concern was attached to the move. It was not, after all, the first time that a relocation of the School had been considered. In 1934 – perhaps coincidentally at a time when Adko was in Australia – the War Office had made a proposal that Kneller Hall should be vacated and the faculty moved to premises in Canterbury. A committee that included the Commandant had visited the venue and agreed that it could be suitable, albeit with some considerable building works, such as the addition of a practice room, bandstand, twelve silent rooms, six class rooms and central heating.

There is little doubt that the scheme was favoured by Whitehall on the perennial grounds of economy (this was at a time when the defence budget was under particular attack), but it foundered on an even more basic problem – Canterbury was simply too far away from London, where most of the professors lived and worked; if they had chosen not to go along with the move, their departure would have seriously damaged the reputation of the institution. The idea was officially dropped on 5 April 1934, just as Captain Adkins was concluding his Australian tour with a series of concerts in Perth.

The move to Aldershot, therefore, though obviously necessitated by the demands of war, must have caused Adko some

Aerial view of Kneller Hall immediately pre-war. Note the four cannons in front

worries that his position at the heart of military music might be under threat. In fact, even with a reduced establishment, Adko's authority was actually strengthened with the re-location, since he was appointed not only Chief Instructor but also Commandant. It was a conflict of roles that was ultimately to prove highly unwise, but at the time it merely enhanced his prestige – in December 1940 Major Adkins was appointed acting Lieutenant-Colonel, to be raised to Brevet Lieutenant-Colonel early the following year.

The size of the establishment had, in any event, long been a matter of some debate. Back in 1927 the permitted number of students had been raised from 42 to 50, but it appears that even this was insufficient for the requirements of the Army, so great were the numbers of bands now dependent upon the School. Certainly it could not have been rigidly adhered to, for a War Office letter dated 25 February 1931 warned Kneller Hall to be mindful of the limit of 50 students and not to exceed it for any length of time.

The consequence was that by April 1934 there were ten regimental bands without bandmasters. The Commandant had long warned of the imminence of this situation, but the restrictions on numbers had prevented him from averting the crisis. The position was not eased by the fact that the

students' course ended on 1 April, out of step with the normal cycle of movements within the Army – a new bandmaster appointed to an overseas regiment could sometimes
wait in Britain for anything up to six months before the
trooping season allowed him passage abroad. The only
alternative was to despatch a bandmaster by private packet,
but this was too expensive to consider in anything but the
most extreme circumstances.

As a result, a number of graduates were left at Kneller Hall
until they could be transferred and they too were included
in the official establishment. The Director calculated that, to
maintain a steady supply of bandmasters, there needed to
be an intake of between sixteen and eighteen students each
year, of whom perhaps three or four would be returned to
their units following their six- month probationary period.
Even with a three-year course this would not involve
exceeding the War Office figures, but the inclusion of
graduates made the calculation impossible to predict. A
more pragmatic and flexible interpretation of the rules was
sought and obtained.

With the smaller number of students and the conditions of
wartime, there were fewer prestigious engagements than
there had been at Kneller Hall, particularly compared to the
'30s when Adko had ensured a regular programme of outside bookings. Predictably the government had got rid of all
bands save for those of the Guards and the Corps at the
outbreak of hostilities (the order was revoked in July 1940
when Winston Churchill became Prime Minister), meaning
that the School had one of the few bands available for the
entertainment of troops: a series of concerts in the Aldershot
area by band and orchestra was undertaken.

There was, however, one highly resonant engagement –
the appearance of the Band in Canterbury Cathedral on the
occasion of the enthronement of William Temple as the
new Archbishop of Canterbury in 1942. William Temple, of
course, was the son of Frederick Temple, formerly Headmaster of the Kneller Hall Training College.

Initially in the new location the students were responsible
for helping teach each other – the post of Professor of
Theory, for example, was taken by the senior student,
George Stunell, later Director of Music of the Royal
Military Academy – but in 1942 a new staff of instructors

arrived at Churchill House, drawn from serving band-masters who now had no musicians to command. Amongst them were Mr L Hicks of the Black Watch, Mr G W Jackson of the Royal West Kent Regiment, Mr D Keeling of the Seaforth Highlanders and, as harmony and aural teacher, Mr C Nalden of the Sherwood Foresters.

Charles Nalden has already appeared in this story during his time as a pupil, but the years since then had seen him establish himself as one of the most gifted musicians in the Army. He had obtained a Bachelor of Music degree at Durham University and was busy studying for a doctorate when he returned to the School; when an essay competition for bandmasters was instigated in 1937 with the subject 'Discuss military music in all its phases in relation to warfare, with ancient history', he won quite easily.

In his excellent autobiography, *Half and Half*, Mr Nalden has painted a vivid picture of the last few months of Adko's time at the School. Whilst giving credit for the Director's admirable exploitation of the ground of Churchill House to provide fresh vegetables for the wartime establishment, he also points out Adko's somewhat inappropriate lifestyle, including lavish dinner parties for which the food was prepared by Private Bertorelli – formerly proprietor of a Charlotte Street restaurant – and at which the orchestra played background music. Mr Nalden believes that it was one of these dinners, attended by the local brigadier, that sowed the seeds of Lt-Col Adkins' downfall.

The fall, when it came, was shockingly sudden. The background to the case – the preliminary enquiries and what prompted those enquiries – has never been revealed, leaving only the bare facts, stripped of the manoeuvrings and politics that must have been involved. Those facts, however, are simple enough: on 30 September 1942 Lt-Col Adkins was placed under arrest, whilst investigations were made into what was believed to be a wide range of offences. A thorough search of Churchill House produced no traces of irregularities in the instruments or library inventories, but even without any fresh evidence (which presumably was what had been anticipated) a total of 21 charges were brought forward. Over a period of three days between 16 and 18 December a Court Martial was held in the Prince Consort Library in Aldershot, with Lt-Col Adkins defended by Henry Maddocks, a leading barrister, and with the prosecution led by Major L R Miller.

The first seven charges were heard on the first day as a

discrete block. All seven related to the approach made by Charterhouse School to Lt-Col Adkins on his arrival at Churchill House: the school wanted a bandmaster, Adko provided one from amongst his students, and for two years it appears that everyone was happy with the arrangement. Until, that is, it was discovered that Charterhouse was paying not only the student but also Lt-Col Adkins; the argument at the Court Martial was that this money – a total of some £146 – should not have been his personal fee but should have been handed over to the Army. Adko's response to the accusations was characteristically bullish:

> I consider that I was absolutely entitled to keep the money because I felt it was for private work which I have always been allowed to do both as a bandmaster and director of music. I have spent money lavishly out of my own pocket on the School of Music, which I regarded as my own particular baby.

Despite the somewhat arrogant tone, his submission was evidently accepted, for he was acquitted on all the charges.

On the second day the remaining fourteen counts were brought. Three of them, however, which concerned an alleged practice of keeping a greater than equitable share of engagement fees, were subsequently dropped by the prosecution. Eight of the remainder charged that official railway warrants were abused, at a cost to the nation of £202; on these counts, Lt-Col Adkins was again acquitted.

With eighteen of the counts now dismissed, only three were left: that he obtained £62 from Glasgow Corporation for travel expenses on an engagement that were not incurred, that he improperly obtained wine and spirits to the value of £171 from the NAAFI by falsely claiming an officers mess establishment of 40 people, and that he fined a Sergeant £1 for not complying with an order. There was no finding on these three charges, though it is believed that Lt-Col Adkins was reprimanded.

Certainly he did not attempt to deny the accusations. He accepted that the money was received from Glasgow Corporation, though he protested his ignorance of the precise arrangements. He further admitted that he claimed an officers mess based on the figures of the entire establishment when in reality he was the only officer on the strength. (It should be noted in this context that he was not alone in consuming the drink thus obtained: there were many others who benefited from the hospitality he was thus able to offer – yet no one else was brought to book for their involvement in the practice.) Perhaps the most controversial issue raised, however, was the £1 fine levied on Sgt Hurst, since everyone knew that the charge was effectively a token one: behind it lay Lt-Col Adkins' entire system of fining those under his authority.

This practice, it appears, had been a regular part of Kneller Hall life for some time, for Mr Nalden describes it as being fully operative when he attended as a student some ten years earlier. As he recalls it, the three years during which he was supposedly studying to become a bandmaster were dominated by the huge number of paid engagements he was expected to play as a member of the Orchestra and the Band, and the main feature of those performances was the terror that one might be fined by the Director of Music, thus eating into one's fee:

> A wrong note (real or imagined, for Adko had the reputation among us of possessing a 'lousy ear'), a split note, a missed or untidy entrance inevitably would result in a fine. And alleged inattention to marks of expression would lead to a mass fine for the whole orchestra.

In an attempt to save money, Mr Nalden took to soaping his violin bow on the basis that if he didn't make a sound, he couldn't play a wrong note.

The money that was collected would be held in a fund, to be spent at the end of each year on a dinner at the Savoy Hotel, attended by all those who had been fined. Also invited were the Commandant, Adjutant and Director, who of course had not made any contribution to the fund. Lt-Col Adkins happily accepted that this was the system he operated, adding that:

> I used to purge my own sins of omission and commission by paying anything over and above the amount we had in the fine fund for the annual dinner at the Savoy. It frequently cost me £20 in tips.

The system of fines in itself was certainly unorthodox, but not one would have thought necessarily a court martial affair; if it were, then one might have expected the various Commandants and Adjutants who attended the dinners to have been similarly reprimanded. Instead Colonel H S Jervis, a former Commandant, appeared at the court martial to give evidence that not only did he know about the fines, but that he thoroughly approved of it and was prepared to take full responsibility for its implementation.

In the absence of the official court martial records – which remain restricted – it is difficult to draw any absolute conclusions from the case. On the basis of the evidence that is in the public domain, however, it is difficult not to feel that the prosecution was simply an attempt to 'get Adko'. Possibly there was a lack of students, former students and others prepared to testify, but it certainly seems that little was revealed that would justify the ending of one of the greatest careers in the history of military music.

For Adko's career was undoubtedly ended by the court martial. He may not have been found guilty on any of the charges, and reprimanded only for relatively trivial matters, but he was unable to continue. Newspaper reports of the time describe him as being 'until recently the Director of Music' and, though this was probably a little premature in official terms, he had been removed from his post as Commandant, and replaced on 15 October 1942 by Major A T B Bignold de Cologan of the Rifle Brigade (TA), who was appointed acting Commandant. Lt-Col Adkins was thus placed in a position subordinate to a junior officer, a situation that was clearly intolerable, and would have been even to one less sensitive to questions of rank than the Director was. He chose to leave the institution that he had so effectively made his own (his 'own particular baby'), and departed soon after the verdict under something of a cloud.

On his retirement, Lt-Col Adkins moved to South Africa where he died on 8 November 1962. A memorial plaque was placed in the School chapel to commemorate perhaps the greatest, and certainly the most influential, Director of Music that Kneller Hall had ever had.

With the departure of the Director, a temporary replacement was found in Bandmaster Charles Nalden, who became the only man to take the psm examination and then sign his own certificate for having passed. (Others have signed their own certificates but without having actually sat the exam.)

One of Mr Nalden's prime concerns on taking over was to re-open friendly relations with the BBC. According to his own account, this relationship – which had commenced back in 1924 with an appearance on the pre-BBC station 2LO from Savoy Hill – had been soured in the early '30s when Hector Adkins had dragged the programmes offered by Kneller Hall ruthlessly down-market. He cites in particular a 1932 broadcast that included a humorous musical sketch entitled 'A Visit to the Dentist', which Mr Nalden contemptuously refers to as 'drivel'. (It is worth noting in this context that Mr Nalden is adamant that Adko was never entirely converted to the kind of high-brow music advocated by Colonel Somerville; with that Commandant's retirement, he comments, 'the respective commands of Brigadiers Bach and Beethoven also lapsed, their successors in office being Jack Payne and Debroy Somers.')

Whether Mr Nalden is right or not in claiming that Adko was more concerned with finding the lowest common denominator of a mass audience, it is certainly the case that the BBC broadcasts, which had become a regular occurrence by 1931 before tailing off, were not resumed until late 1942. In November of that year an audition at Churchill House, supervised by Dr Dennis Wright and Harry Mortimer, was followed on 16 December by the relay of a programme from the Garrison Theatre, Aldershot. On 6 January the following year, the Band broadcast a 30-minute programme from the BBC studios in Delaware Avenue.

Further engagements were also undertaken, for the School Band was in great demand at the time for morale-boosting spectacles. On 30 May 1943 it combined with the Royal Marines (Chatham) under the direction of Lieutenant Francis to play for a march past the King at Windsor Castle, and in June and August it joined the massed bands of the Aldershot district for concerts co-ordinated by the Commandant that included community singing.

But though life was proceeding, the problem remained of who was to be the permanent replacement for Lt-Col Adkins. There were three men shortlisted for the appointment: Captain J A Thornburrow of the Royal Horse Guards, Bandmaster Meredith Roberts of the Royal Artillery (Portsmouth) and Bandmaster Nalden. Given that Mr Nalden was the acting director, that he had impeccable academic qualifications and that (in his words) 'Colonel Adkins had confided that he was seriously considering recommending me as his successor,' some thought that he had the job sewn up. It was not to be. On 8 May 1943 a War Office letter notified Captain Thornburrow that he was to become Director with effect from 15 June.

But even this was not to last, for on 31 May a further letter cancelled the previous appointment. It is believed that the abrupt reversal was prompted by the War Office's realization that Captain Thornburrow was Lt-Col Adkins' nephew, making his appointment a dangerously sensitive choice; instead he was to remain in his post with the Horse Guards until his death in 1947. The consequence for Kneller was a straight swap, with Mr Nalden departing for the Royal Artillery (Portsmouth), and the former Bandmaster of that regiment, Mr Roberts, being promoted to Lieutenant and appointed Director of Music of the Royal Military College of Music.

Mr Nalden has admitted that he felt 'bitterly disappointed' when he did not get the position, but with the benefit of hindsight he was prepared to admit that he might not have been the right man for the job:

> The reforms which I intended to introduce (had I been given the position) would have had me dubbed a reactionary; for however much I disliked the about-turn which military music had executed under the Adkins regime, there can be no disputing the fact that he instituted a form of entertainment which appealed to a vast section of the general public.

✳

The new Director had a long and honourable service record, having joined The Royal Welsh Fusiliers in 1910, with whom he was awarded a Mons Star during the Great War, and

Aldershot Tattoo 1946, conducted by Lt M Roberts (RMSM)

subsequently he had become Bandmaster of the 10th Royal Hussars (his arrangement of their regimental quick march, 'The Merry Month of May', is still officially played) before moving on to the Artillery. He was also a marked contrast to his predecessor; Lt Roberts was above all else a musician, who placed his strongest emphasis on good music and who eschewed gimmicks in the selection and presentation of programmes.

The first year of his directorship, however, presented other concerns, covering as it did the vast mobilizations necessary for the D-Day offensive – it must have seemed at times that the entirety of the British Army was on the move, with the School Band at Churchill House lying uneasily in the eye of the storm gathering across North-West Europe. Concerts were given at Crowborough, Haywards Heath, Haslemere, Chailey, Cooksbridge and Aldershot and a return performance at Windsor Castle with the Royal Marines, this time under the baton of Captain Vivian Dunn. There were even occasional ventures into the more stable world of civilian music, most notably when the trumpeters were invited to play at a luncheon given by the Musicians Benevolent Association to celebrate the 70th birthday of Sir Henry Wood.

But there was still fighting to be done and a war to be won; even though bandmasters were officially non-combatant, the students were expected to be able to defend themselves and rifle-training was a regular part of life. In August 1944 they also manned various Home Guard Sector Headquarters, having been trained as signallers to be employed in case of emergency. Nonetheless, the tide of the conflict had clearly turned by 1944 and there was an attempt to return to something like normality. In late June some 40 boys from various bands arrived in Aldershot to join an unofficial pupils' course that was to last for approximately six months. And the competition for the Worshipful Company of Musicians' silver medal was still as keen as ever, won that year by Student O Birkin of the Rifle Brigade, though as he only won by four marks a second medal was also awarded to Student K A Elloway of the Dorsetshire Regiment.

If 1944 was sometimes unpredictable, 1945 was all the more so, though this time for all the right reasons. Even before the peace celebrations, the trumpeters returned to Canterbury Cathedral for the enthronement of the new Archbishop (William Temple having died the previous year); it was a service they provided again later in the year for the enthronement of the Bishop of London.

The main events of the year, however, began on 9 May when an audience of over 10,000 attended the Victory in Europe Day concert at Aldershot Football Ground. A month later a band of 80 musicians took part in the Victory Parade in London, with the trumpeters taking part in the Thanksgiving for Preservation Service at Canterbury Cathedral in the presence of the King and Queen.

An 80-strong band was also invited by the Société Les Invalides Prévoyantes to participate in the National Fete in Belgium in July. Concerts were given in Brussels, Namur and Knocke during a three-day tour of the country. For Lt Roberts this was the first overseas visit in his new job; a trip further afield was undertaken in September when he flew out to Italy to inspect the bands then active in that zone.

The future of Army bands had become an issue in defence circles earlier in the year. With the imminent end of hostilities, there was clearly going to be an urgent demand for bandmasters, but this was a need that could be met and 1945 actually saw a record 25 appointments. Much more worrying was the potential collapse in numbers of bandsmen when those who had served pre-war, and had been kept on during the conflict, finally left; with recruitment having been restricted to boys for so long, the fear was that many if not most bands would be unable to rebuild their strength. A conference at the War Office, Hobart House on 16 January 1945 saw the Commandant and Director win approval for a scheme whereby musicians could in future be drawn from the ranks of conscripts. This system continued into peacetime National Service, and enabled bands to draw on a wide range of experienced musicians through the '50s. (Its effects could still be felt many years later – it was not until 1993,

Admin Inspection 1946; believed to be at Malplaquet Barracks, Aldershot (RMSM)

with the retirement of Lt-Col Peter Hannam of the Welsh Guards that the last National Service musician left the Army.)

Further conferences were held to determine the post-war establishment of bands and of the School of Music itself. On 14 June 1945 the new establishment was published: the Commandant was to be a Lieutenant-Colonel (this was upgraded in 1950 to Colonel), the Adjutant/Quartermaster to be a Major and the Director of Music to be a Captain, with the opportunity to rise to Lieutenant-Colonel; two weeks later the Director became Captain Roberts.

One other look towards the future should also be noted. The war had brought various new regiments into existence and in May 1945 the Kneller Hall Band paraded at Buckingham Palace, performing the regimental marches of the Reconnaissance Corps, the Parachute Regiment and the Auxiliary Territorial Service.

While these developments were recorded in official accounts, there is some confusion about the last few months spent by the school in Aldershot. The Diary merely states that: 'The School, after an absence of seven years, returned to Kneller Hall from Churchill House.' Elsewhere, however, the same source refers to a Short Course being held at Malplaquet Barracks in Aldershot from 29 March and 26 July. Most of those there at the time, including Major Jimmy Howe – then a student, later the Director of Music of the Scots Guards – confirm that Malplaquet Barracks were used prior to the return to Kneller Hall. The dates for moving into and out of Malplaquet are unknown. All that is certain is that at some point in 1946 approval was given for the homecoming, and that on 1 November the School moved back to Whitton.

CHAPTER 7

BACK
HOME

THE SCHOOL BAND CONDUCTED BY CAPT JEAN MacDOWELL, C.1953 (RMSM)

The Richmond and Twickenham Times dated 2 September 1939, the day before war was declared, had carried a lengthy report under the by-line 'Keynote' of the previous Wednesday's concert, attended by some 1200 members of the public. Pieces played at that final performance included Student W J Hickman's march 'The Sphinx' and works by Massanet, Bridge, Sullivan and Wagner as well as Col Somerville's bête noire, the 'William Tell' overture. It also featured the singing of Douglas Taylor, a baritone who had travelled from Yorkshire for the occasion, and whose c.v. included an appearance at the Hollywood Bowl. Most impressively of all, there had been several numbers in which the band was accompanied by Student R Hurst playing the Hammond Organ, an instrument that had only been invented some four years earlier.

In all this there was nothing to suggest the turmoil to come. Indeed the report ends with the programme for the following week's concert, whilst the correspondent comments that 'nothing seemed more remote than a crisis'. He describes a scene of idyllic, almost elegiac, tranquillity:

> Chancing to look behind me, I saw the moon shining brilliantly in a sky of dense dark blue, between two slight wisps of white cloud, while in the near foreground was the graceful outline of a branching silver birch silhouetted above a string of vari-coloured electric lights.

The piece concludes that 'music matters a great deal to the Army and just as much to the vastly larger number of the civil population. Music and the practice of music should not be scrapped whenever big trouble occurs.' In the event, of course, it almost was scrapped, and certainly for the local population of Whitton, it disappeared altogether from Kneller Hall.

When the School did return in 1946, it was not to the peaceful haven of pastoral bliss that had so soothed 'Keynote' in 1939. In fact the state of Kneller Hall came as something of a shock to those who been pupils there pre-war. It had been taken over by the General Headquarters Home Forces in 1939 and was used in that capacity throughout the hostilities, including a brief period of occupation by Lord Gort, formerly commander of the British Expeditionary Force and one of the few Allied leaders to emerge from the 1939-40 European campaign with any honour. A report in *The Times* many years later even mentions Kneller Hall as being 'the centre from which the Battle of Britain was fought', though the full extent of the wartime operations is far from clear.

In August 1945, following the surrender of Japan, a new use was found for the Hall, and it became a Civil Resettlement Unit, designed to help former prisoners of war re-adjust to peace and to a country that had changed so much since they had last been at home (it should be remembered that many of the prisoners taken in Asia had served overseas for some years even prior to 1939). A maximum of 250 such men could be accommodated on a course that lasted for between four and six weeks and which provided psycho-logical counselling, education and above all training and preparation for civilian employment; in recognition of this latter priority, the centre was renamed the Civil Recruitment Unit, under which title it ran through to 1946. So successful was the initiative that a Civil Recruitment Unit Extension Scheme was later added, as a kind of out-patients depart-ment to provide assistance for veterans living locally.

Because the emphasis of the course was civilian (even allowing for wives and families to attend) Kneller Hall was effectively demilitarized. Amongst other innovations a temporary cinema, theatre and dance hall were erected in the grounds – though the cinema at least was not quite as temporary as intended, for it was still there in the '50s.

By the time that Kneller Hall resumed its normal function, therefore, there had been many changes to the physical environment. The grounds that had been kept in such immaculate condition during the Adkins era were now in a terrible state, and even the lake had dwindled to little more than a pond. There were further new structures to be found on the playing field adjacent to the Commandant's lawn where a circle of Nissen huts with a central wash-house had been erected – again these were supposedly temporary and, it was promised, would be demolished soon, though again they survived, to be used as living accommodation for pupils until the two new blocks were built in 1957.

And the four guns that had stood in front of the main building, relics of previous conflicts, had disappeared at some stage, never to return. Possibly they had been com-mandeered in the wake of Dunkirk when, with so much of the British Army's equipment abandoned in France, there was a desperate need for just about anything that looked like a piece of artillery.

Nonetheless the School had to continue functioning and, though no concerts were held in 1946, there was a season

Sketches of Professors' teaching rooms and of individual practice in living accommodation, 1948
(RMSM)

the following year. On 7 May the first concert since 1939 was attended by an audience of 447 (the total for the season was 26,330):

1. March   'Canada Overseas'   Std J M Gayfer
   conducted by the composer   Mus Bac LRAM

2. Overture   'The Magic Flute'   Mozart
   conductor: Std L P Smith SCM

3. Waltz   'Espana   Waldtenfel
   conductor: BSM G L Bradbury

4. Piccolo solo   'Picaroon'   Green
   soloists: BSM G L Bradbury,
   Pupils L Marks, J S MacLean
   & J C Hewgill
   conductor: Std R Bashford

5.	Excerpts from	'The Song of Norway' conductor: Std J Plant	Grieg
6.	Two pieces	a) 'Sinfonietta' conductor: Std E Jeanes	Curzon
		b) 'The Grasshopper's Dance' conductor: Std R Watkins	Bucalosssi
7.	Selection	'Merrie England' conductor: Std H Balshaw	German
8.	Xylophone solo	'On The Track' soloist: Std A Kelly conductor: Std C H Pike	Simpson
9.		'Slavonic Rhapsody No. 1' conductor: Std T G Prue	Friedmann
		'Rule Britannia' 'God Save The King'	

On this programme are some of the great names of post-war military music: Major Ted Jeanes of The Blues, Captain Cliff Pike of the Royal Signals, Captain Roy Watkins of the Royal Tank Regiment and Lt-Col Rodney Bashford, later Director of Music of Kneller Hall. It was a particularly rich era for Army musicians; others studying at the School around this time included Bill Lemon, Jimmy Howe, Arthur Kenney, Trevor Sharpe and Des Walker.

Many of the students had seen active service during the war and had earned promotion in the field that would not otherwise have been available to them, with the result that the immediate post-war classes were for the most part senior to classes from other times. Typical was Ted Crowcroft, who had been a professional trumpet-player before joining the Royal Artillery (Salisbury Plain) Band in 1940. He had gone on to serve with the Eighth Army in Africa, rising to WO1 and – having been invalided in 1943 – to take over the Royal Artillery (Middle East) Band. He became a student in 1948 and eventually rose to the rank of Captain as Director of Music of the WRAC.

An alternative war experience was that of Keith Boulding, one of the finest cornetists the Army has ever known. He enlisted into the Band of the Royal Army Medical Corps at the age of 15 in 1939 and spent the war years with that band, joining the students course in 1947. Mr Boulding went on to become a Lieutenant-Colonel in the Royal Signals, but those who heard him at the time still remember his cornet solos at Kneller Hall concerts, often performed from the top of the main building, whilst the band accompanied him on

Presentation of bass drum belonging to Dan Godfrey's Band, 1947. Mr Godfrey's grand-daughter in centre, Mayor and Mayoress of Twickenham on either side.
(RMSM)

the bandstand; a particular public favourite was an arrangement of 'Alice Blue Gown', written for him for Student Ted Moon (later Bandmaster of the Ugandan Police).

❄

With such an outstanding intake of students, the routine at Kneller Hall gradually resumed the appearance of stability. On 27 September 1947 the first post-war Garden Party was held on the Commandant's lawn, whilst a further indication of the return to peacetime operations came with the performance of seventeen trumpeters (including Ted Crowcroft) at the wedding of Princess Elizabeth to The Duke of Edinburgh in November; a similar appearance was made at the service celebrating the Silver Wedding Anniversary of the King and Queen at St Paul's Cathedral the following year. 1948 also saw the making of the film *The King's Musick*, much of which was recorded at Kneller Hall, and which was released to a generally favourable critical and public response, both in Britain and overseas.

For Meredith Roberts this was a period that was both rewarding and stressful. Amongst the highpoints, he was awarded the MBE in June 1948 and on 29 July promoted to Major. During the same time he undertook a tour of band inspections in Germany, which was so hectic that – combined with all his other commitments – it proved too much for his constitution; he was taken into hospital, and for nearly four months Major Tommy Chandler (who had retired from the Welsh Guards earlier in the year) stepped in as temporary Director.

That summer, Kneller Hall was visited by Military Attachés and Representatives from eighteen nations – at the request of the War Office, clearly keen to show off the institution – and by the King of Thailand. More unusual was the visit in July 1949 of Major-General Milton Baker, the Commandant of the Valley Forge Military Academy in America. Kneller Hall has often been asked to find bandmasters and directors of music for countries historically close to Britain, but America has traditionally kept its military music to itself; in this instance, however, General Baker had been unable to find a suitable American candidate as Academy Bandmaster, and seemed happy with the choice of Bandmaster D Feltham of the Oxfordshire & Buckinghamshire Light Infantry.

(It is worth noting, however, that there had been one man

who had taken the influence of Kneller Hall to America the previous century: Arthur A Clappe had left the School in the early 1870s to become Bandmaster of the 3rd Battalion, King's Royal Rifle Corps before being appointed Bandmaster of the Governor-General's Band in Ottawa and subsequently moving on to a similar post at West Point Academy in the States.)

After the upheavals of the war and the inevitable period of readjustment that followed, there was at last something of a new beginning in 1950. To start with, the new decade dawned with a new member of staff on the strength: Bandmaster E R Wragg, formerly of the 5th Royal Inniskilling Dragoon Guards, had been appointed on 19 December 1949 as the first ever Bandmaster of Kneller Hall, a post designed to provide an assistant to the Director of Music. Mr Wragg stayed for less than eighteen months, being offered the post of Director of Music in the Royal Canadian Army, but fortunately a highly suitable replacement was found in George Stunell.

RAEC Instructor teaching in a Nissen hut, 1954 (RMSM)

Mr Stunell had been appointed Bandmaster of the 1st Battalion, The Suffolk Regiment early in 1940 and had later been transferred to the Royal Army Education Corps. Arriving at Kneller Hall in 1949 as an instructor, he proved to be a brilliant teacher who was responsible for helping many future bandmasters through the Army First Class Education examination. Although he too did not remain long as School Bandmaster, soon moving on to the Royal Military Academy, Sandhurst, Mr Stunell built on Mr Wragg's contribution, and between them these two established the post as an important and enduring part of the School's establishment.

The Army too was undergoing changes, and in 1950 the Band and Trumpets of Kneller Hall gave a concert at the Royal Albert Hall with a guest appearance by the Band of the Women's Royal Army Corps, under Bandmaster F A G Goddard; this was the debut public appearance of the new women's band. Not all of the School's pupils could be accommodated in the band, but the scale of the production can be judged by the fact that the first movement of Mozart's Clarinet Concerto featured 24 clarinettists, led by Trevor Sharpe. Other pieces played included work by Walton, Borodin, Elgar, Rimsky-Korsakov, Haydn and Tchaikovsky, suggesting that the musical standards called for by Commandant J C Somerville nearly thirty years earlier were still being met. (The organ for the concert was played by Captain F L Stratham, Director of Music of the Welsh Guards.)

A more surprising premiere came with the first performance of the Kneller Hall march. It seems extraordinary that it took nearly a century of existence for the School to acquire its own march but, though there had been talk for some time of replacing 'Rule Britannia' (which was traditionally played at the end of concerts), it was not until 1950 that two tunes were selected and approved: 'Blow Away The Morning Dew' and 'Near London Town'. Major Roberts made an arrangement of the pieces, explaining that the titles referred to the dew on the Kneller Hall field where students and pupils stood for individual practice and to the proximity of Whitton to the capital. The new march was debuted on 26 July.

It was in 1950 too that the title of Student was amended to Student Bandmaster, with the NCO badges of rank replaced by a lyre surmounting the word 'Student' in scroll. The following year the pre-war 'Frocks RMSM' dress for student bandmasters was declared obsolete and replaced with a new uniform:

No. 1 Dress Infantry (Royal Regiments) with the following embellishments:

- (a) Buttons of pre-war design
- (b) Badges of rank to consist of Bandmasters' Lyre with the word 'Student' in scroll underneath
- (c) Shoulder straps to be edged with gold piping
- (d) Crimson waist strap
- (e) RMSM Cap Badge
- (f) Yellow Dress Cord

Permission is granted for gold aiguilettes to be worn in lieu of yellow dress cord if desired.

These changes may not have been of immense significance in themselves, but they were of a piece with the transformation that the whole country was undergoing at a time when the wartime restrictions were being thrown off. Perhaps the most profound development of all in the wider society was the advent of television, an innovation which affected Kneller Hall at an early stage, with the televising of the weekly concert on 19 July 1950.

At the time, however, the most powerful symbol of the new era was the Festival of Britain, staged in 1951. The band and trumpets played at St Paul's Cathedral on 3 May for the opening of the Festival, and the following day at the official opening of the South Bank site. Both ceremonies were attended by the King and Queen.

The last years that 'Taffy' Roberts spent at Kneller Hall saw a clutch of other firsts: an appearance by the band and trumpeters in the Royal Tournament at Earls Court in 1951 (they returned the following year), the arrival of the first female student with Captain J B MacDowell of the WRAC starting the course in 1952, and the attendance of nine Gurkha students later in that year.

But 1952, of course, was dominated by the death of George VI and the accession to the throne of Elizabeth II. Kneller Hall provided 20 trumpeters for the Coronation Service in Westminster Abbey on 2 June 1953, a further 30 trumpeters opposite the entrance to the Abbey to sound fanfares for the arrival and departure of the Queen, and a band of 75 to play in Parliament Square. The following month the Director of Music – now Lieutenant-Colonel Roberts – and the trumpeters took part in the royal visit to Wales and headed the procession at the Water Pageant.

In the Coronation Honours List Lt-Col Roberts was awarded the MVO, a fitting tribute to an outstanding military musician who was due to retire at the beginning of the next year.

❄

Perhaps the greatest tribute to Lt-Col Roberts' period as Director came with the choice of his successor. When he had been appointed back in 1943 he had, like his predecessors, been a regimental bandmaster, but the post had by now become so important – particularly in regard to the inspections of bands – that it was decided that it should in future by occupied by one of the Army's senior directors of music.

To this end the War Office called upon the judgement of Lt-Col Roberts and of the directors of the ten major staff bands: Major Albert Lemoine, Major David McBain, Lt-Col Owen Geary, Major Alf Young, Captain John Judd, Lt-Col Fred Harris, Major Douglas Pope, Major Sam Rhodes, Captain 'Jiggs' Jaeger and Captain Leslie Stratham. It was the first and only time that such an appointment board was convened, but it could hardly have had a more impressive composition: this was perhaps the greatest group of senior musicians that the Army has ever had. It is also perhaps significant that five of the group – Meredith Roberts, Albert Lemoine, Sam Rhodes, Owen Geary and Alf Young – had all been in the same student class, in the Sommerville-Adkins era.

Like the Cardinals gathering in Rome to choose a new Pope, this distinguished group was expected to nominate one of their own number as the new director. The result was a great deal of lobbying and factionalism, as Major Young told his band clerk, the then Lance-Corporal Turner. After a day of discussion, Major Young returned to his band confident that his favoured candidate, Major Rhodes, had won sufficient support to be chosen. The next day, however, Lt-Col Geary telephoned to say that there had been a change of mind by some of the directors and that Captain Jaeger

Retirement dinner for Commander and Adjutant, 1951. David McBain second from left, Meredith Roberts extreme right (D YOUNG)

Maj M Roberts (N ROBERTS)

was now emerging as a rival; like Major Rhodes, Captain Jaeger had a Bachelor of Music degree, but he was younger (he had earlier become the youngest ever Guards Director, taking over the Irish Guards at just thirty-five) and a more charismatic personality. Perhaps fearing the appointment of someone who might potentially stay as long and be as dominant as Lt-Col Adkins, Major Young's grouping threw their weight behind a compromise candidate, Major McBain. Following a further meeting, Major McBain was finally elected.

To many in military music circles, the choice was something of a surprise. Though he had led the bands of the King's Royal Rifle Corps, the Royal Artillery (Mounted) and The Blues, and was a man of immense practical experience, Major McBain lacked the academic qualifications of his rivals, had no reputation as a composer and was the only director of music without a psm, having passed only four of the requisite five subjects. Despite the doubts and misgivings, however, David McBain was to prove one of the finest and most respected directors of music that Kneller Hall has ever known.

CHAPTER 8

CENTENARY

CENTENARY 1957. HM THE QUEEN WITH COL A ABEL-SMITH (RMSM)

The personality of the Director of Music has always had a major impact in determining the atmosphere at Kneller Hall, and the arrival of David McBain undoubtedly marked the dawning of a new era. He was a well built, imposing figure who had never lost his Scottish accent and made no attempt to conceal it. With a military moustache and a dignified bearing, and always immaculately dressed, he was every inch a soldier; he also passed his love of the Army on to his three sons, who all rose to the rank of Lieutenant-Colonel, with The Royal Scots, The King's Own Scottish Borderers and The Light Infantry.

One of Col McBain's first tasks as Director was to appoint a replacement for George Hart, who had moved to the Light Infantry Brigade, thus leaving the post of School Bandmaster vacant. The choice fell to Rodney Bashford, then Bandmaster of the 17th/21st Lancers and a man who had formerly played first horn in the King's Royal Rifle Corps Band, when David McBain was Bandmaster. Re-united again, they made a formidable team that was to influence the School for years to come.

Soon afterwards there was a further change in the senior staff of Kneller Hall with the arrival in January 1955 of Colonel A Abel-Smith as Commandant. Again he was to make a significant contribution to the style of the School, largely in his case through his apparent non-involvement; evidently finding the Director to be more than capable of running the day-to-day establishment, Col Abel-Smith was – at least as far as the student body was concerned – a seldom glimpsed presence, content not to intervene directly.

The ease with which the Commandant was able to work with his Director was reflected in their inspections of bands. Where previously each inspection had taken an entire day, Col Abel-Smith and Col McBain from the outset were clearly determined not to waste time: a ten-day tour of Germany in March 1956, for example, saw them visiting a total of thirteen bands. The same approach prevailed even after Col Abel-Smith's departure, as evidenced by one trip to the North-East of England in 1959: the bands of the 3rd Carabiniers, under Bandmaster Mick Price, and of the 4th/7th Royal Dragoon Guards under Ray Courtnell, were inspected in the morning, after which the Director and Commandant made a quick dash to Barnard Castle to inspect the 15th/19th The King's Royal Hussars (Bandmaster Gordon Turner) in the afternoon, before returning to Twickenham in the evening. (All three bandmasters, coincidentally, had originally come from the Royal Engineers, Chatham.)

The major concern of Col Abel-Smith's time, however, was the 1957 commemoration of the centenary of the School's foundation. The celebrations commenced on 1 March with a Dinner and Ball held in London, followed two days later by a Service of Commemoration in the School Chapel, with an address by the Rev R Yale, Assistant Chaplain-General of Eastern Command.

A week of concerts in June saw the major bands of all three services playing at Kneller Hall in acknowledgement of the beneficial effect that the School had had on military music generally in Britain. The week started with a performance on the afternoon of Saturday 8 June by the massed military bands of the Royal Artillery, the Royal Engineers and the Royal Signals, followed in the evening by an orchestral concert by the same three bands – one of the very few occasions on which the three senior corps in the British Army have come together for such a performance. Later in the week there were concerts by the massed bands of the Royal Marines School of Music and the Royal Air Force, by the massed bands of the Household Brigade and by the massed bands of the Aldershot District. The series of performances culminated on 16 June with an open-air Service of Thanksgiving.

Running concurrently with this week of celebration, there was an exhibition of 'military music, instruments, books, manuscripts, medals &c.' held at Kneller Hall, an exhibition that grew out of the founding some eight years earlier of the School Museum.

Twelve days after the Thanksgiving Service the Queen visited Kneller Hall, where she unveiled a plaque for the centenary of the institution created by her distant relative, which reads:

This stone was unveiled

by

Her Majesty Queen Elizabeth II

on

28th June 1957

to commemorate

the founding of the School

by

H.R.H. The Duke of Cambridge

in

March 1857

The unveiling was followed by the official opening of two new accommodation blocks which had been built to house the pupils (though in fact these were not ready for use until the following April, when a new cookhouse and dining hall were also inaugurated), and by the Queen's attendance at the Annual Garden Party, where the following programme was played:

Concert March	'Welcome the Queen'	Bliss
	Student/Bandmaster C V Wright, ARCM	
Overture	'Vanity Fair'	Fletcher
	Student/Bandmaster F G Firth	
Suite	'Summer Days'	Coates
	Student/Bandmaster W J Best, ARCM	
Centenary March	'HRH The Duke of Cambridge'	Arnold
Fantasy	'Songs of the Gael'	O'Donnell
Waltz	'Festive Days'	Ancliffe
	Student/Bandmaster J Offord	
Suite in F		Holst

  1) March (Morris Dance)   2) Song without Words
  3) Blacksmith's Song   4) Fantasia on the Dargason
        Student/Bandmaster A Pinkney, ARCM

Ballet Music	'Pineapple Poll'	Sullivan-Mackerras
	Student/Bandmaster G Turner, ARCM	
March	'Pomp and Circumstance No. 1'	Elgar
	Student/Bandmaster C V Wright, ARCM	

The entire occasion was a resounding success and the following message was subsequently received by the Commandant from Buckingham Palace:

> I greatly enjoyed my visit to Kneller Hall this afternoon and was much pleased to have the opportunity of listening to the Band and inspecting the Staff and Students of the Royal Military School of Music. Please convey my warm congratulations to the Musicians and to all Ranks under your command, together with my best wishes on the occasion of the Centenary which you are celebrating this year.

Further recognition of Kneller Hall's contribution to music came with the giving of various awards to Col McBain: HonRAM from the Royal Academy of Music, FGSM from the Guildhall School of Music and HonFTCL from Trinity College, London.

Mr Percy Grainger conducting the School Band, 1957 (RMSM)

Though these honorary awards were made on the occasion of the Centenary, they also reflected the high esteem in which Col McBain was held in musical circles. He too was anxious to maintain the good relations that had been built over the years between Kneller Hall and the world of music in London. During his time as Director one of the first guest conductors at a summer concert was Sir Arthur Bliss, the Master of the Queen's Music, and in 1958 he introduced a custom of having prizes awarded on Prize Day by a musician rather than a senior officer; that year the guest of honour was Sir Ernest Bullock, Director of the Royal College of Music, whilst 1960 saw Sir Arthur Bliss return to the School for the occasion.

One of those who had done much to confer musical respectability on Kneller Hall had been Ralph Vaughan Williams, and it was thus appropriate that the trumpeters were invited to play at the Westminster Abbey Memorial Service for the great composer in September 1958; the Commandant also attended, representing the Secretary of State

Prize Day 1961. L-R: Lt-Col D McBain, Sir Arthur Bliss, BM T Le M Sharpe, Col RE Loder, Maj RD Pitt (RMSM)

for War. The trumpeters returned to the Abbey for a happier occasion two years later, playing fanfares composed by Sir Arthur Bliss for the wedding of Princess Margaret and Anthony Armstrong-Jones.

These engagements represented the formal state functions of Kneller Hall, but during this era too there were less traditional events. In the late '50s the first long playing records were made by the Band – a compilation of the more famous regimental marches, followed by a programme of music taken from Gilbert and Sullivan's Savoy operas. There were also frequent broadcasts on radio and television on such variety programmes as 'Billy Cotton's Band Show', and the late '50s saw too an appearance by the trumpeters at the first of the famous concerts staged by Gerard Hoffnung.

In May 1959 Mr Bashford was commissioned and appointed Director of Music of the Royal Armoured Corps at Bovington. His replacement as School Bandmaster was Trevor Sharpe of The Buffs, another of those who had been students in the immediate post-War years under Major Roberts. He did not remain as long in his post as his predecessor (though he did receive the MBE during his time) for within two years he was again succeeding Rodney Bashford, this time at the RAC. The new Bandmaster, appointed in 1961, was Bob Spencer of the Queen's Dragoon Guards.

1961 was also the year of another important departure from Kneller Hall with the retirement of Col McBain. There had been some doubts expressed at the commencement of his period as Director, but he had proved to be an outstanding success. Certainly it is difficult to think of anyone else who could have brought such a sense of gravitas to the Centenary celebrations; the fact that they went so smoothly and presented the School to the world in such a positive way remains his memorial.

❄

The new incumbent was Lieutenant-Colonel Basil Hector Brown, who had succeeded David McBain as Director of Music of the Royal Artillery Mounted Band in 1948, and now followed him to Kneller Hall. He was also stepping in the footsteps of another illustrious musician, for he was the nephew of Col Adkins (after whom he had been named Hector), and his appointment brought some satisfaction to those who felt that Captain Thornburrow, another of Col Adkins' nephews, had been unfairly barred from the job

Lt-Col Basil Brown (RMSM)

because of his family connexions; certainly it must have brought some pleasure to Hector Adkins himself, then spending his twilight years in South Africa.

Basil Brown had been an outstanding success in his days as a student at Kneller Hall, winning the coveted Worshipful Company of Musicians Silver Medal. In the years since he had built a reputation as not only an excellent musician but also one of the finest concert presenters in the Army; one of his ex-bandsmen describes him as 'the ultimate showman', and certainly he was capable of charming the huge audiences he attracted to his performances with just a few words.

Under Col Brown in the '60s the School continued to enhance its status, and much of Col McBain's good work was maintained: the tradition of inviting musicians to be guests of honour, for example, was extended in 1963 to Brigadier H A F Crewdean, Master of the Worshipful Company of Musicians, and in 1968 to Sir Malcolm Sergeant.

Outside engagements too included prestigious events, with the trumpeters in particular much in demand for formal engagements, playing at the consecrations of both Guildford Cathedral and Coventry Cathedral, at the enthronement in 1961 of the new Archbishop of Canterbury and at the memorial service in Westminster Abbey for Dag Hammarskjôld, the Swedish Secretary-General of the United Nations. They also played at Westminster Abbey for services celebrating the independence of various former British colonies: Tanganyika in 1961, Trinidad & Tobago and Uganda in 1962 and Zambia in 1964. And the traditional association with royal weddings was not lost: the trumpeters appeared at the 1963 union of Princess Alexandra of Kent and Angus Ogilvy.

Other ventures of the period included a new album *Nulli Secundis* released in 1963, and a 1966 series of concerts by thirteen major staff bands broadcast from Kneller Hall by the Forces Broadcasting Service. Further broadcasts were made with an appearance on the 1963 BBC TV programme, *Tunes of Glory*, and three years later on the critically acclaimed *Music on Command*, in conjunction with the choir of The Welch Regiment, The Parachute Regiment Steel Drum Band, The Army PT School and Commonwealth Students.

Many in the Army, however, were even more impressed by the appearance of Kneller Hall students on the TV series *Strike a Chord*, a game show in which music students from various colleges challenged the expertise of a panel of professionals. In 1966 the Kneller Hall team of Bob Smith,

Mike Butcher and Ben Titley were the only contestants to beat the experts. The following year Student Bandmasters Bob Smith, Roger Tomlinson and Tony Gomersall repeated the feat, triumphing over the combined knowledge of Ron Goodwin, Dudley Moore and Jack Brymer.

Appearances in films were also made: the full band of 250 players made a film for COI in 1967, and was again featured in a project under the auspices of the National Council of Great Britain.

Larger scale undertakings of the 1960s came with a Gala Concert featuring the whole band at the Royal Albert Hall on 24 June 1962 in aid of the Army Benevolent Fund: this became a regular event, later switching venues to the Festival Hall. Even bigger was the commemoration of the 150th Anniversary of the Battle of Waterloo in 1965, for which a massed band performance was staged on Horse Guards Parade with a total of 1000 musicians.

At Kneller Hall itself, the reconstruction following the war had effectively been completed by the Centenary, and little changed in the physical structure of the place – save for the opening of a new students' mess in 1962 by the Commandant, Col A A N Tuck – until 1967. In that year a new concert hall was built (at a cost of some £50,000) so that indoor performances could be added to the long established programme of summer concerts. On 18 December the first concert of a winter season was staged for the public. The series ran through to March the following year and featured not the full band but performances by the four separate company bands, each comprising 60 players. These events were to become a regular part of School life.

In some ways the most significant development of the era was the return of a Kneller Hall magazine. It had been thirty years since *The Leading Note* had fallen victim to wartime exigencies, but in 1968 a new journal, *Fanfare*, was launched. Privately funded by John Pope, a sub-editor at the *Daily Telegraph*, it has continued through to the present; control of the magazine has now passed entirely into the hands of the School, but Mr Pope continues to advise in his capacity as Editor Emeritus.

The Kneller Hall Diary records that Col Basil Brown OBE ARCM retired on Christmas Day 1968. Nonetheless he was to make one final appearance commanding bands: in 1969 he was the Director of Music for the British Tournament and Tattoo, which toured North America very successfully for three months.

CHAPTER 9

CONSOLIDATION

LT-COL C JAEGER AND THE EARL OF SNOWDEN
AT THE INVESTITURE OF THE PRINCE OF WALES
(RMSM)

The retirement of Lt-Col Basil Brown paved the way for the arrival of Lt-Col C H Jaeger, the man many had tipped for the job some fourteen years earlier. 'Jiggs' Jaeger was one of the outstanding musical talents of the British army in the 20th century and one of its great characters. Having taken over the Band of the Irish Guards in 1949, he had risen to be the Senior Director of Music, Household Division in 1963 – in which capacity he had been responsible for the musical arrangements at the state funeral of Winston Churchill – and had been promoted to Lieutenant-Colonel in 1966.

As a result of having been in such a senior position for so long, Lt-Col Jaeger brought to the School not only his natural ability and aptitude but also a vast experience, particularly in the international field. As a young bandmaster with the 4th Hussars at the end of the war, he had found himself in Austria, where he was invited to conduct the Vienna Symphony Orchestra for a series of five concerts, whilst with the Irish Guards he had played virtually all over the world, touring in North America, South America, Europe, the Far East and Australia. In the period immediately prior to taking up the position at Kneller Hall, he had taken a sabbatical period, visiting the USA and Germany to broaden his experience still further, and had conducted the Band of the United States Army on the steps of the Capitol in Washington. Even after arriving at Kneller Hall, he still had international commitments to meet, including a visit to Belgrade as the guest of the Yugoslavian army.

Lt-Col Jaeger's talent was also appreciated beyond the world of military music, and simultaneously to his appointment to Kneller Hall he was attached to the Royal College of Music, the Royal Academy of Music and the Royal School of Church Music.

With all this wealth of expertise potentially at the School's disposal, it is all the more tragic that Lt-Col Jaeger's period in office should have been so abruptly cut short; on 27 September 1970, less than two years after his appointment, he died at his home in Whitton. What he might have achieved at Kneller Hall had he secured the nomination in 1954 and enjoyed 16 years at the helm of military music will forever remain open to speculation.

During his brief tenure however, he did preside over some spectacular events. In June 1969 he was the Director of Music for the first of the Military Music Pageants at Wembley, revisiting the scene of Hector Adkins' greatest moment. Four years later, under Jiggs' successor, the School again played at Wembley, providing a band of 200 together with 24 trumpeters as part of what was then the largest massed bands event ever staged in Britain, with 1600 musicians.

On 22 May 1970 the full Band of 250 players gave a concert at the Royal Festival Hall, with the School's professor of clarinet, Jack Brymer, appearing as guest soloist performing a rendition of Rossini's 'Theme and Variations for Clarinet' arranged by Jaeger. Also included on the programme was the 'Music for the Investiture of His Royal Highness, The Prince of Wales'. At the Investiture itself the preceding year, Lt-Col Jaeger had conducted the Kneller Hall trumpeters from a position high up in one of Caernavon Castle's towers. And Lt-Col Jaeger's last ever appearance – the day before he died – was conducting the Grenadier and Welsh Guards, together with the antiphonal trumpets, at the Investiture in the Lower Ward of Windsor Castle during the Windsor Festival.

Less than a month after the premature death of Lt-Col Jaeger, his successor as Senior Director of Music, Household Division, Major Rodney Bashford of the Grenadier Guards, was promoted to Lieutenant-Colonel and appointed to Kneller Hall.

The new incumbent came from a family of military musicians. His grandfather, George Bashford, had joined the 17th Lancers as a bandboy back in the 1840s, whilst his father, also named George, had attended the Kneller Hall pupil's course as a trombone-player and at some point had been Band Sergeant of the 21st Lancers. Rodney Bashford himself had joined the King's Royal Rifle Corps in 1932 as a french horn player and seen active service during the Second World War, being taken prisoner at Calais during the 2nd Battalion's heroic defence of that port in 1940. (His father, incidentally, had died at Abbeville in 1916.) In 1950 he had been appointed Bandmaster of the 17th/21st Lancers – the regiment amalgamated from his grandfather's and father's units – before his first stint at Kneller Hall as the School Bandmaster.

Amongst Lt-Col Bashford's engagements were as guest conductor for the 1971 Military Music Pageant at Wembley, where he returned with the Band two years later, as director of music for the Westminster Festival of Music in 1970 and 1972. In November 1971 the Band played at a concert in Chester Castle to mark the closing down of Western Command, whilst the trumpeters played that month for the opening of the National Army Museum in Chelsea.

Changes were still being made to the physical structure of Kneller Hall. In the late 1960s, as we have seen, a Concert Hall had been built and on 2 March 1972 a new practice room adjoining the hall, named The Morris Hall after Brigadier Charles Morris (Commandant 1967-70), was opened. Less than a fortnight later, however, disaster struck. Some 150 bandsmen were in the Concert Hall rehearsing for a charity concert when the roof – which was being re-felted – began to cave in. Fortunately the band, which was just about to start 'Fanfare and Soliloquy for Band', was not playing at the time, otherwise the noise might not have been heard. Sixteen men were treated in hospital, including one knocked out by a falling girder, and several instruments were damaged, but the potential loss had been much greater than the reality. As the *Daily Telegraph* reported:

> Student Bandmaster Alan Clarke of the Lancashire Regiment had just raised his baton when a loud creak came from the roof. The bandsmen dropped their instruments and ran for cover as tons of masonry came crashing from the roof.

The wreckage of the new concert hall, 1972 (RMSM)

The Air Dome (RMSM)

The incident was reported through the national press in its usual range of styles, from *The Sun*'s jokey 'Army Band Brings The House Down' to *The Times* with its more sober 'Bandsmen escape in Kneller Hall roof fall'. The latter included an account from Edwin Brooks, who had been working on the roof: 'The roof just gave way beneath me. I fell 25ft and landed on top of a bandsman but neither of us was injured.'

The School, having been thus left without an indoor concert venue, was obliged to consider how best to construct a replacement. As a temporary solution an inflatable air dome costing £7000 was erected on 14 July 1972, though the problems inherent in such a structure were clear even before its erection, with the Adjutant, Col F A D Betts, commenting that 'inflation at the stated time will depend on weather conditions, as a semi-inflated air structure is susceptible to high winds.' Queries over planning permission were partly answered by the fact that the air dome was coloured green and therefore blended in with the sports field, but the more serious problem remained of the acoustics of the new hall – many were convinced that the best effect was gained by having the band inside with the audience listening from the outside, which somewhat defeated the point of the thing existing at all.

Despite these internal structural problems, Kneller Hall

113

continued to add to the ceremonial life of the nation, with the trumpeters playing at Westminster Abbey twice in 1972 – firstly for a memorial service for the late King of Denmark and then for a Service to commemorate the silver wedding anniversary of the Queen and the Duke of Edinburgh – and again in 1973 for the marriage of Princess Anne and Captain Mark Phillips. For the latter two occasions the Director of Music wrote new fanfares: 'The Silver Trumpets' and 'Toccata for Trumpets' respectively.

During this period, too, the School acquired one of its most sympathetic Commandants, Colonel R G Style, who was appointed in November 1971. Commissioned into the Coldstream Guards, he was a keen amateur musician who played both the piano and saxophone. During the Second World War he had served in France, where he had formed a dance band for the famous Guards Armoured Division. Even more impressively, he could boast of having played piano with the great Edmundo Ros at the Coconut Grove in London.

The Director officially retired on 18 June 1974, though he had been given a memorable send-off earlier in the year. Following the annual conference for directors of music and band-masters, Lt-Col Bashford and his wife, Beryl, were driven in a decorated Land-Rover from Kneller Hall along a route lined with the four company bands; the music played reflected his service: the quick marches of the King's Royal Rifle Corps, the 17th/21st Lancers, the Grenadier Guards and the School.

But though no longer serving, Lt-Col Bashford did not leave Kneller Hall, continuing to be employed at the School in the newly created post of Assistant Director of Music. He was also the Professor of Conducting and Curator of the Museum, and even found himself called back to active service in 1976 when his old regiment, the Grenadier Guards, were without a director of music; Lt-Col Bashford returned to uniform for several months as acting director. In 1982 he did finally retire, but he remains a familiar and important figure at Kneller Hall, taking a great interest in the School museum and archives. He was awarded the OBE in the 1974 Queen's Birthday Honours.

Lt-Col R Bashford (RMSM)

With Lt-Col Bashford installed as Assistant, the post of Director of Music was awarded to Major Trevor Sharpe, a fine musician who had distinguished himself both as regimental bandmaster of The Buffs and then as Director of Music of the Coldstream Guards; he remains one of the few military musicians whose name is regularly seen on television, thanks to his arrangement of the closing theme of Dad's Army. As had now become standard, Major Sharpe was promoted to Lieutenant-Colonel on his appointment. He was to remain as Director for four years and then, like Lt-Col Bashford, to take up a civilian post at Kneller Hall, in his case as Professor of Instrumentation, in which capacity he continued until finally retiring in March 1988.

Between them Rodney Bashford and Trevor Sharpe have had a greater influence on the music of the British Army than anyone since Hector Adkins; both were and still are prolific arrangers and composers, whose works continue to be played regularly, whilst virtually every current bandmaster or director has served under one or other of them at some point in their career.

Memories of the era of the late Dr Adkins were stirred early in Lt-Col Sharpe's period as Director, when Imogen Holst – who had presented the prizes two years earlier – returned to the School for a televised Grand Concert on 17 July 1974, at which she conducted her father's 'Suite in Eb'. The prizes that year were presented by the widow of another of Kneller Hall's old friends, Ursula Vaughan Williams.

Other engagements in 1974 included a programme at Westminster Hall, featuring Rodney Bashford's arrangement of Verdi's 'Requiem' for band and choir, an appearance by the trumpets at the Albert Hall for the St Cecilia Concert and a concert on 30 November at the Royal Festival Hall. That year too saw the first ever visit of the Inspectorate of Army Bands to the Gurkha Staff Band, during a trip to the Far East. Student Bandmaster Hastabahadur Thapa of the Gurkhas was also to score a significant first in 1974 when he was awarded the MBE by the Queen.

1975 saw a visit by Lt-Col Sharpe to Dundee University to lecture and conduct, and a concert at Kneller Hall by the massed bands of the Foot Guards, but it was principally notable as the start of three years dominated by anniversaries and celebrations. In April a brass ensemble played at St George's Chapel at Windsor to celebrate the 500th Anniversary in a service attended by the Queen and many other members of the royal family, whilst the trumpeters played at the Albert Hall to mark 150 years since the opening of the

Stockton-Darlington railway, the world's first passenger rail service; for the latter occasion an original fanfare was composed by Malcolm Arnold.

The following year was, of course, the Bicentennial of American Independence and, in a spirit of forgiving past disagreements, Lt-Col Sharpe flew to America to direct the British contribution to the celebrations, whilst the trumpeters took part in a service at Westminster Abbey.

Lt-Col T Le M Sharpe (RMSM)

These events were, for Kneller Hall, effectively a warm-up for the big occasion of the late '70s: the Queen's Silver Jubilee. The Band and Trumpets were in great demand throughout 1977, performing at a huge number of events and venues, including the Royal British Legion Festival in Margate, the BBC's *Friday Night is Music Night*, Portsmouth Guildhall, Glasgow Cathedral, Covent Garden, the BBC Light Music Festival at the Royal Festival Hall, the Royal Jubilee Service at Westminster Abbey, a Thanksgiving Service at St Paul's Cathedral, and Yorke House in Twickenham. The Band and Trumpeters also performed at a Grand Spectacular in the Albert Hall on 7 June, alongside the bands of The Royal Artillery (Woolwich), the Grenadier Guards, the Irish Guards and the 3rd Battalion Royal Green Jackets, the pipes and drums of the Scots Guards, the Caledonian Scottish Dancers and the London Symphony Orchestra; for this occasion a new work for string band by the celebrated composer John Gardiner was commissioned.

Even more spectacular was the Silver Jubilee Pageant at Wembley over three nights from 30 June to 2 July, which was produced by Major Aubrey Jackman and Lt-Col Sharpe and which was the largest massed band pageant ever staged in Britain with a total strength of 2014 performers drawn from all three services.

Despite these major commitments, life at the School – both in terms of teaching and performing – continued much as normal. The final concert of the 1976 season featured Lieutenant-Colonel Sir Vivian Dunn, formerly Director of Music in the Royal Marines, whilst a visit by the Band of St Olaf's (Minnesota) in January 1977 saw a combined concert given at the Fairfield Hall, Croydon with Imogen Holst as guest conductor.

The Silver Jubilee had a generally positive effect on the public perception of military bands and 1978 began with a flurry of performances by the School Band in collaboration with various other ensembles: with the Concordia Choir at the Fairfield Hall in January, with the Irish and Welsh Guards

The School Band, 1934 (RMSM)

at the Dome in Brighton and with the London Welsh Choir in the Acton Hill Methodist Chapel.

On 1 March 1978 a further combined concert was staged, this time in the Kneller Hall air dome that had been erected on a temporary basis some six years earlier. The occasion was the retirement from active service of Lt-Col Sharpe and the performers included the Band of the Women's Royal Army Corps, the pianist Robert Docker, solo singers Patsy Gilland and Robert Bowman and the Ambrosian Singers. Ten days later Lt-Col Sharpe handed over the baton to Lieutenant-Colonel George Evans of The Blues and Royals.

CHAPTER 10

THE DEMISE OF
REGIMENTAL BANDS

VISIT OF HM THE QUEEN TO KNELLER HALL, 1990 (RMSM)

The next fifteen years were to produce a transformation more rapid and more radical than military music had yet seen, precipitated by the election in 1979 of a government even more set on reform than that of Gladstone in the late-19th century. Since the Great War the position of the Army – and by implication its bands – had endured a steady erosion by cost-conscious politicians; in the 1980 and '90s the drip of cuts was to turn into a torrent.

In 1978, however, there was no immediate sign of the changes to come; the main concern was the confusion caused by the advent of Lt-Col Evans since the School Bandmaster at the time was also called Mr Evans. The latter, however, soon departed to be commissioned into the King's Own Royal Border Regiment, becoming the Director of Music of The King's Division, and was succeeded by Bandmaster Roger Swift of the Queen's Royal Irish Hussars. Other major changes in personnel during this period came with the arrival of a new commandant in Colonel Everard Ivor Windsor-Clive (late Coldstream Guards) and a new adjutant in the form of Major Selwyn Charles Seelhoff (of The Royal Scots Dragoon Guards).

Col Windsor-Clive – known affectionately as 'Lump' – had a reputation as a motorbike fanatic and it became a familiar sight to see him roaring out the gates dressed in biker's leathers, often accompanied by other enthusiasts, both students and pupils. When he retired in 1980, he was escorted from the School by a motorcade of the most powerful machines that could be found, with Col Windsor-Clive trailing along behind in a Landrover. At a farewell concert on 19 June, the Corps of Drums of his old regiment, the Coldstream Guards, marched on to join the Kneller Hall Band to play some of his favourite tunes: 'Pretty Polly Oliver', 'San Lorenzo', 'Radetsky March' and finally his regimental march, 'Milanollo'.

The successful running of an institution like Kneller Hall naturally depends not only upon such senior personnel as the Commandant and Director of Music, but also upon the endeavours of a whole host of less celebrated individuals. The School gardener of this era, for example, was Mr Roberts who could proudly boast that, 'We produced 4000 plants in 1978'; his efforts were rewarded that year with the award of a Britain in Bloom Certificate of Excellence from the London Tourist Board.

Another such 'back-of-house' hero was Charlie Brown, the cook of the Students' Mess who had joined the staff of the School back in 1946, whilst it was still at Aldershot; when he finally retired in 1980, a social evening was organized for some of the many hundreds of friends he had made over the years. He was made a life member of the Students' Mess and was presented with a colour television set (complete with a two year licence) and a clock, both of which were inscribed: 'To Charlie Brown for 35 years' loyal service, from directors of music, bandmasters serving and retired and ex-members of the Students' Mess and Staff of The Royal Military School of Music.'

Lt-Col G Evans (RMSM)

1980 also saw a less lamented departure from School life with the closing down of the air dome, which had been erected on a temporary basis in 1972 and which had some-how survived for the best part of a decade. The inadequacy of the structure had been amply demonstrated time and again over the years: the 1978 winter concert season, for example, had been reduced to just two performances, since the cold weather had precluded any further use, and even on those occasions a battery of very powerful heaters had to be left on all day just to bring the temperature up to an endurable level. The fact that the air dome was disappearing was celebrated by the Commandant, Colonel Tim Beath, in the 1981 edition of *Fanfare*, though he also pointed out that this didn't solve the problem of the lack of an indoor venue:

> After eight years of valiant but barely satisfactory service this vast, panting, hippopotamus-like creature, increasingly held together by masking tape and with an ailing heart (or engine) has finally been borne away. The trouble is that its demise has not coincided with the birth of our new Concert Hall. The cold eye of the Financier lit upon the plans and in the present straightened circumstances that was that – for the time being. We live in the hope that this essential new facility will soon be given the go-ahead, but for the present the facilities at the Home of Military Music are slim indeed; we have even had to apply for authority to use the former RSMs Quarter as practice rooms.

Regrettably – but one has to add, somewhat predictably – the School is at the time of writing this history still obliged to 'live in hope'. The plans for a new concert hall, to which Col Beath refers, were approved in 1978 with completion estimated to be three and a half to four years away; a start has yet to be made.

Despite the inability of Kneller Hall to provide an indoor concert venue appropriate for its status as a musical insti-tution, prestigious and highly successful performances continued through the late '70s and early '80s. In 1978 Lt-Col Evans, who thirty years earlier had been the principal cornet-player in the Morris Motors Band under the baton of the great Harry Mortimer, invited his former conductor to the School to be the guest of honour at prize-giving.

More controversial was his endorsement of the moving of the summer concerts from Wednesday to Thursday in 1980. The argument behind the move was that the strength of television schedules on Wednesday nights, including the popular 'Sportsnight', was proving too strong for Kneller Hall to compete with. The average audience for the 1980 season was some 100 up on the previous year, which certainly seemed to support the decision, but there was much dissatisfaction amongst regular concert-goers at such tampering with tradition; typical was the reaction of Clive Folkard, a regular attender who, writing in the 1995 edition of Fanfare about his memories of 33 years of Kneller Hall concerts, noted: 'During Lt-Col Evans' time we had those peculiar years of the Thursday concerts, but happily in 1984 they reverted to Wednesdays.'

Std BM J Huggins (J HUGGINS)

Outside engagements during the 1978-79 course year included concerts at the Central Hall, Westminster and at the Royal Festival Hall, the latter in aid of the Army Benevolent Fund, and an appearance in the Military Music Pageant at Wembley.

The trumpeters and percussionists returned to Wembley two years later for the 1981 Military Music Pageant, when 1600 musicians under Lt-Col Evans played in the presence of Prince Charles and Lady Diana Spencer. When the couple were married in July of that year, the trumpeters were again invited to play for a royal wedding, whilst the next day a celebratory summer concert at Kneller Hall attracted an audience of nearly 6000.

The following year – 1982 – saw the retirement of Lt-Col Evans to become instead the Assistant Director of Music, following the simultaneous retirement of Rodney Bashford; his successor as Chief Instructor (as the post had now been re-named) was Lieutenant-Colonel Duncan Beat of the Scots Guards. In his final months, however, there was one last task for Lt-Col Evans: overseeing the celebration of the 125th anniversary of the founding of the School. A highly successful Gala Concert was staged at the Royal Festival Hall, featuring a new work for wind band, 'The Duke of Cambridge Suite', commissioned from Adrian Cruft with financial contributions made by the Arts Council, the Household Division and the London Borough of Richmond-on-Thames. Also performed that night was a composition by Geoff Richards, 'The Soldier', which had commissioned by the Army Benevolent Fund. The fact that the programme included these premieres of new music was, of course, in the best traditions of Kneller Hall.

✳

Even while these celebrations of Kneller Hall were being staged, however, the music of the British Army was being thrown into the most tempestuous period in its history. The recession of the early '80s had seen an attempt by the Conservative government to find economies in public spending, and military bands were clearly seen as a possible area of saving. In 1981 a decision was taken to cut staffing levels by 550 to leave an overall establishment of just under 2000 musicians – a reduction of more than 20%. On 8 December the cuts were announced: one Royal Artillery band, one Royal Engineers band, the Royal Army Medical Corps Staff Band and the Royal Military Academy Band (Sandhurst) were to be abolished; the three bands of the Royal Tank Regiment were all to lose their directors of music and their staff band status, being reduced to just a bandmaster and 21 men; the Foot Guards and the Gurkhas were to lose ten men each and most of the other bands were to be reduced by six, seven or eight musicians. In response the Queen's Regiment, the Royal Regiment of Fusiliers, the Light Infantry, the Royal Green Jackets and the Parachute Regiment all opted to have two bands apiece of 35 men, rather than endure three bands of 22 musicians each.

These reductions were severe enough, but far from being a one-off cut, they were merely the beginning of what was to be a thorough and continuing programme of slashing the music of the Army. In 1985 the posts of divisional directors of music in the infantry – established in the early '70s to oversee the work of the depots, supervise recruiting and act as musical staff officers to the divisional brigadiers – were axed, to be replaced by just two directorial posts, to be known as Director of Music Infantry North and Director of Music Infantry South. On a brighter note, the Royal Armoured Corps managed to retain its one and only Director of Music.

These sweeping changes were even to threaten the School itself. We have seen that as long ago as 1934 proposals had

Kneller Hall trumpeters in State Dress at Coronation of Edward VII, 1901 (RMSM)

been put forward to vacate Kneller Hall and relocate the School; nearly fifty years later, in 1981, the issue was to return to the political agenda with a finance-driven decision to merge the schools of music for the three services – Kneller Hall, the Royal Marines school at Deal and the RAF school at Uxbridge. What ensued was a five-and-a-half year struggle to defend the independence of the services that ended in 1987 with a decision that the Royal Military School of Music was to remain at Kneller Hall.

Normally such processes are hidden under the cloak of government secrecy, but in this case we have the benefit of an account by the former civil servant, Clive Ponting, who was part of the Ministry of Defence team charged with finding savings in the music budget. In his fascinating and revealing book *Whitehall: Tragedy and Farce* Mr Ponting records his impressions on first visiting Kneller Hall:

> By the 1980s it was run-down and decaying. The old house needed repair, the barracks accommodation was spartan, music practice facilities were almost non-existent, there was no concert hall, and worst of all it was directly under the flight path to Heathrow with large jets passing overhead every few minutes. It was just about the worst possible place to put a music school …

Neither Uxbridge nor Deal met with Ministry approval either and a new site was proposed at Eastney near Portsmouth, in an old Royal Marines barracks. (It will be remembered that it was at Eastney that a Royal Navy School of Music had been founded under the guidance of Edward Stretton in 1903.) Mr Ponting had no doubt that this was the most cost-effective option, but his report on the subject coincided with the Argentinian invasion of the Falkland Islands, and any decision was inevitably postponed until the cessation of hostilities.

When the proposal was re-floated in late 1982, a fierce opposition to the suggested closure of Kneller Hall was mounted on two fronts: pressure was brought behind the scenes by the senior levels of the Army, whilst a public campaign was led in the House of Commons by the local Conservative MP for Twickenham, Toby Jessel, who declared, 'I will fight like a tiger to save Kneller Hall'. This was no over-statement; by 1987 Mr Jessel could proudly boast that he had spoken in support of Kneller Hall seventeen times in the Commons, had met Defence Ministers on eleven occasions, had rallied the support of 164 Conservative MPs for an Early Day Motion and had presented a petition of over 18,000 signatures to the Prime Minister. His endeavours were recognized by all sides in the debate from Margaret Thatcher, who

Sir Yehudi Menuhin and Std BM John Brigden, pictured at a performance of Beethoven's Ninth Symphony in Strasbourg, featuring Mr Brigden playing the Jingling Johnny from the Kneller Hall Museum (J BRIDGEN)

congratulated him 'on his valiant campaign in support of the excellent military bands', right through to Mr Ponting, who commented pointedly that he was 'remarkably well briefed'.

Whilst these campaigns were progressing, it appears that there was an equally intense political struggle at Cabinet level. Michael Heseltine, who had become the Secretary of State for Defence in the wake of the Falklands War, chose to reject the Eastney proposal in favour of an Army site in Edinburgh, presumably as part of a continuing attempt to spread government money around the country. Meanwhile, however, the Chief Secretary to the Treasury, Peter Rees, was espousing the cause of Deal – where coincidentally he was the local MP – as the location of any unified School.

Deal it was that in December 1984 ultimately emerged as the government's choice. It was a muddled decision and one that was clearly based more on political considerations than on the quality of music that a new School would be able to offer the Services, or even on the initial objective of saving money, as *The Times* reported on 5 December 1985:

> Sir Clive Whitmore, Permanent Secretary at the Ministry of Defence, told the public accounts committee last night that there was little difference between the cost of continuing with the existing schools and going to Deal.
>
> Under highly critical cross examination from angry Conservative and Labour MPs, he indicated standards at the new school could drop.

Mr Ponting went even further, estimating that, rather than saving four million pounds, the Deal option would actually cost two and a half million more.

Those who opposed the proposal were in no mood to yield to the confused messages emanating from the MoD; further representations were made within the defence establishment, whilst the public debate continued to rumble on for more than two years, with Mr Jessel in particular seizing every opportunity to raise the issue. In February 1986 the Public Accounts Committee produced its report, which was highly critical of the Government's flawed economic arguments, and it became evident that the battle was turning in the School's favour; Lord Tregarne, the Minister of State for Defence Support, told the House of Lords:

It is already clear that the original date of 1988 for establishing a Defence School of Music can no longer be met, and I can tell your Lordships, therefore, that there is no prospect of Kneller Hall or the RAF school of music at Uxbridge being closed before 1989.

The following month the government threw in the towel altogether, and announced that Kneller Hall had been reprieved. Amongst the many guests at that year's concert season were George Younger and Roger Freeman – the Defence Ministers responsible for taking the decision – Viscount Tonypandy, the former Speaker of the House of Commons, and of course Mr Jessel.

Elsewhere, however, there was no such reprieve: the junior bandsmen training establishments at the divisional depots were closed down and replaced by an Army Junior School of Music (AJSM) at Bovington, where previously only the junior bandsmen of the Royal Armoured Corps had been trained, and an AJSM at Pirbright.

1988 saw changes at the top of the School hierarchy. Colonel Sandy Ewing, who as Commandant had fought extremely hard to keep Kneller Hall open, handed over to Colonel David Lewis of the Welsh Guards, whilst Malcolm Torrent, The King's Own Royal Border Regiment, was appointed School Bandmaster in place of Geoff Kingston, who was commissioned to take up one of the recently created posts as Director of Music, Infantry North. Even more significant was the arrival of Lieutenant-Colonel Frank Renton as Director of Music.

Lt-Col Renton was to do more than perhaps anyone else in recent years to modernize the School. He was anxious to keep the best in military music, but also believed that changes needed to be made to re-establish Kneller Hall's leading position in the military and wind band world. Within months of his appointment he had set in motion the building of a comprehensive reference library, a facility that astonishingly had not existed previously, and was successful in eliciting the financial support of Boosey & Hawkes for the purchase of new books and scores. He also used his powers of persuasion to convince the Royal Tournament to donate £5000 over a period of five years to help commission new works for bands, and then set up a tri-Service committee chaired by himself to select suitable composers to approach.

Elsewhere he adapted the Bandmasters' Examination to include such projects as arranging a selection of popular tunes, recognizing the need to stay in touch with the general public. Perhaps most innovative of all, he added a computer laboratory to the facilities at the School; this proved to be an enormous and rapid success, so that by 1991 he could report that:

> The computer room, and its two Midi workstations, is now in constant use. Many of our students are computer-literate and a great deal of composition work is now done directly on the computer.

This development has of course continued in the years since.

Partly this rapid programme of modernization stemmed from Lt-Col Renton's experience beyond the world of military bands. Having started his career as a cornetist with the famous Black Dyke Mills Band, he had always maintained his links with a wider musical environment, and was in great demand as a conductor, adjudicator and broadcaster in the brass band world; for some considerable time he was the professional conductor of the Grimethorpe Colliery Band, and was also extremely active with BASWE (the British Association of Symphonic Bands and Wind Ensembles), eventually being elected Chairman in the early '90s.

Even whilst at Kneller Hall, Lt-Col Renton continued these commitments, somehow fitting in appearances as guest conductor with the Concert and Radio Orchestras of the BBC, the British Concert Orchestra and the British Chamber Orchestra, and presenting programmes on Radio 2 and Radio 3. In the brass band world he steered the Scottish Band, Kirkentilloch, to the European Championships and helped Grimethorpe win the BBC Band of the Year Award. He also conducted the first performance of the Army Concert Orchestra – an outfit that brought together 50 musicians from some 15 regiments and corps – in a charity variety show at the Palace Theatre, Manchester. And though he was never a prolific composer, he emulated Lt-Col Sharpe's achievement in writing the theme tune to a successful BBC comedy series: in his case a fife and drum march for *The Brittas Empire*.

The connexions with the wider musical scene were reciprocated. Guests at the 1988 Prize Day were Ursula Vaughan Williams and Sir Vivian Dunn, with Sir Malcolm Arnold attending the following year. Another of Britain's most distinguished contemporary composers, Arthur

Butterworth, visited in 1991 to examine the Somerville Competition, whilst the prizes that year were presented by Lady Trudy Bliss, widow of Sir Arthur. Other visitors during this period included Donald Hunsberger, the conductor of the Eastman Wind Ensemble of America, Timothy Reynish, principal horn player with Sadler's Wells and the City of Birmingham Symphony Orchestra, and two of the country's leading instrumentalists: the percussionist Evelyn Glennie and the trumpeter Maurice Murphy.

Apart from these musical guests, the highlights of the period were two royal visits in 1990. In June Prince Charles attended a concert, when the guest band was that of the Brigade of Gurkhas, whilst in November the Queen returned for the first time since the centenary celebrations of 1957. Curiously both occasions coincided with other events: Prince Charles travelled to Kneller Hall straight from the Queen Mother's 90th Birthday Parade, whilst the Queen's visit was slightly disrupted by the resignation that day of Mrs Thatcher as Prime Minister, necessitating a certain number of messages being posted back and forth to Whitehall.

One other event from Lt-Col Renton's era should be mentioned. To commemorate the 175th anniversary in 1988 of the Fort Henry Guard in Baltimore USA, a competition

The School Band led by BM T Griffiths marching to Twickenham to see the film The Queen's Music, 1971 (RMSM)

was held with the challenge of writing a march in the style of the 18th century that could be played by the fife and drum corps at Fort Henry. The winner was Student Bandmaster Colin Hicks, subsequently Bandmaster of the King's Royal Hussars; the prize was £500 plus a trip to Fort Henry.

For some time Lt-Col Renton had felt some conflict between his service career and the possibilities offered by civilian music. Having achieved all that there was to achieve in the Army, and having unmistakably left his imprint upon Kneller Hall, he decided to leave to concentrate on a career as a broadcaster, conductor and teacher of conducting. His successor was Lieutenant-Colonel Roger Tomlinson of The Blues and Royals, who took over in September 1992.

❄

By this stage the uncertainties that had plagued the military music establishment for the last decade had returned in force with the government's Options For Change programme in 1991. The need for a re-appraisal of Britain's defences in the aftermath of the Cold War was unquestionable, but for the bands and for Kneller Hall it was an unwelcome further stage of disruption.

The School was affected almost immediately. The AJSMs were closed and permanent staff from them were brought to Kneller Hall to fill posts that had previously been the responsibility of students: Bandmasters Dave Thompson, John Winterflood and Tony Hodgetts arrived as company commanders and instructors, and WO2 'Spike' Wilkins became Band Sergeant Major. Meanwhile Captain Malcolm Torrent succeeded Kevin Lamb as Deputy Chief Instructor, and Ian McEllicott of the Royal Green Jackets was appointed School Bandmaster. In addition, a new department called Training and Development – comprising Captain Lamb, Bandmaster Dennis Burton and WO2 Roy McCluskey – was set up to supervise training of musicians throughout the Army.

These modifications were but the start of yet another phase of the transformation facing Army bands. In July 1991 a Review Committee was formed to consider the future organization of military music, chaired by Brigadier Charles Bond, who had taken over as Commandant earlier in the year. Writing in the 1992 edition of *Fanfare*, Brigadier Bond reported that the restructuring was:

to be carried out in two Phases. The aim of Phase One was to identify options for the reorganization of bands within a new ceiling of 1400 all ranks (a reduction of 591 from the current overall strength) and to make recommendations on their size and cap badge affiliation.

Phase Two was to concentrate on improvements to the career management of musicians.

The major recommendation amongst the Committee's findings, and certainly the one that was to have the most immediate impact on the public debate, was that the minimum establishment for a dismounted band should be 41 men. The logical consequence was that while the sixteen larger staff bands would face little change, the 53 smaller regimental bands would cease to exist. The Report of the Committee therefore concluded that the number of bands should be reduced from 69 to just 32: eight State Bands (comprising two mounted Household Cavalry bands of 35 apiece, and the Royal Artillery and five Foot Guards Bands of 49 each) and 24 others, each of 41, to be allocated to the various regiments and corps.

Perhaps equally far reaching was the recommendation that a single authority should be established at Kneller Hall, responsible for recruitment and staffing duties that had previously been the preserve of commanding officers, Personnel Branches and Manning & Record Offices. Kneller Hall would also take over band finances and the coordination of band engagements. To assist this process it was suggested that the Commandant should be appointed Director (or Inspector) of Army Music and be given a staff to carry out the new duties.

The Report naturally became the centre of a heated debate within the military establishment, with the major line of division coming not surprisingly between those who would be largely unaffected if the proposals were to be implemented and those in the Royal Armoured Corps and the Infantry who were likely to lose their bands. With the parties concerned unable to reach agreement, and with new requirements due to come from other Committees looking into Army Medical Services and into Public Duties, the Adjutant General called for a further report in March 1992.

Three options emerged from the new enquiry. First, to continue along the path that had been suggested by the earlier Report; second, to allocate bands in varying sizes from 31 men upwards to as many regiments as resources would allow; third, to create a Band Corps which, though

Final concert of Lt-Col F Renton
(M FARNHAM)

suitable in musical terms, would not necessarily give the Army the support it required. This third option was subsequently to return to the agenda, but the first tangible effect of Options For Change came in the form of a signal issued on 16 March 1993, in which the Chief of the General Staff announced that the following structure was to be implemented:

Corps/Regiment/Division	Number of bands	Size	Musicians
Household Cavalry	2	35	70
Royal Armoured Corps	4	35	140
Royal Artillery	1	49	49
Royal Engineers	1	35	35
Royal Signals	1	35	35
Foot Guards	5	49	245
Scottish Division	2	35	70
Queen's Division	2	35	70
King's Division	2	35	70
Prince of Wales's Division	2	35	70
Light Division	1	49	49
Parachute Regiment	1	35	35
Royal Irish Regiment	1	35	35
Army Air Corps	1	35	35
REME	1	35	35
Royal Logistic Corps	1	35	35
Adjutant General's Corps	1	35	35
Total	29		1113

There was also to be an establishment of 20 musicians to be employed at Kneller Hall, giving a total of 1133 musicians in the British Army. Prior to Options For Change the overall establishment had been 1991; prior to the 1981 reductions it had been over 2500. In just twelve years therefore the number of military musicians had been slashed by more than 50%.

Looking back still further, to the golden age of both the Empire and of musical music, one finds the War Office letter of 1876 quoted in Chapter Three, which talked of nearly 120 Kneller Hall bandmasters and 35 civilians, a total of over 150 bands; even then there were more to come at the end of the century when many infantry regiments added third and fourth battalions, reaching a total of more than 200 bands. There were now to be just 29, plus the Gurkhas.

Figures for bandsmen are more difficult to obtain, but the bands of last century were undoubtedly larger on average than those of today: as long ago as the 1860s the Artillery could boast an establishment of 80 (albeit including 14 boys), the Grenadiers had 57 men, whilst even a line cavalry regiment such as the 4th Hussars was 39-strong.

Inevitably the numbers of bands and bandsmen have declined over the years, as the technology of the Army has changed and its overseas commitments have reduced – none but the most blinkered traditionalist could expect anything else – but perhaps the most distressing aspect of the early '90s cuts was the loss of regimental bands. The Household Cavalry, the Foot Guards and the Corps retained their bands, but a proud regiment such as The Royal Fusiliers – to take but one example – has suffered heavily: within a period of 75 years The Royal Fusiliers went from having four bands of their own to sharing two bands with the other regiments of The Queen's Division. And elsewhere there was something particularly poignant about the final parade of the Band of The Duke of Wellington's Regiment; recently returned from active service in Bosnia, the men were presented with United Nations medals for their work, prior to marching off for the last time.

The only surviving regimental bands beyond the Guards were those of The Parachute Regiment and the Royal Irish Regiment – though it should be noted that the Royal Armoured Corps did assign one of their four bands specifically to the Royal Tank Regiment (and even kept the first RTR battle honour of Cambrai alive in its title).

It is hard to escape the conclusion that the cuts in numbers were motivated more by political considerations than by any genuine desire to achieve efficiencies. Mr Jessel's plea in the House of Commons in 1987 that 'if it ain't bust, don't fix it,' unfortunately came some years too late – most of the damage had been done in 1982 – and in any event few of his colleagues seemed inclined to heed his advice.

It is worth at this stage remembering the evolution of military music. Bands had originally been created by cavalry regiments and by infantry battalions in response to their own needs. Ignoring the strictures of the central authorities at Horse Guards, regimental officers had recognized that music could assist recruitment, could raise spirits within a fighting body of men and could ease the relationship between the Army and an often downright hostile civilian population; the consequence was the rapid spread of music throughout the Army in the late 18th and early 19th century. Initially those in power over the military had been suspicious of the development and had tried to minimize its

Finale of Kneller Hall concert
(M FARNHAM)

effects; then in the mid 19th century, as we have seen, the Duke of Cambridge had led the move to institutionalize the decentralized, almost anarchical structures that had been built. Over a period of more than a century Kneller Hall had worked to create a situation where British military music had, like the British Army itself, come to be seen throughout the world as the standard to which others would aspire; now it seemed as though that very success was threatening the existence of military music as it had come to be. The fact that bands had become – for civilians, and therefore for politicians – the most visible symbol of the armed forces in a country that has always prided itself on the separation of military and political functions made music even more vulnerable than other sections of the Army.

In 1915 at the height of the Great War Rudyard Kipling, a man who perhaps understood the British Army better than any other poet or philosopher, said:

> No one, not even the adjutant can say for certain where the soul of the battalion lives, but the expression of that soul is most often found in the band. A wise and sympathetic bandmaster – and the masters I have met have been that – can lift a battalion out of depression, cheer it up in sickness, and steady and recall it to itself in times of almost unendurable stress.

Henceforth the battalions would have to do without such support. One could only hope that the soul of the Army would survive despite the politicians.

CHAPTER 11

ANOTHER NEW BEGINNING

MR TOBY JESSEL MP CONDUCTING ON THE KNELLER HALL BANDSTAND, 1996
(RICHMOND & TWICKENHAM TIMES)

The changes that Kneller Hall and the wider world of military music experienced over the 1980s and '90s were as revolutionary as the centralization process instigated by the Duke of Cambridge, and such profound transformations in well-loved and long-established institutions tend to leave one looking nostalgically back to better days. As we approach the new millenium, however, there is also a great deal about which a military band enthusiast can feel optimistic, and it seems appropriate to end this history of Kneller Hall with a brief account of the more beneficial changes that have occurred in recent years.

In the first place, the contribution of Brigadier Charles Bond can hardly be over-stated. Arriving as Commandant in May 1991 he was plunged immediately into the maelstrom of Options For Change; as he commented the following year: 'Since my arrival at Kneller Hall, I have been involved – sadly to the exclusion of all else – in both the future of Army Bands and the future training and career progression of Army musicians.' Perhaps no Commandant since Major-General Whitmore himself had faced so many external pressures and demands on his time, and Brigadier Bond's ability to turn adversity into progressive thinking was remarkable.

The loss of regimental bands, whilst regrettable, has to be balanced against the situation that prevailed prior to the Options For Change programme. The 1982 reductions had left many line bands with just 21 musicians – a staffing level that all agreed was intolerable. In the context of these pitifully small ensembles a decision to establish a minimum of 35 men was a sensible and necessary rationalization; those bands that do now exist are at least in a position to acquit themselves in the best traditions of Army music.

Furthermore, although the number of bands was reduced, the number of directors of music was actually increased, since every band was to include both a director and a bandmaster in its establishment; this also meant that bands such as those of the Foot Guards now had the benefit for the first time of a bandmaster on their strength to support the director. The possibilities for promotion, both to bandmaster and thence to director of music, have not diminished with the changes, and the opportunities for talented musicians to rise within the structure are arguably as strong today as they have ever been.

Perhaps the greatest change in this context came with the creation of the Corps of Army Music. This, it will be

Col TPB Hoggarth inspecting the Life Guards, 1996. This is believed to be the first ever Kneller Hall inspection conducted on horseback. (RMAM)

remembered, was an option originally floated in 1992; it re-emerged in October 1993 and, following a period of consultation, was adopted in 1994. The first Director of the Corps was Colonel T P B Hoggarth, formerly of the Royal Artillery, who had succeeded Brigadier Bond as Commandant in 1994; in the 1995 edition of *Fanfare* he explained the new concept:

> The logic behind the formation of the Corps has been driven by the need to set in place an efficient administrative arrangement to best direct the recruitment, training and career management of army musicians. This measure had the aim of establishing a coordinated management structure specifically designed to enhance army musicians' careers.

Bandsmen and bandswomen are now therefore members of a separate unit within the Army; at present the cap badges of the various regiments and corps are worn, and the traditional associations remain, but the official status of the musicians is at variance with these allegiances.

Combined with the inauguration of the Corps of Army

Music has come the Director of Army Music, a post that had been mooted in the original report of Options For Change. There had also been a recommendation that he should be given a staff to assist him in his work, and this too has been implemented in recent years. Kneller Hall is now home to no less than six Directors of Music: the Principal Director of Music (Army) with a rank of Lieutenant-Colonel, Senior Instructor (RMSM) in the rank of Major, and four Captains responsible respectively for the Foundation Course, Training & Development, the Bursary Scheme and Projects. These positions are intended to build a team that will exercise ever greater influence on the operations of military music.

Together with the 29 British bands and the Gurkhas (who, unique as ever, have two Directors: one British and one Gurkha) these six posts mean that there are now 36 directors of music in the British Army, more than at any other time. Colonel Hoggarth has stated his intention to increase recruitment amongst the brightest and best young musicians in the country, explaining that he wants 'to tap into the wealth of talent produced by some 56 colleges up and down the country who graduate around 4000 musicians annually'. The enhanced chances of promotion now available should in the course of time assist this effort. Col Hoggarth, building on Brigadier Bond's work, has also placed on record his wish 'to extend an orchestral capacity into all our bands', a welcome re-affirmation of the double-handed tradition within the Army that dates back to the foundation of the Royal Artillery band.

And finally one must turn to Kneller Hall itself. The 1986 reprieve was immediately followed by a refurbishment programme that saw a complete renovation of the building so scathingly described by Mr Ponting on his visit there just a few years earlier. A sum of £2.5m was laid out, with the roof and facings virtually replaced and the balustrade restored; the Queen's visit in November 1990 was partly in recognition of this work, and saw her unveil a brass plaque to commemorate this symbol of the School's survival.

As a final touch, on 5 June 1996, a new bandstand was officially opened. A composite band, conducted by Lt-Col Cliff Ross and comprising serving directors of music, bandmasters and bandsmen in addition to the Kneller Hall Band, performed Sir Malcolm Arnold's centenary march 'HRH The Duke of Cambridge' and a piece that had been specially commissioned by *Fanfare* magazine: 'Pride of

Place' composed by Ray Steadman-Allen. The Band was also conducted by Mr Toby Jessel in a performance of Harold Walters' 'Instant Concert'.

The commitment demonstrated by this injection of government money into the fabric of Kneller Hall was something of a reassurance over the ensuing years, for the future of the School has remained the subject of political attack despite the sterling efforts of the 1980s defence campaign. As recently as 1994, with the new MoD policy document 'Front Line First' suggesting that a new process of change might be attempted, Mr Jessel again initiated an adjournment debate on the future of Kneller Hall. He was answered by the Minister of State for the Armed Forces, Jeremy Hanley, who also happened to be the MP for the neighbouring constituency of Richmond and Barnes; Mr Hanley paid due tribute to the tradition of British military music and cited in particular one of the enduring images of recent times, from the ravages of the former Yugoslavia:

> There could have been no better example of just why [Army bands] are held in such high esteem, and no better demonstration of the skill, dedication and imagination of our Army bandsmen than that incredibly uplifting sight of the Coldstream Guards marching on to the football stadium in Sarajevo … When historians come to chronicle the 20th century, the images of that event will be hard to ignore. I certainly suspect that only a British Army band could have put on such a display.

Nonetheless he also issued a warning that in the continuing review of defence spending 'no sacred cows should be safe from consideration.'

Perhaps most importantly of all, changes have been made to the courses of training at Kneller Hall. A trial bursary scheme has been launched to enable would-be bandsmen to study for two years at college, whilst negotiations with Kingston University have been successfully completed that ally the School to that institution: from 1996 onwards, student bandmasters will graduate from Kneller Hall with a Bachelor of Arts degree in the performing arts. From the later days of Lt-Col Stretton onwards there had been an attempt to encourage students to study for diplomas at civilian colleges to broaden their musical education, and the proportions of graduates with additional qualifications from the Royal College of Music, Guildhall School of Music, Trinity College London and the London College of Music had risen steadily from the end of the Great War onwards:

Lt-Col C Ross after receiving his Honorary Doctorate of Music from Kingston University, 1996
(RMSM)

now for the first time students would graduate with the initials BA after their names.

The size of the military band establishment may have fallen – and may yet fall still further – but the band of the future will have the potential to be better trained and better educated than at any stage in the two-hundred-and-fifty year history of music in the British Army. And Kneller Hall, the brainchild of the Duke of Cambridge, will be even more central to that training and education than ever before.

THE CHAPEL

THE CHAPEL (J TULIP)

Though the exterior of Kneller Hall has remained largely unchanged since the house was rebuilt in 1848, the interior has undergone repeated refurbishment and restructuring to such an extent that it is doubtful whether much of the floor layout or style of decoration remains from Frederick Temple's time. The one major exception to this is the Chapel, which has survived virtually intact, and indeed has been enhanced by its use through the generations and by the history it has acquired.

Situated above the main entrance to the Hall, the Chapel is a double volume room on the first floor, extending into the second with a gallery. The atmosphere is dominated by the striking wood furnishing, essentially plain in style but with simple decorative flourishes, and by the wooden ceiling supported by carved wooden brackets.

The external wall is to the rear and is adorned with stained glass windows, which were added in 1909 (it is probable that the windows, when first constructed, were plain). The central panes have an inscription which reads: 'The funds with which this window was purchased were subscribed by the Bandmasters of the Army past and present.' On either side the windows tell the basic history of the Hall; one panel reads 'On this site was built in 1709 the mansion of Sir Godfrey Kneller, court painter, rebuilt in 1848', and the other reads 'School of Music founded 1857 by General HRH The Duke of Cambridge Commanding in Chief'.

The remainder of the stained glass lists the names of all the Commandants, Directors of Music and Adjutants who have served at Kneller Hall since its inception as a school of music.

The main body of the Chapel comprises rows of wooden pews, arranged so that they face each other in the manner of the choir of a church. Those to the right, as one faces the altar, are headed by a seat reserved for the Commandant, whilst those on the left have a seat for the Director of Music. The walls behind the pews bear a number of plaques, similarly separated by military and musical function according to the senior officer heading each side: thus the right side contains memorial plaques for commandants and the left those of various directors and others.

The following Commandants are commemorated by plaques (reading from the front of the Chapel to the rear):

Lt-Gen Francis Lockyer Whitmore
T B Shaw-Hellier
Col F O Barrington-Foote

Col L M Gregson
Brig-Gen Sir Alfred G Balfour
Brig E H Collins OBE
Col V S Baily OBE
Brig R F Loder CBE
Col F J Jefferson MA
Col D J St J Loftus OBE

These plaques are for the most part similar to each other and very simple in style, forming an orderly display, almost as though on parade. The one exception is that of Lt-Gen Whitmore, which is more decorative and which adds to the bare name and dates the description: 'Commandant of Kneller Hall for the first 23 years of its existence as a Military School of Music.' This, it will be noted, is not strictly accurate since Lt-Col H S Stephens preceeded General Whitmore, if only for a few months.

The plaques on the other side of the Chapel – perhaps appropriately for the more artistic element of the School – are arranged without regard to continuity of design, and are distinctly less orderly in their arrangement. They even lack a unifying theme, for although they are predominantly in memory of Directors of Music, there are other names here as well. The two nearest the altar are straightforward enough and commemorate two of the great Directors – Lt-Col David McBain OBE and Lt-Col Hector E Adkins – but thereafter the regularity ceases.

Above the door is a plaque 'erected by members of the Kneller Hall Club' which is 'In memory of the following Directors of Music and Bandmasters who died as a result of enemy action during World War II 1939-1945':

Major J C Windram, Director of Music of the Coldstream Guards
Bandmaster E E Manley, The East Surrey Regiment
Bandmaster H Jordan, The Royal Scots
Bandmaster W E J Kifford, The Middlesex Regiment
Bandmaster R Ashton, The Gordon Highlanders

Though none of these men had actually served at Kneller Hall, all had of course been students at one time or other, and the bandmasters who subscribed to the memorial were more than conscious of the loss. There must have been a feeling of 'there but for the grace of God go I', for though bandmasters were not officially called upon to fight, there are no guarantees of safety in war. In particular, those bandmasters serving in regiments that were stationed in the Far

Memorial tablet: Carl Mandel
(J TULIP)

East in the late '30s and early '40s took their risks alongside the other men. Thus of the five musicians commemorated in the Chapel, two – Mr Jordan and Mr Kifford – were killed during the Japanese capture of Hong Kong in December 1941, whilst two others died in captivity: Mr Manley as a prisoner-of-war in Japan in January 1945, and Mr Ashton in Siam, working on the notorious railway to Burma. But even those at home were not free from danger: Major Windram was conducting the Coldstream Band for a service in the Guards Chapel, Wellington Barracks, London, on 18 June 1944 when a German V-1 rocket scored a direct hit – amongst the dead were Major Windram and five other members of the Band.

Immediately next to this stone is a memorial which pre-dates the arrival of the School of Music and commemorates a student teacher from Dr Temple's era. It reads:

> Samuel Hunt, student of Kneller Hall who died here 23rd September 1854 aged 21 years. This stone has been erected by his fellow students who knew and loved his simple and affectionate nature.

Regrettably nothing further is known of the unfortunate Mr Hunt.

The next six plaques again commemorate Kneller Hall Directors: Lt-Col Jaeger OBE, Lt-Col Meredith Roberts MVO MBE, Lt-Col A J Stretton MVO, Carl Florian Mandel esq, Charles Cousins and Lt Samuel Charles Griffiths. The inscriptions include, for Mr Mandel: 'This tablet was erected by Band masters of the Army Past and Present as a mark of esteem and regard'; and for Mr Cousins: 'As a mark of esteem and regard the staff Royal Military School of Music the Bandmasters and bandsmen of the Army caused this tablet to be placed here'. The most notable of this group, however, is the stone for Lt-Col Jaeger ('erected by students of 1970-71-72 classes'); it is believed that this is the only plaque behind which lie the ashes of the man commemorated.

Each of the remaining three stones is unique: Francis Hawkins (died 1903) is the only School Sergeant Major represented here, WO1 I Thompson (died 10 July 1981), the only School Bandmaster, and Dominic G A Indelicato (died 7 November 1987), the only pupil. Each of these men died whilst at Kneller Hall, and represented a great loss to the School: Ivor Thompson had been bandmaster of the 13th/18th Royal Hussars for six years and passed away less than six months after his appointment to Kneller Hall, whilst

Memorial Tablet: Charles Cousins (J TULIP)

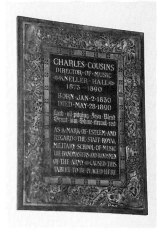

Dominic Indelicato of the Royal Army Ordnance Corps was a talented percussionist who was held in high regard by his fellow pupils – they subscribed to the plaque and many attended a Requiem Mass held for him in Bristol.

The altar and its ornaments, together with other items, are also simple in style. Most have been presented by officers who have served at Kneller Hall; the Diary notes in 1906, for example, that:

> Colonel T B Shaw Hellier [former Commandant] presented a Cross, two large and six small candlesticks for use in the Chapel; also a banner for the Kneller Hall Branch of the Guild of the Holy Standard.

Curiously, however, this last item is crossed out in the typed script and a hand-written comment has been added: 'This banner was removed by Col Shaw Hellier on 19 September 1906.' The story behind this removal is unknown. An alms plate also rests on the altar, donated by the Guild of St Helena in 1910.

In January 1911 a portable stone font, provided from public money, and a brass font ewer, purchased out of Chapel funds, were added, whilst Colonel Gregson (Commandant 1929-31) and his wife Lady Violet Gregson donated the pulpit.

The final major addition to the decoration of the Chapel came after the coronation of the present Queen. The altar cloth used for that coronation service was cut into several pieces and given to the various institutions who participated: a section of the cloth now hangs behind the altar at Kneller Hall.

Choir Gallery, Std BM J Brush conducting rehearsal c.1966
(RMSM)

✳

As a working institution, the Chapel has always played a central part in School life, just as church parade has always been integral to the official military culture beyond. For generations of Army bandmasters, the Kneller Hall Chapel has been an important training ground for their future duties, and for generations of students and pupils it has been a regular part of the weekly routine.

In July 1906 the Right Reverend Bishop J Taylor Smith, the Chaplain General, visited the School and, in the words of the then Commandant, 'expressed himself as more than pleased with the manner in which Divine Service is conducted in Kneller Hall Chapel'. The Chaplain General was to make an early return, conducting a service on 27 September 1906 when he confirmed three students and twenty pupils. These confirmation services appear to have become an annual event, with the numbers increasing each year so that by 1910 a total of forty-one confirmees attended the service. That year too saw a memorial service for Edward VII.

The status of the Chapel was recognized in 1936 when it was officially licensed for the publication of banns and marriages. Interestingly, however, there had already been at least one marriage conducted, for on 10 September 1927 Miss Tarrant – the daughter of the Adjutant, Colonel E V Tarrant – was married in the Chapel; it is believed that this was the first wedding to have been solemnized in the Chapel since the opening of the School.

There were to be other such celebrations. On 26 August 1939, barely a week before the outbreak of war, Donald Keeling was married in the Chapel to Enid Green. Mr Keeling had been appointed Bandmaster of the 1st Battalion, The Seaforth Highlanders less than a month before and was, reported the *Richmond and Twickenham Times*, 'Britain's youngest Army bandmaster', whilst Miss Green was a local woman from Whitton. The paper added that a reception for 130 guests was held in the students' mess.

Thirty years later the Chapel saw a notable first, with the marriage of Robert Smith and Zara Bowness, a couple who had met whilst students at Kneller Hall. Mr Smith was Bandmaster of the 3rd Battalion The Royal Anglian Regiment, and Captain Bowness was Director of Music of the Women's Royal Army Corps: this was the first (and so far the only) union of two serving bandleaders in the British armed services.

Appendix A
THE COMMANDANTS

1857	Captain (brevet Lieutenant-Colonel) Henry Sykes Stephens
1857	Lieutenant-General Francis Locker Whitmore
1880	Colonel Robert Thomas Thompson
1888	Colonel T B Shaw Hellier
1893	Colonel George Brooke Meares
1894	Colonel Farquar Glennie
1900	Colonel Sir F O Barrington Foote
1905	Sir Alfred Granville Balfour
1910	Colonel Cameron Somerville
1920	Colonel John A C Somerville
1925	Colonel Sir Francis N Elphinstone Dalrynple Bart CBE DSO
1929	Colonel Lancelot M Gregson OBE
1931	Colonel Herbert S Jervis MC
1935	Colonel Reginald H R Parminter DSO MC
1939	Colonel John A A Griffin DSO
1940	Lieutenant-Colonel Hector E Adkins D Mus LRAM ARCM
1942	Lieutenant-Colonel A T B Bignold de Cologan TD
1946	Colonel Robert G W Callaghan
1949	Colonel Edmund H Collins OBE
1951	Colonel D C Campbell Miles MBE
1955	Colonel A Abel-Smith OBE
1958	Colonel Robert E Loder
1961	Colonel Alasdair A N Tuck MBE
1964	Colonel Vincent S Bailey OBE
1965	Colonel Henry N Hoare
1967	Colonel Charles Morris CBE
1970	Colonel Francis J Jefferson MA
1973	Colonel R Gerald Style
1975	Colonel Michael ff Woodhead OBE
1978	Colonel Everard I Windsor-Clive
1980	Colonel Tim Beath
1982	Colonel David J St J Loftus OBE
1985	Colonel Charles Ewing OBE
1988	Colonel David Lewis
1991	Brigadier Charles H Bond OBE
1994	Colonel Tim P B Hoggarth

Appendix B
THE DIRECTORS OF MUSIC

Since 1992 the post has been known as Principal Director of Music (Army).

Lt-Col D McBain (RMSM)

1857-1859 SCHALLEHN, Henry. Born 1815 died 1887. Civilian bandmaster 17L 185?-1854; Bandmaster Crystal Palace 1854-1857; Civilian DoM RMSM 1857-1859.

1859-1874 MANDEL, Carl Florian. Professor of Flute, Oboe and Bassoon RMSM 1857-1859; Civilian DoM RMSM 1859; died whilst serving 19/9/74.

1874-1890 COUSINS, Charles. Born 1830 died 1890. Enl 1LG 1848; Sgt (BM) The Bays 30/9/63; Civilian DoM RMSM 31/10/74; died 23/12/90.

1890-1896 GRIFFITHS, Samuel C. Born 1847 died 1896. Enl 2/1 Ft 17/2/62; Sgt (BM) 2/1 Ft 31/3/74; WO (BM) 1/2 Ft 1/7/81; WO (BM) RMC 3/5/90; Lt (DoM) RMSM 24/12/90; died whilst serving 24/3/96.

1896-1921 STRETTON, Arthur John MVO. Born 1863 died 1947. Enl RA (Wool) 12/10/75; WO (BM) 2 Cheshire 2/9/93; Lt (DoM) RMSM 25/3/96; retd 21/9/21 in rank of Lt-Col.

1921-1942 ADKINS, Hector Ernest Mus Doc (Edin) LRAM ARCM psm. Born 1885 died 1963. Enl 2 Glosters 8/5/1900; WO (BM) 2 Suffolk R 8/3/13; Lt (DoM) RMSM 22/9/21; retd 14/4/43 in rank of Lt-Col.

1942-1943 NALDEN, Charles Mus Doc LRAM ARCM psm. Born 1908. Enl RA(Mnt) 31/10/22; WO1 (BM) 2 Foresters 7/4/35; WO1 (Acting DoM) RMSM 1/10/42; WO1 (BM) RA (Port) 26/8/43; retd 17/11/47.

Lt-Col D Beat (RMSM)

1943-1953 ROBERTS, Meredith MVO MBE LRAM ARCM psm. Born 1895 died 1954. Enl 1RWF 25/8/10; WO1 (BM) 10H 18/2/26; WO1 (BM) RA (Port) 24/10/37; Lt (DoM) RMSM 30/8/43; retd 25/11/53 in rank of Lt-Col.

1954-1961 McBAIN, David OBE HonRAM FGSM HonFTCL ARCM psm. Born 1901 died 1963. Enl 2RS 1917; WO1 (BM) 2KRRC 8/11/27; WO1 (BM) RA (Mtd) 12/12/38; Lt (DoM) 11/8/47; Capt (DoM) RHG 14/1/48; Lt-Col (DoM) RMSM 20/1/54; retd 22/4/61.

1961-1968 BROWN, Basil Hector OBE (MBE) ARCM psm. Born 1909. Enl 2 S Stafford R 30/4/23; WO1 (BM) 2 Kings Own R 15/12/48; Lt (DoM) RA (Mtd) 19/1/48; Maj (DoM) RE (Chat) 17/3/58; Lt-Col (DoM) RMSM 23/4/61; retd 21/1/68.

1968-1970   JAEGER, Cecil Harry OBE Mus Bac LRAM ARCM psm. Born 1913 died 1970.   Enl 1 KOYLI 6/10/27; WO1 (BM) 4H 21/7/42; Lt (DoM) RMA (Sand) 6/3/48; Lt (DoM) IG 9/4/49; Snr DoM Bde Gds 1963; Lt-Col (DoM) RMSM 2/12/68; died whilst serving 27/9/70.

1970-1974   BASHFORD, Rodney Bowman OBE LRAM ARCM psm. Born 1917.   For full details see under School Bandmasters.

1974-1978   SHARPE, Trevor Le Mare, LVO OBE (MBE) LRAM ARCM psm.   Born 1921.   For full details see under School Bandmasters.

1978-1983   EVANS, George Edwin OBE ARCM psm.   Born 1926. Enl Ox & Bucks LI 7/12/44; demobbed 1947; re-enl 3rd DG 17/10/49; WO1 (BM) The Royals 28/9/56; Lt (DoM) RA (Mtd) 5/4/66; Capt (DoM) RHG/D 21/6/73; Lt-Col (DoM) RMSM 10/3/78; retd 5/1/83; Ass DoM/Prof Conducting RMSM 1983-91.

1983-1988   BEAT, Duncan Ritchie LVO ARCM psm.   Born 1931. Enl RA (Wool) 8/1/47; WO1 (BM) BW 9/2/59; WO1 (BM) Highland Bde 2/4/65; Capt (DoM) RAOC 14/6/68; Capt (DoM) SG 28/8/74; Lieut-Col (DoM) RMSM 1/12/82; retd 28/2/88; DoM Metropolitan Police 1988.

1988-1992   RENTON, Frank Anthony ARCM psm.   Born 1939. Enl RHG 19/1/59; WO1 (BM) Gordons 29/7/69; WO1 (BM) King's Div Depot (badged DWR) 6/8/76; Capt (DoM) Para Bde 8/5/78; Capt (DoM) RA (Mtd) 10/11/82; Capt (DoM) RA (Alan) 26/7/84; Capt (DoM) RA (Wool) 30/1/85; Lt-Col (DoM) RMSM 7/1/88; retd Sept 1992.

Lt AJ Stretton (RMSM)

1992-1994   TOMLINSON, Roger Grenfell BA FTCL LGSM ARCM psm.   Born 1939.   Enl R Signals 25/2/57; WO1 (BM) A&SH 4/2/69; WO1 (BM) 16/5L 28/12/70; WO1 (BM) PoW Div (badged RWF) 17/2/75; Capt (DoM) RAC Jnr Ldrs (badged 16/5L) 21/2/79; Capt (DoM) RTR (Cam) 20/4/82; Capt (DoM) RAC 1/4/84; Capt (DoM) RHG/D 18/6/86; Lt-Col Principal DoM (Army) 24/8/92; retd 1994.

1994-   ROSS, Clifford James Hon Mus Doc ARCM FISM psm.   Born 1942.   Enl 1 BW 8/4/58; WO1 (BM) Kings Own Border 19/3/73; Capt (DoM) PoW Div (badged RRW) 2/3/81; Capt (DoM) REME 18/11/85; Maj Snr DoM BAOR 3/2/91; Maj (DoM) WG 22/2/93; Lt-Col Principal DoM (Army) 4/7/94.

Lt-ColCH Jaeger (RMSM)

Senior Instructor

1992-1994   WATTS, Stuart Alastair LRAM psm.   Born 1945.   Enl RHG/D 6/9/60; WO1 (BM) 3 R Anglian 14/1/74; WO1 (BM) Queen's Div 1980; Capt (DoM) Para 1/11/82; Capt (DoM) Guards Depot (badged RHG/D) 8/7/85; Capt (DoM) Gurkhas 16/3/87; Capt (DoM) Gren Gds 18/7/88; Maj Snr Instr RMSM 31/8/92; Maj (DoM) WG 7/94.

1992   MAYCOCK, Raymond Edward William LRAM ARCM LmusTCL LGSM psm.   Born 1944.   Enl 1st Bn RRF 21/4/61; WO1 (BM) 4/7DG 9/12/74; WO1 (BM) RA (Wool) 1979; WO1 (BM) BW 6/1/84; Capt (DoM) Para 16/8/85; Capt (Dep Ch Inst) RMSM 27/1/86; Maj (loc) AJSM (Bov) 4/5/87; Capt (DoM) RCT 3/9/90; Maj (DoM) Snr Instr RMSM 7/94.

Appendix C
THE ADJUTANTS/
QUARTERMASTERS

Until 1993 there was a single post of Adjutant/Quartermaster.

1881	Lieutenant R T McIllwham
1889	Captain F H Mahoney
1901	Major J MacLellan Bett
1918	Lieutenant Colonel G Wilson DSO
1922	Major C Henson DCM
1925	Lieutenant Colonel E V Tarrant
1928	Lieutenant Colonel A R Newlins
1934	Major R C Jones
1939-1945	no Adjutant/Quartermaster
1945	Lieutenant Colonel A G Bent MBE MM
1951	Lieutenant Colonel W H Mabbot OBE
1956	Major J Garcia MBE
1959	Lieutenant Colonel R D Pitt OBE
1967	Lieutenant Colonel F A D Betts MBE
1973	Lieutenant Colonel R Maddison MBE
1978	Lieutenant Colonel S C Seelhoff MBE
1983	Major B T Eastwood
1984	Lieutenant Colonel G Oakley MBE
1990	Major J G Savelle MBE
1993	Major R Hicks

Adjutant

1993	Major Jeffries
1995	Lieutenant Colonel M Turner OBE

Appendix D
THE SCHOOL BANDMASTERS

1949-1950   WRAGG, Ernest Reginald ARCM.   Born 1906.   Enl
1Suffolk 16/8/24; WO1 (BM) 5DG 27/3/45; WO1 (BM) RMSM 19/12/49;
Retd 28/5/51; BM 1951 Canadian Army; retd 196?

1950-1953   STUNELL, George Herbert ARCM psm.   Born 1910.
Enl 1 R Sussex R 24/2/27; WO1 (BM) 1 Suffolk R 3/1/40; WO1 Instructor
RAEC (att RMSM) 29/9/49; WO1 (BM) RMSM 29/5/51; Lt (DoM) RMA
25/2/54; retd 30/12/64 rank of Maj.

1953-1954   HART, George Dennis.   Born 1920.   Enl 2 Devon R
4/9/35; WO1 (BM) 1 Rifle Bde 17/9/52; WO1 (BM) RMSM 25/2/54; WO1
(BM) LI Bde 18/8/54; WO1 (BM) Libyan British Military Mission 1/9/55;
WO1 (BM) Aden Protectorate Levies 20/8/59; retd 28/1/62.

1954-1959   BASHFORD, Rodney Bowman OBE LRAM ARCM psm.
Born 1917.   Enl 2 KRRC 2/8/32; WO1 (BM) 17/21L 5/2/50; WO1 (BM)
RMSM 27/10/54; Lt (DoM) RAC JLR (badged 17/21L) 1/9/59; Lt (DoM)
Gren Gds 16/7/60; Snr DoM Household Div 1968; Lt-Col (DoM) RMSM
19/10/70; retd 17/6/74; RO2 (Ass DoM) RMSM 18/6/74.

1959-1961   SHARPE, Trevor Le Mare, LVO OBE (MBE) LRAM ARCM
psm.   Born 1921.   Enl 1 Loyal R 2/9/35; WO1 (BM) The Buffs 4/4/50;
WO1 (BM) RMSM 10/9/59; Lt (DoM) RAC Jnr Ldrs (badged RTR)
26/10/61; Lt (DoM) Coldm Gds 27/7/63; Lt-Col (DoM) RMSM 5/4/74;
retd 11/3/78; Profesor of Instrumentation RMSM 1978-88.

1961-1963   SPENCER, Robert Hamilton, ARCM.   Born 1923 died
1968.   Enl RA (Mtd) 9/2/38; WO1 (BM) KDG 1/10/53; WO1 (BM) QDG
1/1/59; WO1 (BM) RMSM 26/9/61; retd 3/7/63; DoM Hong Kong Police
1/8/63 until death 13/12/68.

1963-1968   MORGAN, Frederick ARCM.   Born 1918.   Enl 2 Bedfs
& Herts R 23/8/33; WO1 (BM) 1 Para 10/3/51; WO1 (BM) RMSM 31/7/63;
Capt (DoM) Brunei Malay Regt 7/68; retd 20/3/73.

BM T Griffiths (RMSM)

1968-1969   TAYLOR, Derek Noel MBE LTCL ARCM psm.   Born
1929.   Enl 1 R Ir Fus /12/44; WO1 (BM) 16/5L 30/9/55; WO1 (BM)
RMSM 5/5/68; Capt (DoM) RMA (Sand) 25/4/69; Capt (DoM) WG 8/74;
retd 19/2/86.

1969-1971   GRIFFITHS, Thomas MBE ARCM psm.   Born 1929.
Enl 1   Lincoln R 7/1/46; WO1 (BM) 2/1/63; WO1 (BM) RMSM 1969;
Capt (DOM) RAC JLR (Bov) (badged 17/21L) 25/11/71; Capt DoM
RAOC 27/8/74; Maj (DoM) JMW Pirbright 7/7/79; retd 13/8/86.

1971-1974   MACKAY, Douglas Hunter LGSM ARCM psm.   Born
1931.   Enl RS 4/12/46; WO1 (BM) The Royals 19/1/66; WO1 (BM)
KOSB 29/3/69; WO1 (BM) RMSM 16/8/71; Capt (DoM) RAC Jnr Ldrs
Regt 4/9/74; Capt (DoM) RA (Alan) 6/3/79; retd 26/7/82 rank of Maj.

1974-1975   JAMES, Stuart Everard Munday ARCM LGSM psm. Born 1932.   Enl 3 Para 18/7/49; WO1 (BM) KSLI 8/1/67; WO1 (BM) 3 LI 10/7/68; WO1 (BM) LI Depot 29/1/74; WO1 (BM)   RMSM 2/9/74; Lt (DoM) Iranian Land Forces 2411/75; A/Maj (DoM) Brunei Malay Regiment 15/12/75; retd 11/4/81.

1975-1976   PLATTS, Trevor ARCM psm.   Born 1936.   Enl 2 Para 18/12/54; WO1 (BM) 1 PWO 22/4/68; WO1 (BM) Yorkshire Bde 8/9/72; WO1 (BM) King's Div 11/9/75; WO1 (BM) RMSM 24/11/75; Capt (DoM) (R Anglian) Queen's Div 8/11/76; Capt (DoM) RTR (Rhine) 2/7/79; retd 5/80.

1976-1979   EVANS, Philip Robertson LTCL AmusLCM psm.   Born 1940.   Enl KSLI 23/9/59; WO1 (BM) 15/19H 1/11/71; WO1 (BM) RMSM 11/10/76; Capt (DoM) King's Own Border (King's Div) 15/5/79; Capt (DoM) RE (Ald) 10/5/82; Capt (DoM) RA (Alan) 24/1/85; Maj (DoM) RE (Chat) 14/3/86; promoted Lt-Col 7/11/89; retd 28/4/95.

1979-1981   SWIFT, Roger Graham LRAM LTCL ARCM psm.   Born 1938.   Enl RE (Ald) 20/1/60; WO1 (BM) QRIH 4/11/74; WO1 (BM) RMSM 4/79; Capt (DoM) HQ Light Div (badged LI) 11/2/81; Capt (DoM) RAOC 1/11/83; Capt (DoM) Coldm Gds 4/11/85; retd 3/9/90 rank of Maj; Professor of Conducting RMSM 1991.

1981   THOMPSON, Ivor.   Born 1944 died 1981.   Enl 3 Para 1/12/59; WO1 (BM) 13/18H 22/3/75; WO1 (BM) RMSM 11/2/81; died 10/7/81 whilst serving.

1981-1985   MARSHALL, David John ARCM LTCL BBCM psm. Born 1944.   Enl SCLI 12/1/60; WO1 (BM) WFR 11/11/75; WO1 (BM) RMSM 8/9/81; Capt DoM RAC (badged RTR) 15/8/85; Capt (DoM) RCT 18/8/87; Capt (DoM) Coldm Gds 4/9/90.

1985-1987   HILLS, Phillip Elven, FLCM psm.   Born 1947.   Enl RA 5/6/63; trans WG 1972; WO1 (BM) 1 Queens 29/6/78; WO1 (BM) Albuhera 31/3/84; WO1 (BM) RMSM 10/9/85; Capt (DoM) Infantry (North) badged BW 2/1/87; Capt Senior DoM BAOR 15/1/88; Capt (DoM) AJSM (Bov) 2/7/88; Cpt (DoM) RA (Alan) 9/10/89; Capt (DoM) Gren Gds 10/8/92; Maj (DoM) 30/9/93.

1987-1988   KINGSTON, Geoffrey Arthur psm.   Born 1949.   Enl Staffords 23/3/64; WO1 (BM) RWF 25/6/79; WO1 (BM) PoW Div 17/12/84; WO1 (BM) RMSM 1987; Capt DoM Inf (N) (badged Kings Own Border 8/12/87; Capt (DoM) RA (Alan) 20/7/92; Capt (DoM) AAC 1/12/93.

1988-1989   TORRENT, Malcom John LGSM LTCL psm.   Born 1950. Enl RA 18/4/68; WO1 (BM) King's Own Border 2/2/81; WO1 (BM) AJSM 26/1/87; WO1 (BM) RMSM 4/1/88; Capt (DoM) AJSM (badged King's Own Border) 18/9/89; Capt (DoM) Course Director RMSM 9/91; Capt (DoM) AGC 14/4/93.

1989-199   OWEN, Robert John ARCM.   Born 1954.   Enl LG 1/10/71; WO1 (BM) QLR 30/4/83; WO1 (BM) AJSM(Bov) 28/4/88; WO1 (BM) RMSM 4/9/89; Capt (DoM) Inf South 13/4/92; Capt (DoM) L Div 6/6/94.

1992-1994   McELLIGOTT, Ian David LRAM ARCM psm.   Born 1957.   Enl RAOC 4/5/74; WO1 (BM) RGJ (Normandy) 17/12/85; WO1 (BM) RMSM 27/4/92; Capt (DoM) Para 6/6/94.

1994-1995   STEWART, Ian.   Born 1955.   Enl 2RGJ 17/6/73; WO1 (BM) QOH 7/1/86; WO1 (BM) RMSM 12/5/94; retd 24/5/95.

Appendix E
THE PROFESSORS

Dates of appointment and retirement are as accurate as records allow. At times there may have been an overlap period not shown in the school ledgers. During the Second World War when the school was situated at Churchill House, Aldershot, virtually all teaching was done by serving bandmasters.

FLUTE

1857-1859	Mr Carl Florian Mandel
1859-1866	Mr Hartmann
1866-1890	Mr Henry Chapman
1890-1918	Mr J Wilcocke
1918-1939	Mr Alfred Henry Whittaker
1946-1963	Mr R Boddington
1963-1982	Mr George Crozier
1982	Mr Graham Mayger

OBOE

1857-1859	Mr Carl Florian Mandel
1859-1882	Mr Apollon Barret
1882-1890	Mr James Alfred Smith
1890-1902	Mr F Varness
1902-1928	Mr W H Haywood
1928-1939	Mr John Haywood Field
1946-1956	Mr Jack Hardy
1956-1982	Mr George F Morgan
1982	Mr Robert Cattermole

CLARINET

1857-18??	Mr Thomas Sullivan
1857-1859	Mr Carl Florian Mandel
1858-18??	Mr Henry Lazarus
1861-1905	Mr Robert Martin
1863-18??	Mr James Parke
1890-1905	Mr Julian Egerton
1898-1910	Mr A E Ingham
1900-1913	Mr George A Clinton
1905-1939	Mr Richard G Owen
1913-1919	Mr Charles Draper
1914-1916	Mr H W Stutely
1919-1936	Mr A O Smith
1921-1939	Mr Louis Booth
1946-1949	Mr Alfred Carr
1947-1969	Mr Henry G Pipe
1948-1969	Mr George Garside
1948-1973	Mr J B G O'Keefe
1969-1995	Mr Paul Harvey
1969-1973	Mr Jack Brymer
1973-1981	Mr Thomas Kelly
1974-1996	Mr Michael Farnham
1995	Mr Frank Slack

SAXOPHONE

1910-1919	Mr Richard G Owen
1919-1928	Mr A O Smith
1928-1930	Mr C H Goddard
1930-1939	Mr Walter Lear
1948-1969	Mr Henry G Pipe
1961-19	Mr Patrick Dixon
1969-1995	Mr Paul Harvey
1995	Mr Frank Slack

BASSOON

1857-1859	Mr Carl Florian Mandel
1859-1882	Mr James T Snelling
1882-1900	Mr John Nelsom Hardy
1900-1914	Mr W Wallis
1914-1918	Mr W James
1918-1921	Mr W T Scott
1921-1939	Mr E W Hinchcliff
1947-1970	Mr Frank Rendell
1970	Mr Ronald Waller

HORN

1859-1862	Mr Hudson
1862-1897	Mr Thomas E Mann (also Althorn)
1897-1908	Mr J H Colton
1908-1930	Mr H F Thornton
1930-1936	Mr Edward A Chapman
1936-1939	Mr Alfred J Cursue
1946-19??	Mr Alfred J Cursue
1978-1990	Mr Denzil Floyd
1991	Mr Tony Randall

Professors' lunch in the Kneller Hall Museum, 1961 (RMSM)

CORNET

1857-1869	Mr Carl Zeiss
1869-190?	Mr A McEleney
1901-1916	Mr William O'Keefe
1910-1934	Mr Charles Leggett
1911-1915	Mr J Lloyd Simon
1915-1922	Mr A W Lamb
	also taught Baritone
1934-1939	Mr Jack Mackintosh
1946-1976	Mr Jack Mackintosh
1947-1973	Mr Joseph Hudson
1973-1989	Mr Ian Mackintosh
1976-1981	Mr Denis Clift
1981-1984	Mr John Wilbraham
1985-1995	Mr Norman Archibald
1990	Mr John Hardy
199?-1995	Mr Paul Archibald
1995	Mr Simon Ferguson

TROMBONE

1857-1859	Mr Thomas Sullivan
1859-1860	Mr Hanks
1860-1866	Signor Cioffi
1866-1900	Mr Albert Cousins
1900-1914	Mr Albert Matt
1914-1917	Mr T H Guttridge
1918-1922	Mr J Stamp
1918-1939	Mr Frank Taylor
1946-1949	Mr Harry Johnson
1949-1969	Mr William J Teskey
1969-1988	Mr Dennis Bayton
1988	Mr Cliff Jones

EUPHONIUM

1857-1859	Mr Hughes
	(also Ophicleide)
1859-18??	Mr Alfred James Phasey
18??-1915	Mr J H Geary
1915-1923	Mr Edmund P Edwards
	(also Tuba)
1923-1939	Mr Charles Bryant
1947-1966	Mr John L Wilson
1966-1982	Mr Victor Saywell
1982-1987	Mr Peter Wise
1987-1991	Mr Paul Lawrence
1991	Mr Cliff Jones

TUBA

1857-1866	Mr Thomas Sullivan
1866-18??	Mr Albert Cousins
18??-1923	Mr J H Geary
1923-1939	Mr Charles A Bryant
1947-1966	Mr Charles H Brewer
1966-1978	Mr Charles Luxon
1978	Mr Patrick Harrild

PERCUSSION

1954-1969	Mr Denis Brady
1969-1984	Mr Bernard Harman
1984-1989	Mr John Cave
1989	Mr Paul Cameron

Jack Mackintosh with cornet pupils (RMSM)

HARP

1911-1912	Miss Florence Hudson
1919-1928	Mrs Florence Fremantle
1930-1932	Student E J Webb *
1934-1936	Student Charles Nalden*
1937-1939	Mrs Thorpe
1949-1952	Miss Gwendoline Mason
1959-1964	Mr J Haywood
	Mrs Sarah Duller

*Students Webb and Nalden were paid the normal professors fees in addition to their army pay.

Dr Norman Richardson (RMSM)

PIANOFORTE

1895-1918	Mr J Wilcocke
1918-1925	Mr F G Darbey
1925-1929	Mr Robert Head
1929-1939	Mr Robert Stannard
1947-1974	Mr Richard Tulip
1974-19??	Mrs Dorothy Harvey
19??-1988	Mr G Jones
1988	Miss Veronica Clayton

KEYBOARD HARMONY

1985	Mrs Yvonne Clarke

VIOLIN AND VIOLA

1857-1875	Mr Thomas Sullivan
1875-1900	Mr F W Barnard
	(all strings)
1895-1939	Mr Charles Parker
1905-1909	Mr S J Waud (Viola)
1910-1939	Mr F G Daubey (Viola)
1947-1948	Mr E Mathews
1948-1955	Mr E Yonge
1955-1975	Mr Tom Jones
1975-1988	Mr Malcom Henderson
1988	Mr Barrie Townsend

VIOLINCELLO

	Mr F W Julian
1912-1939	Mr Sydney Arthur Forest
1946-1955	Mr Sydney Arthur Forest
1921-1929	Mr F Momber
1955-1962	Mr Maurice Westerby
1962-1986	Mr Stanley Mant
1986	Mrs Jo Fitzgerald

Alfred Cursue (RMSM)

Alfred Cursue(Hrn)

DOUBLEBASS
1910-1922   Mr Charles Winterbottom
1922-1939   Mr Claude Hobday
1946   Mr Charles Cheeseman
1946-1982   Mr Ernest Ineson
1982   Mr Richard Driver
             (also Bass Guitar)

GUITAR
1982   Mr Terry Walsh

DANCE BAND
1989-1993   Mr John Sands

HARMONY AND AURAL
1859-18??   Mr Charles Mandeville
18??-1925   Dr Ambrose Porter
1925-1929   Mr Robert Head
1929-1939   Mr Robert Stannard
1947-1950   Mr Hubert Dawkes
1950-1969   Dr Norman Richardson
1969-1986   Mr Gordon Reynolds
1986-1994   Mr Peter Byrne
1994   Mr Mark Uglow

INSTRUMENTATION
1910-1929   Mr Frank Winterbottom
1929-1959   Mr William Duthoit
1959   Dr Norman Richardson
1959-1966   Major Alfred Young
1966-1979   Lieutenant-Colonel
             Douglas A Pope
1979-1988   Lieutenant-Colonel
             Trevor le M Sharpe
1988   Major Gordon Turner

CONDUCTING
1969-1978   Mr Maurice Miles
1978-1983   Lieutenant-Colonel
             Rodney Bashford
1983-1991   Lieutenant-Colonel
             George E Evans
1991   Major Roger Swift

HISTORY OF MUSIC
1991   Mr Michael Short

Gordon Reynolds(Harmony)

Left: Gordon Reynolds (RMSM)
Below: Gordon Turner (RMSM)

Appendix F
THE GRADUATES

As far as we have been able to ascertain, this is a complete list of all those students who have graduated from Kneller Hall, together with their certificate numbers and the regiment to which they were first posted. Prior to 1880 numbered certificates were not awarded, and even thereafter there is sometimes no record of the certificate number of graduates; in some cases the same number was given to two students. An asterisk next to the certificate number indicates that the individual was already serving as a bandmaster when he took the examination.

We are aware that this list is likely to contain some errors, since the records are not always wholly reliable, and we would like to apologize in advance to any graduates whose details are incorrect or who have been omitted altogether.

1858
W Van Den Heuvel
1 R Norfolk R
W Marshall
6 DG
W Doulton
1 DWR
J Green
2 S Lan R

1859
J McEntee
2 Sher For
J London
The Bays
WJ Savage
2 R U Rifles
A Brown
The Bays

1860
J Miller
1 DCLI
AG Crowe
14 H
W McHugh
1 Conn Rang
G McPherson
1 Somerset LI
T Haines
7 H
W Lawson
1 S Stafford R

1860 cont.
G McQuade
2 R S Fus

1861
JCJ Lee
5 Innis DG
F Moran
2 R North'd Fus

1862
T McArdle
1 Welsh R
P Kelly
1 A&SH
W Cleary
2 R Fus
C Barry
1 Somerset LI

1863
H Fitzpatrick
11 H
R Sweeny
2 The Buffs
W Hutchinson
St Helena Regt
EH Lay
1 Ox & Bucks LI
C Barthmann
2 Queen's R
WC Lamont
2 Welsh R

1863 cont.
J Gready
1 Queen's R
J Cooke
2 R Mun Fus
S Traise
2 R S Fus
E Ford
2 Worc R
W Perrie
2 Midd'x R
C Cousins
2 DG

1864
T Wheatley
2 E Lan R
W Barry
2 Hamps
J Colman
3 KRRC
W Creighton
2 North'n R
FJ Moore
2 Somerset LI
W Wallace
2 Suffolk R
J Arkell
4 DG
W James
8 H
G Rudolphson
18 H

1864 cont.
W Davies
1 Devon R
D Mahony
2 Wilts R
JT Fenton
1 Lincoln R
A Vlacco
2 R Norfolk R
JB Browne
1 Sher F
G Farrugid
1 Essex R

1865
A Cavallini
2 S Stafford R
S Ricks
1 Green Howards
F Brim
2 Leicester R
G Ehrman
2 RWF
C Hynes
2 R Berks R
C Moore
1 Midd'x R
A Morelli
2 DWR
F Nixon
21 L
P Waters
2 S Wales Bord

1865 cont.
J Croker
1 R Fus
W Dunlop
19 H
C Murray
6 DG
F Mandel
2 R W Kent R
W Allen
2 E York R
W Bonicolli
1 R Norfolk R
C Jennings
17 L
F Beyer
10 H
W Woodcock
2 KRRC
F Beardhall
1 W York R
JJ Murdock
1 Seaforth
M Walsh
1 Leins R
J Emmings
2 Suffolk R

1866
WA Wallace
1 Worc R
T Griffin
3 W India R

1866 cont.
C Somner
2 R U Rifles
T Ring
2 Manch R
J McDonald
1 RWF
P Branigan
1 Conn Rang
W Guiran
2 R Dub Fus
W Wright
11 H
M Quinn
2 R Ir R
W Neuzerling
1 Durham LI
J Sommar
1 Leicester R
T Martin
8 H

1867
J Relli
1 Glosters
J Hecker
2 York & Lanc R
A McEleney
1 Essex R
BF Bell
2 Inniskilling Fus
J Gibbon
1 R Berks R
D Connor
2 KSLI
S Lindenberg
13 H
J Vevers
1 Somerset LI
JS Jones
5 Innis DG
G Pashley
4 W India R
T Brophy
1 R S Fus
J Harford
4 H
C Glennon
1 DCLI
B Hull
1 W India R
HT Embury
2 Ox & Bucks LI

1868
J Hartmann
12 L
J Flaners
2 KOYLI
JW Sawerthal
2 King's Own R
J Lohrisch
2 Green Howards
J Conroy
2 RWF

1868 cont.
T Pitchell
7 DG
J Wilson
1 BW
C Fitzpatrick
1 R Ir R
W Cole
2 Wilts R
A Green
1 KOYLI
T Gordon
1 Wilts R
J Brown
2 Dorset R

1869
E Briggs
16 L
WG Buck
2 BW
W Collender
1 Gordons
T Carbett
1 R S Fus
W Vines
1 E Surr R
HA Rattray
1 S Wales Bord
C Mangelsdorf
2 R War R
T Broady
2 Manch R
F Daniels
2 R S Fus
J Deacon
15 H
T Moran
1 R Fus
W Davies
2 KOSB
JG Light
1 Dorset R
C Farrell
2 Gordons
J Moran
2 North'n R

1870
JA Browne
RHA
J Buchanan
2 HLI
G McNerney
2 Essex R
A Hartmann *Mus Doc*
17 L
M Kleinstuber
2 R Berks R
T Barry
2 Lanc Fus
E Welding
2 R Irish Fus
J Tyson
2 Dorset R

1870 cont.
R Kearns
2 Queen's R
M Salew
1 R Hamps
WS Smith
4 DG
G McLaren
2 Inniskilling Fus

1871
A Frayling
5 L
C Murdock
1 Seaforth
HC Boehmer
2 Bedfs & Herts R
J Holt
2 R Leic
C Luschwitz
1 R Dub Fus
JH McBeath
2 KRRC
M Curry
2 King's Own R
W Beyers
1 Essex R

1872
R Urff
1 S Stafford R
C Richards
2 KOYLI
B Skelton
1 Durham LI
D McInnes
1 HLI
J Antcliffe
1 Green Howards
EP Hurst
1 Glosters
C Young
2 Lincoln R
J Hogan
1 Loyal R
H Dowdall
1 Ox & Bucks LI
Robert Hook
15 H
A Paterson
1 Worc R
J Douglass
1 The Buffs
W Jones
9 L
Richard Hook
2 Sher For
J Quinn
1 R U Rifles
J McDonald
1 Camerons
J Lewis
1 S Lancs R
J Smith
11 H

1872 cont.
S Rowlandson
1 Welsh R
J Stroyan
13 H
B Smith
2 Conn Rang
L Werner
1 Inniskilling Fus
S Barritt
2 N Stafford R

1873
WW Frayling
2 S Stafford R
WC Quinn
4 Rifle Bde
PH Mahony
1 York & Lanc R
TW Ford
2 R Fus
A Clappe
3 KRRC
JB Rubil
2 R Lincoln R
WT Trump
2 Loyal R
C Mansbridge
15 H
W Dencer
1 R North'd Fus
M Troy
1 Lan Fus

1874
T Barley
2 Welsh R
SJ Plant
1 R Leic
G Battershall
2 KOYLI
SC Griffiths
2 R Scots
G Hewson
1 R S Fus
A Neuzerling
2 R Norfolk R
C Barthmann
2 Glosters
A Sims
14 H
EC Matthews
12 L
W Leeson
1 King's Own R
C Poole
7 DG
G Ramplin
19 H
H Edwards
2 Oxs & Bucks LI
G Light
4 KRRC
BM Brophy
3 DG

1874 cont.
HT Dunkerton
1 R Mun Fus
G Clarke
2 Suffolk R
AP Crawley
2 Rifle Bde
J Clancy
1 Loyal R

1875
WH Wilcox
2 Leins R
W Courtney
2 R Sussex R
J Engelfield
18 H
WG Fricker
3 H
O Dunn
4 KRRC
GJ Miller
2 Bedfs & Herts R
W Orton
1 DG
W Smith
2 DG
W Healy
1 Leins R
T Kershaw
1 W India R
J Waldron
1 Kings
CW Hewitt
1 R Sussex R
G Woods
21 L
M Gould
1 DCLI
JA Bunch
2 Seaforth
N Coleopy
1 Midd'x R
M Shepherd
1 Dorset R
C Ford
1 DWR
HA Maxwell
1 Seaforth
WH McEwan
1 KOSB

1876
G Hatfield
1 W York R
J Sharpe
The Greys
JG Stevenight
2 Leicester R
P Madden
2 R Irish
JD Langlands
1 Border R
A Stringer
16 L

1876 cont.
G Voller
1 The Buffs
J Campbell
2 DCLI
CF Frazer
2 W India R

1877
G Sage
2 R Norfolk R
J Wright
1 S Lan R
J Chapman
4 H
H Dimmer
2 Lan Fus
W O'Keefe
2 R Irish Fus
A Walker
3 KRRC
WJ Castle
16 L
E Stubbings
1 Devon R
P O'Brien
1 Green Howards
JW Wood
5 L
J Strudwick
1 R S Fus
J Farrell
2 Kings
ST Webber
6 DG
W McGinn
2 W York R
JG Joyce
The Greys
J Burton
2 Wilts R
JM Barnes
13 H
D Goring
6 DG
WJ Scott
1 BW
H Furner
9 L

1878
S Barley
1 Border R
C Joiner
2 E Surr R
J Davis
2 Durham LI
T Howard
1 R U Rifles
J Simpson
1 HLI
E Holland
1 North'n R
A Morelli
2 R War R

1878 cont.
A McLaughlin
2 DWR
H Bullard
2 S Wales Bord
J Arbuckle
2 Border R
T Hirst
1 Sher For
F Brown
2 Leinster R
EJ Richardson
3 Rifle Bde
J Munday
1 E Lan R
W Walker
2 Essex R
TJ Quigley
2 R North'd Fus
A Templemann
8 H
C Hazell
12 L

1879
PF Bultitude
1 Durham LI
JP Hansen
2 Essex R
BS Green
10 H
J Sangwell
1 Oxs & Bucks LI
H Cannar
11 H
H Quinn
2 The Buffs
F Oakley
RDG
T Carbury
2 Sher For
G Haswell
1 Border R
J King
2 Gordons
W Gidney
1 Queens
R Brown
2 R U Rifles
AJ Rowe
2 Somerset LI
C Zoeller
7 H
H Coole
2 York & Lanc R
C Antony
2 KRRC
R Goodings
2 S Wales Bord

1880
A Robinson
3 DG
WJ Birkby
1 Cheshire

1880 cont.
ER Stebbing
1 R Warwick R
GH Barnes
2 W India R
JT Reardon
1 R S Fus
W Winter
9 L
J Murphy
1 KSLI
J Edmonds
1 Essex R
W Wilson
2 Devon R
A Wilkin
1 Leinster R
1 – M Memsley
1 R Irish
CT Hurst
2 Cheshire
J Gecks
1 RWF
2 – J Fairburn
1 Lan Fus
3 – C Kelly
1 R U Rifles
4 – M Larter
2 R Berks R
5 – W Kelly
1 R U Rifles
6 – J Read
2 Midd'x R
7 – J Mullholland
1 W India R
8 – WH Kierton
2 R Hamps
9 – S Gardner
1 Queens
10 – J Evans
2 Conn Rang
11 – W Chapman
1 E Surr R
12 – J Phillips
2 R Irish
13 – FJ Coleman
2 R Fus
14 – WD Peachey
1 Rifle Bde

1881
15 – J Legrove
2 KOYLI
16 – A James
1 KOSB
17 – S Mowbray
2 HLI
*18 – GJ Miller
RMC (Sand)
19 – J Hickey
17 L
20 – E Wallace
1 R Innis Fus
21 – G Richards
2 Ox & Bucks LI

1881 cont.
*22 – JP Clarke
SG
*23 – D Godfrey
Gren Gds
*24 – C Thomas
Coldm Gds
*25 – L Zaverthal
RA (Wool)
*26 – JP Hansen
2 Essex R
*27 – JA Bonnisseau
The Greys
28 – R Jones
2 Worcester R
29 – CJ Bampton
1 Worcester R
30 – A Neuzerling
1 York & Lanc R

1882
*31 – JB Browne
2 R Dublin Fus
32 – S Grainger
2 R Lincoln R
*33 – J Lawson
RA (Mounted)
34 – ET Quinn
1 Manchester R
35 – JM Rogan
2 Queens
36 – J Hetherington
1 S Stafford R
37 – F Gidney
1 N Stafford R
38 – LM Simms
2 Sher For
39 – JC King
8 H
41 – WJ Fitzgerald
2 Cameronians
42 – P Ayers
1 Leins R
*43 – CT Hurst
2 Cheshire
*44 – J Gecks
1 RWF
47 – R Hancock
1 R S Fus
46 – T Martin
1 Dorset R
48 – W Gildea
1 R Munster Fus
49 – WJ Quord
1 W India R
40 – CG Burck
1 SWB
*51 – C Zoeller
7 H
50 – TJ Marshall
2 DG
52 – L Barker
The Greys
45 – G Raineri
1 KRRC

1882 cont.
55 – W Coen
2 Kings Own R
53 – J Anderson
1 HLI
54 – JJ Smith
1 DG

1883
57 – R Francis
1 R Berk R
56 – AT M'Gill
1 RS
58 – RE Overall
7 DG
59 – W Jones
2 Kings

1884
70 – J Wheeler
2 R Mun Fus
74 – A Preece
2 S Wales Bord
75 – F Tyler
1 KRRC
76 – G Ross
1 Loyal R
77 – F Gregory
2 RWF
78 – J Heron
2 N Stafford R
79 – L Bishop
2 Lan Fus
80 – P Ryan
1 R Ir Fus
81 – R Broster
1 R W Kent R
82 – CWH Hall
1 RD
83 – J Ancliffe
2 Suffolk R
84 – H Wilby
1 R Dub Fus
87 – P O'Donnell
2 SWB
85 – J Grant
2 A&SH
86 – E Croft
3 KRRC
91 – J Kelly
2 The Buffs
88 – A Johnson
2 Leicester R

1885
90 – J Hinds
20 H
89 – TW Bennett
1 RWF
JSJ Lee
RMC (Sand)
92 – A Marks
1 Glosters
94 – E Sharpe
1 R Norfolk R

1885 cont.
93 – J Buckingham
1 E York R
95 – AC Strugnell
2 Green Howards
96 – WJ Stevens
2 Dorset R
97 – C Birkhead
1 The Buffs
98 – WR Moody
1 Devon R
99 – E Bartoli
R Malta Artillery
100 – H Sims
Cavalry Depot Canterbury
101 – R Dunn
3 DG
102 – RW Tucker
1 Lan Fus
103 – C Thomas
1 Suffolk R
104 – RBB Wakelin
1 Camerons
105 – W Hisgrove
2 R Hamps
*106 – C Godfrey
RHG
110 – C Gornell
2 W India R
107 – R Pocock
1 Bedfs & Herts R
109 – CJ Brenner
2 Ox & Bucks LI

1886
108 – W Prosser
19 H
113 – TA Mitchell
1 Somerset LI
112 – G Pickles
5 DG
111 – WG Hallewell
1 DCLI
115 – I Keely
1 Conn Rang
114 – GP Robertson
2 Midd'x R
117 – CWC Lee
4 DG
118 – A Shackleford
2 Welsh R
119 – J Forrest
2 KSLI
116 – L Wallace
2 R North'd Fus
120 – W Rafter
1 KOSB
121 – FG Cunningham
2 E York R
122 – J McKinnon
1 A&SH
123 – D Healy
2 Durham LI
124 – D Lorden
2 R Hamps

1886 cont.
125 – R Fairbrother
Cavalry Depot Canterbury

1887
126 – JJ Harvey
7 H
127 – AJ Butler
2 R Sussex R
128 – T O'Connor
2 Rifle Bde
132 – W Barrett
2 R S Fus
129 – GR Blogg
2 S Stafford R
130 – W Guyton
1 Green Howards
131 – J Graham
2 R W Kent R
133 – F Bradley
2 Ox & Bucks LI
134 – WA Pepperill
1 North'n R
135 – F McChesney
2 Seaforth
136 – T Grant
6 DG
137 – WJ Brown
2 R Norfolk R
138 – EJ Bradley
1 Sher For

1888
139 – A Williams
10 H
140 – AA Wilson
2 KOYLI
141 – W Saunders
1 Kings
142 – S Wright
1 Leins R
143 – FC Russell
1 E Lan R
144 – FB Martin
4 H
145 – T Finnigan
2 W Yorks R
147 – JJ Carroll
8 H
146 – E Shields
5 L
148 – J Kelly
1 W India R

1889
149 – M Hill
1 A&SH
150 – F Millman
1 R Fus
152 – HL Cooke
2 Wilts R
151 – H Bampton
2 Devon R
154 – J Kean
2 Glosters

1889 cont.
153 – W Robinson
1 Border R
155 – G McLaughlin
2 York & Lanc R
156 – J Matthews
1 S Stafford R
157 – IS Dunlop
The Greys
158 – JA Caborn
1 S Wales Bord
160 – WA Ramsey
2 S Lan R
159 – A Henderson
2 R U Rifles
161 – S Dore
2 R Berks R

1890
162 – T Clear
2 Border R
164 – R Elliott
1 R Dub Fus
165 – RJ Hill
2 Essex R
163 – J Birmingham
1 Cameronians
167 – A Stewart
1 R W Kent R
166 – RT Chandler
1 R Irish R
168 – A Hurst
2 Lincoln R
169 – A Light
21 L
170 – W Cawley
2 RS
171 – H Bach
11 H
175 – SJ Howarth
2 Sher For
173 – J Vince
2 Loyal R
172 – A Lamb
1 Ox & Bucks LI
178 – JM Pilton
17 L
174 – G Alexander
1 Midd'x R
176 – FJ Inkster
1 Queen's R
177 – C Franklin
1 R U Rifles
179 – J Harvey
1 Loyal R
180 – HG Hedges
18 H
178 – FW Wood
1 York & Lan R
181 – SJ Edwards
2 E Lan R
184 – J Robinson
2 R Dub Fus
182 – G Perdue
1 Devon R

1891
183 – WC Windram
2 Gordons
186 – T Blench
1 DCLI
185 – R Willis
2 Bedfs & Herts R
187 – W Thompson
2 Leicester R
188 – E Gallway
2 North'n R
189 – GH Clifford
1 Inniskilling Fus
190 – E Hughes
1 Leicester R
193 – CB Frayling
2 Inniskilling Fus
191 – J Snell
2 Durham LI
192 – J Prosser
6 D
194 – D McNeil
1 R War R

1892
195 – T Scott
10 H
196 – S Pope
1 Wilts R
197 – J Ferry
1 S Lan R
198 – EO Davies
4 H
198 – R Owen
2 Glosters
199 – T McFarlane
1 E York R
200 – CH Hassell
4 KRRC
201 – T Barker
5 DG
202 – WR Cooper
2 KOSB
203 – J Griffiths
2 The Buffs

1893
204 – H Carr
3 H
205 – FJ Harris
4 Rifle Bde
206 – J Markey LRAM
16 L
207 – E Rogers
1 Lan Fus
208 – HL Collins
2 Ln Fus
209 – WGJ Bentley
1 W York R
210 – S Liddle
1 Durham LI
212 – WJ Agness
1 R Mun Fus
211 – AJ Stretton
2 Cheshire

1893 cont.
213 – AV Barwood
1 R Berks R
216 – J Harwood
1 R Hamps
217 – W Clark
1 E Surr R

1894
218 – E O'Neill
2 Suffolk R
219 – R Jones
2 BW
220 – E Elford
2 Norf R
221 – J Livingstone
2 R Mun Fus
222 – F Haines
2 King's Own R
223 – RH Smith
2 S Stafford R
225 – JT Cocking
2 R War R
224 – WH Field
13 H
226 – W Brunt
1 S Lan R
227 – T Lane
2 Leins R
228 – HJ Pipe
1 E York R
229 – JB Runciman
1 Gordons
230 – GA Williams
1 R U Rifles

1895
231 – W Davies
2 A&SH
232 – F Ward
2 N Stafford R
234 – JW Monk
1 Welsh R
235 – JP Mullins
2 R Dub Fus
233 – AVR Laverock
2 Cameronians
236 – B Wingrove
2 Manch R
237 – A Hind
1 Durham LI
238 – W Wille
1 Seaforth
240 – W Froud
2 Suffolk R
239 – D Neill
1 DWR
241 – WEE Edwards
2 DWR
242 – A Hazell LRAM
2 Dorset R
243 – WH Moss
1 KSLI
244 – J Tyrrell
1 Kings Own R

1895 cont.
252 – PF Battishill
2 Queen's R
245 – J Kirwan
1 Bedfs & Herts R

1896
247 – JW Tucker
19 H
246 – AE Joiner
6 DG
248 – A Ivermee
1 R North'd Fus
249 – RW Ramsey
2 Inniskilling Fus
250 – WJ Applin
2 Cheshire
251 – HA Broughton
13 H
253 – AJ Cunningham
2 R U Rifles
254 – GB Bartlett
1 R Norfolk R
255 – A Turner
1 Inniskilling Fus
256 – G Marsh
1 Seaforth
257 – LL Worthington
1 Kings
258 – C Wright
1 Lincoln R
259 – G Walsh
1 RWF

1897
265 – JH Sage
2 KRRC
269 – CRR Hackney
1 The Buffs
261 – WJ Imbusch
1 Midd'x R
262 – AE Imbusch
1 Midd'x R
263 – WRJ Leeson
1 R Sussex R
264 – JG Hewett
2 DCLI
265 – J Murphy
Duke of York's School
266 – JE Beever
1 Wilts R
267 – F Levy
2 E York R
268 – SW Harman
1 Essex R
269 – A Graham
1 N Stafford R
270 – R Wade
10 H
273 – WB Wiltshire
2 Loyal R
271 – H Elcox
1 R Mun Fus
272 – WR Reilly
2 RS

1897 cont.
274 – AJ Dunn
1 R Irish Fus
275 – TW Payne
18 H
276 – AJ Norris
5 L

1898
277 – JG Crossley
2 R Sussex R
278 – A Hendry
20 H
279 – JV Richardson
1 Wilts R
280 – RG Evans
2 HLI
282 – JH Harward
3 R War R
284 – WH Keefe LRAM
3 R Fus
285 – JG Worms
3 Lan Fus
281 – A Weyer
1 North'n R
283 – TH Rich
1 RSF
286 – E Blake
2 Gordons
287 – WJ Gutteridge
2 W India R
288 – M Fisher
2 Camerons
M Ryan
3 W India R
289 – GJ Miller
1 DCLI
293 – SFJ Small
1 Glosters
291 – H Bradley
1 R War R
290 – J Gruar
12 L
292 – G Strong
1 Dorset R

1899
294 – G Davis
1 R W Kent R
295 – C Gregory
2 Conn Rang
296 – E Whelan
1 Queen's R
297 – EJ Else
3 KRRC
298 – JH Ploughman
1 W India R
299 – C Wingrove
2 Essex R
300 – C Atherley
1 R Irish R
304 – JH Moir
2 RWF
301 – HB Mitchell
2 R Ir Fus

1899 cont.
302 – R Wood
2 Rifle Bde
303 – HP Edwards
2 KSLI
305 – B Grinter
2 W India R

1900
306 – CE Stretton
1 York & Lancs R
307 – ER Pallant
1 Gordons
308 – CH Price
1 R Dub Fus
309 – W Robertson
2 RSF
313 – J Durham
2 E Surr R
310 – AJ Wilson
1 KOSB
311 – JR Calthorpe
3 Kings
312 – J Matthews
4 R War R
314 – AO Smith
4 R North'd Fus
321 – W Cox
1 Devon R
316 – A Harris LRAM
2 S Lan R
317 – GE Pitt
4 Lan Fus
318 – RJ Shepherd
3 R North'd Fus
319 – R Wright
4 R Fus
315 – JW Faulkner
2 DG
320 – RT Stevens
3 Rifle Bde
325 – AW Ellis
1 RS
322 – WF Hawkins
4 Midd'x R
323 – G Refoy
4 Kings
324 – JG Roberts
4 Manch R
326 – TP Brown
2 N Stafford R
327 – A Parkes
4 KRRC
328 – CW Ancliffe
1 SWB
329 – EA Barrett
3 Manch R
330 – AG Varnfield
1 Suffolk R

1901
331 – S Swain LRAM
4 Worc R
332 – JH Amers
2 Devon R

1901 cont.
333 – GJ Crosbie
11 H
335 – J Dought
2 Worc R
334 – J Slattery
3 KRRC
336 – F Andrews
2 Green Howards
339 – J Sheehan
1 RD
337 – F Ripp
2 R Gar R
338 – WG Taylor
3 R Gar R
340 – WJ Gibson
9 L

1902
341 – J McClurg
1 A&SH
342 – CH Barry
4 Rifle Bde
343 – C Murrell
1 Green Howards
344 – T McKelvie
2 R W Kent R
345 – CB Hewitt
2 The Buffs
346 – EAH O'Keefe
1 R Fus
349 – CS Witt
1 Leicester R
347 – F Ferguson
1 DG
350 – J Ward
2 S Stafford R
348 – JJ Dunn
2 KOSB
351 – FW Frayling
The Greys
354 – H Cooper
2 Loyal R
352 – H Jones
1 Manch R
353 – J Brady
4 Rifle Bde
355 – J Gandee
1 N Stafford R
356 – W Arnold
2 KOYLI
357 – J Fowles
2 Seaforth
358 – HJ Bartram
1 HLI
359 – HW Alden
8 H

1903
360 – E Hinton
21 L
361 – A Graves
2 Cheshire
362 – WE Eden
2 Wilts R

1903 cont.
363 – JW Cole
2 R Sussex R
364 – C Cornfield LRAM
7 DG
365 – WA Featherstone
2 R U Rifles
366 – CR Bicks
2 HLI
367 – HM Reilly
1 DCLI
370 – R Banbury
1 Worc R
368 – J Walsh
2 A&SH
371 – A Fawcett
1 R Dub Fus
369 – JJ Connors LRAM
2 W York R
372 – E Butler
1 W York R
373 – EA Baxter
2 Bedfs & Herts R
375 – A Graham
1 York & Lanc R
374 – ET Murrey
1 BW
376 – CO Saunders
1 Camerons
377 – T Brown
1 KRRC
378 – FR Holt
1 RD
379 – HWC Pearce
1 R Hamps R

1904
380 – TA Adams
1 S Lan R
381 – WH Richardson
17 L
382 – J Ollerenshaw
1 R Sussex R
383 – THF Freeman
1 RSF
384 – JW Newton
2 Durham LI
385 – G Dean
1 R Norfolk R
386 – H Baxter
2 Sher For
387 – EE Berry
1 E Lan R
388 – G Landrock LRAM
2 Conn Rang
389 – AF Hawkes
1 Glosters
390 – GW Elvin
1 The Buffs
391 – A Stock
2 Queen's R

1905
392 – RB Harwood
1 R U Rifles

1905 cont.
393 – EE Beechey
2 North'n R
394 – F Burnell
2 R Irish R
395 – JLT Hurd LRAM
2 E York R
396 – HW Simpson
1 KOYLI
397 – WT Roberts
2 DCLI
398 – SJ Brown
2 Glosters
399 – AE Halford
1 King's
400 – G Martin
2 King's
401 – E Brambleby
1 Wilts R
402 – PSG O'Donnell
2 BW
403 – F Horton
3 DG
405 – EN Miles
1 Lan Fus
404 – RE Collier
20 H
406 – G Elliott
1 R Mun Fus
407 – FW Sylvester
1 Ox & Bucks LI
410 – WF Gidney
1 RSF

1906
408 – H Melville
2 R Hamps R
409 – G Salter
2 Rifle Bde
411 – AN Moss
1 R North'd Fus
412 – R Jones LRAM
1 W India R
413 – EU Lane
2 N Stafford R
414 – EJ Dunn MC
2 KRRC

1907
415 – AH Dawsall
1 Sher For
416 – GE Turner
1 E York R
418 – H Borland
1 Bedfs & Herts R
417 – AW Mining
2 York & Lanc R
420 – D Parfitt
1 R Mun Fus
419 – W Scragg
2 R Dub Fus
421 – GT Acres
1 DG
422 – GA Loftus
2 R Mun Fus

1907 cont.
423 – WH Abbott
1 Camerons
427 – H Dudley
4 DG
424 – GO Walker
2 North'n R
425 – J Vickers
2 R Fus
426 – TM Duffy
1 Oxs & Bucks LI

1908
428 – E Adams
6 D
429 – RA Cooke
2 Midd'x R
430 – WH Owen
2 Leicester R
432 – HR Lovell
3 KRRC
433 – H Stockey
1 HLI
431 – HE Facer
1 Essex R
434 – H Norris
1 Inniskilling Fus
435 – FJ Ricketts
2 A&SH
436 – AE Noble
2 Cheshire
437 – A Macdonald
2 Somerset LI
438 – HLC Funcane
2 E Lan R
439 – A Scates
1 W York R
440 – S Hays
1 RWF
442 – TJ Hillier
1 Midd'x R
441 – A Douglas
1 Durham LI
443 – GL Gecks
1 R Irish R

1909
446 – FJ Goodered
12 L
444 – W Carleton
2 KOSB
447 – AL Wallace
1 R Fus
445 – W Carbury
2 R Lincoln R
448 – C Hindemarsh
1 R Sussex R
449 – LL Hoyle
2 Manch R
450 – J Moull
2 Sher For
451 – AE Shaw
1 Welsh R
452 – AD Hancock
2 DWR

1909 cont.
453 – C O'Neill
Canadian Horse Artillery
454 – EM MacDonald
1 A&SH
455 – CE Caulfield
1 R Dub Fus

1910
456 – EJ MacDonald
1 Conn Rang
457 – RP O'Donnell
21 L
458 – CA Hartmann
1 R Warwick R
459 – SJ Freeman DCM
1 S Lan R
460 – RE Cahill
2 S Lan R
461 – KS Glover LRAM
2 Welsh R
462 – J McNichol
1 Dorset R
463 – G Quick LRAM
1 Border R
464 – H Eldridge
2 Durham LI
465 – WM Robinson
LRAM
14 H
467 – WH Bartlett
2 Gordons
466 – CC Hartley
20 H
468 – W Cheeseman
8 H
469 – FG Moss
1 KOYLI

1911
470 – SJ Young
2 Rifle Bde
471 – WH Orbinski
2 R Hamps R
472 – GE Hudson
3 Midd'x R
473 – CS Moon
2 KOYLI
474 – EA Stebbing
2 R Warwick R
475 – CE Richardson
LRAM
2 King's Own R
476 – CV Richardson
7 H
477A – Hatherley
3 H

1912
480 – WJ Clancy
2 RWF
478 – AE Hopkins
13 H
481 – J Hansen
2 S Stafford R

1912 cont.
487 – G Hendren
R Malta Artillery
479 – GW Grayson
LRAM
1 Seaforth
482 – HS Dobinson
4 KRRC
483 – JES Vince
1 Bedfs & Herts R
484 – H Langtry
1 DWR
485 – NRC Neville
2 Ox & Bucks LI
486 – F Adams
2 HLI
489 – T Wilson
2 KOSB
488 – C White
1 R Berks R
490 – W Gumbley
1 R Hamps R
491 – W Richards
1 Dorset R
492 – FA Bradey
LRAM
5 L
496 – B Beale
1 Suffolk R
493 – HE Dowell
LRAM
1 Cameronians
497 – TH Wheeler
4 Worc R
498 – TBF Wiltshire
2 Seaforth
494 – AF Bultitude
1 S Stafford R
495 – AJ Wilson
1 KSLI
499 – RL Seymour
2 Cameronians
502 – WH Jenkins
2 E Surrey R

1913
501 – JW Eatson
2 Wilts R
500 – SS Smith
1 RD
504 – WF Brown
4 Rifle Bde
503 – WJ Dambmann
Mus Bac
2 Leicester R
505 – HE Adkins LRAM
2 Suffolk R
509 – E Nash
2 W India R
506 – W Bradshaw
1 E Surr R
508 – JE Grace LRAM
2 RS
510 – RR Ricketts
2 Essex R

1913 cont.
511 – LP Bradey
LRAM
2 R Irish Fus

1914
512 – JC Windram
LRAM
1 R North'd Fus
513 – ADW Hunt
2 R W Kent R
514 – FE Minns
2 R Sussex R
516 – F Shearing
2 W York R
515 – LK Harrison
LRAM
1 DCLI
517 – W Cresswell
LRAM
1 North'n R
519 – FL Wood
1 R Fus
518 – E Smith
1 Ox & Bucks LI
520 – W Sayer
1 E Lan R
521 – GE Friend
1 Inniskilling Fus
523 – EA Weaver
LRAM
2 R Berks R
522 – BW
O'Donnell ARAM
7 H
524 – GA Herniman
LRAM
2 Devon R
525 – HJ Matthews
1 R U Rifles
529 – J Garrett
1 A&SH

1915
526 – JJ Buckle
1 Queen's R
527 – WH Hildyard
2 DCLI
528 – M Prindeville
1 E York R
530 – F Willis
7 DG
531 – SG Owen
1 W India R
532 – TW Stopford
2 Loyal R
533 – W Millett
2 R U Rifles
534 – HE Austing
2 BW
537 – H Fenner LRAM
2 SWB

1916
535 – W Steffen
2 North'd Fus

1916 cont.
536 – T Adams
2 Noth'n R
538 – SF Fricker
1 Durham LI
539 – RC Hanney
LRAM ARCM
1 Dorset R
542 – JW Clark
1 Midd'x R
540 – W Allen
LRAM ARCM
1 R U Rifles
541 – WM Fryer
2 E Lan R

1917
543 – WP Graves
2 R Dub Fus
544 – EC Griffin
1 Worc R
545 – F Spencer
7 H
546 – JJ Burkmann
1 Somerset LI

1918
547 – ATS Chandler
LRAM ARCM
2 King's Own R
549 – JP Walmsley
1 R W Kent R
548 – A Stone DCM
1 R Irish Fus
550 – ECH Burgess
2 R Norfolk R
551 – MW Geoghegan
1 HLI
552 – CM Gordon
5 DG
553 – CW Griggs
2 Inniskilling Fus
554 – A Evans
1 Somerset LI
555 – WN Campbell
1 Gordons
556 – H Gilbert
2 Border R
557 – T Taylor
1 SWB

1919
558 – R Moir
1 King's Own R
559 – R Scarlett
3 Worc R
560 – AW MacDonald
2 RS
561 – EH Hedges
1 Leicester R
566 – AW Woodham
1 KSLI
563 – HT Whittingham
2 York & Lanc R
568 – JE Fox LRAM
15 H

1919 cont.
562 – T Francis
LRAM ARCM
1 Green Howards
565 – G Passelow
1 King's
570 – MP Flannery
2 E York R
564 – H Grout
2 Leicester R
567 – E Ovington
1 DWR
569 – T Underhill
2 Cheshire
573 – EJ Rees
2 Sher For
571 – EV Barwood
18 H
576 – WC Compton
4 R Fus
577 – HA Rowe
1 BW
572 – S Laing LRAM
16 L
575 – AV Barwood
19 H
575 – S Yorke DCM
4 Rifle Bde
578 – OE Marshall
21 L

1920
579 – WF Bryant
1 N Stafford R
581 – A Grice
2 Durham LI
584 – EJT Haywood
2 Lan Fus
585 – HD Hemsley
RAM ARCM
2 King's
587 – DW Jones LRAM
1 Camerons
586 – EA Parrott
1 Loyal R
582 – W Doloughan
1 E York R
583 – FW Saunders
ARCM
5 L
580 – E Spiteri
R Malta Artillery
588 – CS Trowt
1 Lincoln R
591 – EA Bethell
1 Rifle Bde
590 – H Carrotti
20 H
589 – CLP Ward
2 Welsh R
592 – CA Friend
2 HLI

1921
593 – A Pullinger
3 Rifle Bde

1921 cont.
595 – GV Vince
4 H
594 – HA Collier
1 Wilts R
596 – GL Cooke
2 Green Howards
598 – VRS Wright
2 DWR
597 – R Winters
2 Camerons
600 – WG Yates
1 Manch R
601 – G Hart
1 York & Lanc R
599 – J Turtle
1 S Stafford R
602 – GJ Froude
3 R Fus
604 – FG Lewis ARCM
2 Suffolk R
603 – RG Mark
4 Midd'x R

1922
605 – JE Needham
LRAM ARCM
1 R Berk R
606 – SA Guilmant
1 R Sussex R
607 – TK Jarvis
1 KOSB
608 – HL Butt ARCM
1 R W Kent R

1923
610 – SW Henwood
2 R Warwick R
609 – T Stenning ARCM
11 H
612 – JW Duthoit ARCM
2 S Stafford R
611 – J Nichol
2 Manch R
614 – FW Coleman
ARCM
1 S Lan R
613 – TW Turner
1 W India R
619 – AE Harvey
2 Sher For
615 – JR Bell ARCM
2 N Stafford R
617 – WC Withers ARCM
1 RSF
616 – HJ Coombes
1 R Norfolk R
618 – A Stringer ARCM
2 Lincoln R
620 – GF Wooley MM
1 DG
621 – FL Leach ARCM
1 The Buffs
623 – JC Hitch
LRAM ARCM
1 Cheshire

1923 cont.
624 – DJ Plater
LRAM ARCM
2 SWB
625 – ST Webber
ARCM
2 Seaforth

1924
622 – R Marshall
2 KOSB
626 – BS Gumbley
2 Glosters
627 – B Glibbens
ARCM
2 Midd'x R
628 – LJ Pay
LRAM ARCM
2 Leicester R
636 – C Spanholtz
2 KOYLI
629 – BH Gubbins
LRAM ARCM
1 Suffolk R
635 – PJ Ryan ARCM
2 S Lan R
633 – WH FitzEarle
ARCM
2 KOSB
637 – HTJ Gebbels
ARCM
1 DCLI
632 – AE James
2 Somerset LI
630 – HC Jarman
ARCM
1 HLI
631 – JR Fleckney
2 Queen's R

1925
634 – GO Bixley
2 Worc R
638 – HPG Perdue
ARCM
1 RWF
639 – RB Heggie
5 DG
640 – RC Jones ARCM
4 H
643 – BG Pipe ARCM
2 Oxs & Bucks LI
645 – FH Pomphrey
2 R Sussex R
641 – DB Dowle
1 E Surr R
642 – WC Windram
ARCM
1 Inniskilling Fus
644 – G Smith ARCM
1 Sher For
646 – RW Tulip
2 R Fus
647 – FJ Allisebrooke
MM
17/21 L

1925 cont.
648 – REG Grimes
14/20 H
649 – R Botting
DCM MM ARCM
E Essex R

1926
650 – M Roberts
LRAM ARCM
10 H
651 – AJ Butt ARCM
1 R Fus
654 – EJ Woollcott
1 Somerset LI
656 – JB Lockton
1 Dorset R
652 – A lemoine
12 L
653 – S Rhodes ARCM
1 RS
655 – OW Geary
ARCM
1 Border R
657 – GH Willcocks
2 SWB
661 – R Gough ARCM
2 DWR
658 – EP Courtnell
ARCM
8 H
659 – CE Raison
ARCM
1 JOYLI
660 – A Young ARCM
2 DCLI

1927
662 – D McBain
ARCM
2 KRRC
663 – FM Marks
ARCM
4/7 DG

1928
664 – CS Beat ARCM
2 A&SH
666 – H Perry ARCM
1 Queen's R
667 – H Ivemey
LRAM ARCM
2 York & Lanc R
665 – G Hardy
LRAM ARCM
2 Rifle Bde
669 – JP Howson
1 S Lan R
670 – H Hope ARCM
1 North'n R
668 – GW Hespe
LRAM ARCM
1 Seaforth
671 – HE Hull MM
1 R Fus

1928 cont.
672 – LJ Halloway
2 R W Kent R
673 – A Coventry
1 King's Own R
674 – RFA Howard
ARCM
1 R Norfolk R
675 – E Kleinstuber
1 E Lan R
676 – AH McPherson
ARCM
2 Gordons
677 – GAV Lawes
LRAM ARCM
3 H

1929
678 – GH Potter
1 King's
679 – WB Salmon
LRAM ARCM
1 The Buffs
680 – JA Thornburrow
LRAM ARCM
2 DG
681 – ER Hooper
LRAM ARCM
2 Green Howards
683 – J Baxter
2 S Stafford R
682 – PA Purcell
LRAM ARCM
1 Bedfs & Herts R
684 – LN Dunn ARCM
1 Cameronians
685 – T Gray ARCM
1 Manch R
686 – B Howe ARCM
1 Essex R

1930
687 – FJ Harris ARCM
2 E York R
689 – AB Yule
2 E Lan R
688 – H Johnson ARCM
2 N Stafford R
689 – JA Dalrymple
2 Wilt R
690 – WB Foster ARCM
2 The Buffs
691 – A Hibbert
LRAM ARCM psm
1 KRRC
692 – FJ Davidson
1 Welsh R
693 – R Barsotti ARCM
2 Queen's R
694 – HA Hole ARCM
1 R U Rifles
696 – EG Underhill
ARCM
2 S Lan R
695 – JJM Watts
2 W York R

1930 cont.
697 – JL Judd
LRAM ARCM
2 HLI
698 – A Hollick ARCM
1 R North'd Fus

1931
699 – WH Lawton
ARCM
1 R War R
699 – AW Crofts
ARCM
The Greys
700 – FW Dennett
ARCM
2 KSLI
702 – WEN Sherratt
1 Worc R
701 – LW Lee ARCM
1 N Stafford R
706 – A Aquilina
R Malta Artillery
703 – AE Judge
1 Midd'x R
704 – AJF Allen ARCM
9 L
705 – NM Richardson
LRAM ARCM
5 DG
707 – FW Barber ARCM
2 R U Rifles
708 – EGR Palmer
ARCM
1 Loyal R
709 – AA Singer
ARCM
1 RD
710 – V Stadden
2 Devon R
711 – GTH Holley
ARCM
1 R Hamp R

1932
712 – EJ Webb ARCM
1 Dorset R
713 – EWT Cox ARCM
2 Sher For
714 – F Burnett ARCM
2 RWF
715 – WA Elliott ARCM
1 Lan Fus
716 – JL Evans ARCM
2 North'd Fus
717 – DA Pope ARCM
1 Camerons
718 – A Brundsen
ARCM
2 Seaforth
719 – EE Manley
ARCM
2 E Surr R
721 – L Bradley ARCM
1 Devon

1932 cont.
725 – AG O'Connor
ARCM
1 A&SH

1933
724 – HWV Roberts
ARCM
2 RSF
726 – JBH Thorpe
ARCM
2 Bedfs & Herts R
720 – TG Dought
ARCM
1 KSLI
723 – LJ Maiden LRAM
ARCM
1 BW
728 – CE Dennis ARCM
2 Midd'x R
727 – JAG Mantz LRAM
ARCM
2 R Leic
729 – CM Brooks
ARCM
1 Queen's R
730 – E Baker ARCM
1 Seaforth
732 – J Longstaff
2 Suffolk R

1934
734 – JCJ Martin
2 KOYLI
733 – FH Rose ARCM
2 Durham LI
735 – JR McKenna
ARCM
1 R W Kent R
736 – H Gould ARCM
2 Border R
737 – AJ Caldicutt
ARCM
2 DWR
738 – R Williams LRAM
ARCM
2 Lincoln R
739 – WJ Gibbs ARCM
1 Glosters
740 – FH Reid ARCM
1 W York R
741 – JBG O'Keefe
2 R berk R
742 – CS Evans
1 York & Lanc R
743 – LP Austing
2 Loyal R
762 – C Eldicott ARCM
1 SWB
744 – AE Neale ARCM
1 Leicester R
745 FA Jones ARCM
1 DWR
746 HB Jordan ARCM
2 RS

1934 cont.
749 – HF Brown ARCM
2 S Stafford R
752 – CF West ARCM
1 Rifle Bde

1935
753 – RG Ashton
ARCM
2 Gordons
754 – SH Hills ARCM
2 RWF
747 – W Atkins ARCM
1 Wilt R
750 – LD Brown
LRAM ARCM
1 E York R
751 – AL Streeter
ARCM
13/18 H
755 – R Lester ARCM
1 Green Howards
756 – G Savage
LRAM ARCM
2 R Warwick R
757 – C Nalden
LRAM ARCM
2 Sher For
748 – RW Griffett
ARCM
1 Lincoln R
758 – A Carr ARCM
2 Dorset R
761 – JA Gilbert ARCM
2 R Hamp R
759 – G Irvin ARCM
1 DCLI
760 – EL Statham
ARCM
2 Manch R
763 – EA Eames ARCM
2 DG
764 – BH Brown
ARCM
2 King's Own R
766 – GC Hensby
ARCM
7 H
767 – HC Macpherson
ARCM
1 RS
768 – ME Thatcher
ARCM
1 S Stafford R
769 – JPC Bailey
LRAM ARCM
2 R Sussex R
770 – RHE Jarvis
ARCM
1 DG
771 F Buckmaster
ARCM
1 Cheshire
776 JH Dought ARCM
1 E Lan R

1936
765 – GWT Perry
11 H
775 – CH Marriott
ARCM
2 North'n R
772 – C Nel ARCM
4/7 DG
773 – EF Rippon
ARCM
1 Durham LI
774 – EGH Irving
ARCM
1 S Lan R
777 – JL Wallace
ARCM
1 Border R
780 – EF Bagwell
ARCM
1 R Hamp R
781 – WH Moore
ARCM
1 SLI

1937
778 – SV Hays
LRAM ARCM
2 SWB
779 – RC Ridewood
ARCM
4 H
782 – J Laing ARCM
Nigerian Regt
783 – JW Brown
ARCM
2 R Ir Fus
784 – HF Ottway
ARCM
2 Inniskilling Fus
790 – RAN Marsh
ARCM
1 Inniskilling Fus
785 – CO Parker
ARCM
1 R War R
786 – GCB Quick
LRAM ARCM
1 R Fus
787 – AHH Swift
LRAM ARCM
10 H
789 – WM Kendall
LRAM ARCM
2 KOSB

1938
788 – HE Roberts
ARCM
12 L
791 – HCF Monk
ARCM
1 Essex R
792 – PV Walsh
ARCM
2 King's

1938 cont.
793 – LH Hicks
LRAM ARCM
2 BW
794 – FAG Goddard
LRAM ARCM
1 Bedfs & Herts R
795 – SW Ord-Hume
ARCM
1 North'n R
798 – DK Feltham
LRAM ARCM
1 Ox & Bucks LI
796 – CEF Marriott
ARCM
1 E Surr R
797 – GE Jackson ARCM
2 R W Kent R
799 – WHW Mills
LRAM ARCM
1 DCLI
809 – A Chaffoo
LRAM ARCM
Iraq Army
801 – WEJ Kifford
ARCM
1 Midd'x R
800 – GJF Dean ARCM
2 DCLI
802 – W Williams
ARCM
1 Gordons
803 – B White ARCM
2 W York R
804 – VE Webster
ARCM
2 Camerons
808 – AW Jarvis
LRAM ARCM
2 KRRC

1939
805 – SA Baker ARCM
1 KRRC
806 – JA Carrick ARCM
1 HLI
807 – LR Bayly ARCM
1 N Stafford R
810 – SW Pennell ARCM
1 Cameronians
811 – CA Bolt ARCM
The Greys
812 – WG Taylor ARCM
2 Worc R
813 – EP Martin
LRAM ARCM
2 Cheshire
814 – RA Lawson
LRAM ARCM
1 R U Rifles
815 – D Keeling ARCM
1 Seaforth
816 – HW Holyoak
ARCM
2 RSF

1939 cont.
817 – ST Vinnciombe
ARCM
13/18 H
818 – T Coleman
2 Somerset LI

1940
819 – GH Stunnell ARCM
1 Suffolk R
821 – FL Wright ARCM
2 Lan Fus
820 – LE Cox LRAM
ARCM
15/19 H
825 – HL Appleby
ARCM
1 Sher For
822 – G Idris Jones
ARCM
2 N Stafford R
823 – L Fereday ARCM
1 R Hamp R
826 – FJ Brooks ARCM
1 R Ir Fus
824 – RA Newman
ARCM
3 H

1941
827 – GA Bennett ARCM
2 RWF
829 – JC O'Reilly ARCM
2 RS
830 – F Vallas ARCM
2 Dorset R
831 – T Davies ARCM
1 King's
832 – ES Smythe ARCM
1 R Norfolk R
833 – EE Snape ARCM
1 Glosters
834 – WJ Hickman
ARCM
1 SWB
836 – R Hurst ARCM
14/20 H
837 – FJ Gallagher
ARCM
2 Ir Fus
838 – T Clegg ARCM
1 Welsh R
840 – J.H Hempstead
ARCM
17/21 L
841 – T Noble ARCM
16/5 L
842 – RW Soars ARCM
1 R U Rifles
843 – LR Morley ARCM
1 King's Own R

1942
828 – J Purcell ARCM
2 Leicester R

1942 cont.
839 – D Seed ARCM
2 DWR
835 – CA Adams ARCM
1 RS
845 – CT Beare ARCM
2 KOYLI
849 – RE Selley ARCM
2 Suffolk R
848 – FE Taylor ARCM
3 DG
847 – JM Thritle ARCM
1 Midd'x R
846 – AJ Wilson LRAM
ARCM
2 HLI
844 – CH Jaeger LRAM
ARCM
4 H
850 – CD Jarrett ARCM
2 Green Howards

1943
852 – CP Arnell ARCM
2 Sher For
851 – DV Start ARCM
1 Camerons
853 – WT Brown ARCM
1 Lincoln R

1944
854 – MV Young ARCM
1 Border R
855 – JC Wood ARCM
8 H
856 – JR Hands
2 DCLI
857 – RE House ARCM
2 Glosters

1945
858 – A Underwood
ARCM
1 W York R
859 – ER Wragg ARCM
5 DG
861 – W Jackson ARCM
1 N Stafford R
860 – D Harvey ARCM
2 Norf R
863 – LR Barnett ARCM
1 BW
873 – MR Davis
2 R U Rifles
870 – HL Burge ARCM
2 E York R
867 – CWG Hey ARCM
1 KSLI
871 – O Birkin LRAM
ARCM
2 Rifle Bde
864 – FE Hays LRAM ARCM
1 Worc R
866 – HB Clarke
9 L

1945 cont.
874 – E Gaines
2 Queen's R
862 – J Haworth ARCM
2 E Lan R
868 – WJ Adams ARCM
2 Cheshire
872 – KA Elloway ARCM
2 Bedfs & Herts R
869 – A Mitchenall ARCM
2 S Lan R
876 – EJ Moore ARCM
1 E Lan R
865 – EG Spooner ARCM
2 Manch R
875 – WH Freeth
1 R Berk R
877 – GE Young
2 York & Lanc R
878 – GR Freeth
2 Worc R
879 – DS Pooke1
S Lan R
880 – GR Crowhurst
2 Durham LI
881 – FA Payne1
E York R
882 – WGJ Lemon ARCM
2 Gordons

1946
883 – AF Trythall
1 RD
884 – FW Roy ARCM
15/19 H

1947
885 – GA Craig ARCM
1 KOYLI
886 – T Geggie1
Cheshire
890 – M Scott LRAM
ARCM
R Canadian Regt
891 – H Balshaw
1 KOYLI
888 – J Plant
1 Dorset R
889 – JM Gayfer
Mus Bac LRAM ARCMR
Canadian Artillery

1948
892 – LP Smith DCM
South Rhodesia Staff Corps
893 – G Magri ARCM
R Malta Artillery

1949
894 – JH Howe LRAM
ARCM
A&SH
895 – GL Bradbury
LRAM ARCM
10 H

1949 cont.
896 – HA Kenney
LRAM ARCM
Ox & Bucks LI
897 – GR Hall ARCM
Inniskilling Fus
898 – SH Price LRAM
Sher For
899 – CH Pike LRAM
ARCM
Cameronians
900 – HW Vince ARCM
5 DG

1950
901 – EW Jeanes
LRAM ARCM
1 KRRC
902 – LE Stockham
LRAM ARCM
KOSB
903 – RB Bashford
LRAM ARCM
17/21 L
905 – HF Stone
Gold Coast Regiment
904 – JW Pearson
Sierra Leone Regiment
906 – TL Sharpe
LRAM ARCM
The Buffs
907 – RG Watkins
LRAM ARCM
R.W Kent R
908 – FA Jackson
LRAM ARCM
Midd'x R
909 – E Crowcroft
LRAM ARCM
W York R
910 – RF Hilling ARCM
R War R
911 – AW Brown
LRAM ARCM LGSM
12 L
912 – KRR Boulding
LRAM ARCM
Devon R

1951
913 – AR Kelly LRAM
ARCM
R Sussex R
914 – CE Smith
RS
915 – EG Featherstone
RWF
916 – F Morgan ARCM
1 Para
HV Woollaston
6 King African Rifles
917 – RF Rodgers
ARCM
2 KRRC

1951 cont.
918 – WA Lloyd
4 H
919 – JH Cooper
8 H
920 – EA Moon
12 L
921 – JA Baker LRAM
ARCM
BW
922 – AB Brown
Royal Canadian Army
923 – H LePage
Royal Canadian Army
924 – BJ Lyons
Royal Canadian Army
925 – JC Smith
R Ir Fus

1952
926 – CF West
Border R
927 – AE Hollowell
ARCM
2 Para
928 – DK Walker ARCM
Leicester R
929 – DW Turner ARCM
The Greys
930 – GEE Plummer
ARCM
Glosters
931 – CH Churchill
Inniskilling Fus
932 – FJ Blaber ARCM
T Fus
933 – GHJ Hurst ARCM
S Stafford R
934 – PF Cane
2 RWF
937 – W Babbs
2 BW
938 – WGT Stevens
2 Green Howards
939 – SR Peacock
2 Durham LI
940 – R Quinn
2 Inniskilling Fus
935 – GD Hart
1 Rifle Bde
936 – RA Verrall
Welsh R
941 – AWE Davis
1 R U Rifles

1953
942 – RAY Mitchell
ARCM
HLI
943 – LF Marke
2 Lan Fus
944 – W Snowden ARCM
E Surr R
945 – G Fidoe
R Hamp R

1953 cont.
946 – RW Spencer ARCM
1 KDG
947 – AG Henderson
Seaforth

1954
949 – F Sutton ARCM
Loyal R
948 – DP Cole
Sher For
950 – W Allen
RSF
952 – E Thompson
R Nor R
951 – PW Parkes
LRAM ARCM
DCLI
954 – EH Wade
3 H
953 – D Snowden ARCM
1 Rifle Bde
955 – RW Brown
Essex R
956 – EG Horabin
LRAM ARCM
7 H
957 – EC Harris
17/21 L
958 – G Gagnier
Royal Canadian Army
959 – A Ferland LRAM
Royal Canadian Army

1955
960 – JB MacDowall
LRAM
WRAC
961 – LS Camplin ARCM
N Stafford R
962 – RA Mott
14/20 H
964 – CH Buck
Camerons
963 – LCW Bently
LRAM ARCM LGSM
Manch R
965 – NF Hirst
Somerset LI
969 – RD Ford
Gordons
970 – RAJ Pritchard
North'n R
966 – DA Bayton
Lincoln R
967 – OR Whiting
SWB
973 – FJ Francis
ARCM LGSM
11 H
972 – P Russell ARCM
King's Own R
971 – GA Holben
ARCM
Suffolk R

1955 cont.
974 – RE Courtnell
4/7 DG
975 – DN Taylor
16/5 L
968 – HA Jeffrey
ARCM LGSM
Royal Canadian Army

1956
978 – FT Avery ARCM
Loyal R
977 – C Blackburn ARCM
North'n R
976 – CA Maile ARCM
Wilt R
979 – AJ Richards ARCM
Lan Fus
980 – BW Crossman ARCM
3 Para
981 – WC Lyne
Queen's R
982 – GS Martin
DWR
985 – RR Greening
York & Lanc R
983 – JL Long
Worc R
984 – GE Evans ARCM
The Royals

1957
986 – C Adams LRAM
ARCM
Can Signals
987 – NM Wise ARCM
India Navy
988 – MN Pryce
3 DG
989 – KS Mohamed
Ceylon Police
991 – RA Ridings ARCM
KSLI
990 – BT Keeling ARCM
12 L
992 – TA Konteh
Sierra Leone Police
993 – CV Wright
LRAM ARCM
Border R
994 – FG Firth
KOYLI

1958
995 – DG Suttnil
RS
996 –
E York R
998 – MA Pope ARCM
A&SH
1000 – FR Jones ARCM
6 King's African Rifles
999 – GA Rutherford
ARCM
Cheshire

1958 cont.
1001 – TC Higgins
LRAM ARCM
Royal Canadian Dragoons
997 – SK Swanwick
ARCM
3 King's African Rifles
1003 – B Bowyer LRAM
DWR
1002 – G Turner ARCM
A(Mus)TCL
15/19 H
1004 – WJ Best ARCM
2 Para
1006 – PJ Fuller
R Fus
1005 – TA Kenny ARCM
Welsh R
1008 – JA O'Brien ARCM
11 H
1007 – R Hibbs
R Berk R
1009 – J Offord
KOYLI

1959
1012 – DR Beat ARCM
BW
1010 – RA Hunt LRAM
ARCM
Staffords
1011 – DR Kimberley
LRAM ARCM LGSM
R War R
1013 – HCR Bently ARCM
RWF
1014 – HRG Currie
ARCM LTCL
Royal Canadian Army
1016 – FR Fitch LRAM
ARCM
10 H
1017 – JE Battye ARCM
Leicester R
1018 – DE Pryce
R Sussex R
1020 – Alies Bin Arshad
LRAM ARCM
Malay Police
1019 – AF Kershaw
13/18 H
1021 – JC Mutlow
Sierra Leone Regiment
1022 – WT Purnell
King's
1025 – HC Eagles
Canadian Black Watch
1026 – CA Villeneuve
LRAM ARCM
Royal Canadian Army
1024 – SW Patch LRAM
ARCM
4/8 H
1023 – BE Simpson
1 RGJ

1960 cont.
1027 – Hassan Bin Din
ARCM
Malayan Army
1028 – JH McShane
ARCM
Midd'x R
1029 – Ridzwab Bin
Mulck LRAM ARCM
Singapore Police
1030 – RJ Sandwell
LRAM ARCM
Lan Fus

1961
1031 – R Tonks
4 King's African Rifles
1033 – GJ Peiris LRAM
ARCM
Ceylon
1034 – Abdulsulam J
Franco
Iraq Army
1035 – Ibrahim A
Mustapha
Iraq Army
1036 – Mohamed
abdul Razak
Iraq Army
1037 – GA White
LRAM ARCM
6 King's African Rifles
1032 – B Skelton
LRAM ARCM
3 King's African Rifles
1038 – AL Lee ARCM
*Canadian Horse
Artillery*
1039 – JR Howe ARCM
5 DG
1040 – RC Berry ARCM
Durham LI
1041 – CM Williams
LRAM ARCM
1 QDG

1962
1043 – MM Clark
LRAM ARCM
R U Rifles
1042 – TA Cunnell
Aden Prot. Levies
1044 – GT Cooke
LRAM ARCM
RHF
1046 – BE Hicks
LRAM ARCM
R Fus
1045 – HL Johnson
ARCM
Loyal R
1047 – AR Henderson
ARCM
*Royal Australian
Infantry*

1962 cont.
1048 – B Storey LRAM
DCLI
1049 – JT Dowell
LRAM ARCM
Royal Canadian
Artillery
1051 – F Cockcroft
AMusTCL
3 E Anglian
1050 – RW Benson
D and D
1052 – K Jackson
LRAM ARCM
Green Howards
1053 – CE Gregory
R Hamp R
1055 – BM Thomas
ARCM
14/20 H
1056 – MRG Sumber
York & Lanc
1054 – T Charlton
Cameronians
1058 – RHF Wait
LRAM ARCM
QOH
1057 – FEW Short
ARCM
QR Surr

1963
1059 – T Griffiths
ARCM
17/21 L
1062 – W Bibby ARCM
3 Para
1060 – GR Daniels
KOSB
1063 – D Stannard
LRAM ARCM ARCT
Royal Canadian
Regiment
1064 – AM Rahuma
Tripoli Police
1065 – Shamsudin
bin Ismail ARCM
Malay Police
1066 – R Larbi ARCM
Ghana Army
1061 – BV Langton
QO Hldrs
1067 – RG Baker
4/7 DG
1068 – W Wroe
1 Para
1069 – CA Harper
ARCM
Gordons
1070
J Pope ARCM
R North'd Fus
1071 – JH Pearson
ARCM
A&SH

1963 cont.
1072 – D Carson
Glosters

1964
1075 – PJ Herrington
Sher For
1077F – W Fairbairn
ARCM
The Greys
1073 – MG Lane
ARCM
10 H
1074 – Bin Arshad
Mahmoud
Malay Regiment
1076 – A Prospect
ARCM LRSM LTCL
Trinidad Police
1078 – A Oduka
Uganda Police
1079 – AP Meek
LGSM
RS

1965
1080 – RG Richards
PWO
1081 – BW Kingsbury
R Ir Fus
1082 – G Small ARCM
LGSM
British Guiana Forces
1083 – GC Naylor
Mus Bac GRSM LRAM
ARCM LTCL
Can LI
1084 – JF Pierret
ARCM
22 Regiment of Canada
1085 – K Swanwick
BBCM
Can Signals
1086 – Ashine Raile
Ethiopian Forces
1087 – CI Herbert
ARCM
3 DG
1090 – F Hayes ARCM
1 RGJ
1091 – EB Smith
D and D
1089 – FH Lamb
2 Para
1088 – JM Parkinson
ARCM
R War R
1093 – Abdullah bin
Ahmed
Singapore Military
Forces
1094 – BG Bogisch
ARCM ALCM
Royal Canadian
Army

1965 cont.
1092 – SP Holmes
ARCM ALCM
BW
1095 – WK Spry
ARCM
The Buffs
1096 – PM O'Connell
2 R Anglian
1097 – JT Poole
King's
1098 – AT Jamal
Jordan
1099 – B Dawson
ARCM ALCM
Welsh R

1966
1100 – SC Wood
DWR
1101 – DK Mackay
ARCM LGSM
The Royals
1102 – AI Chowd-
hury
Pakistan
1103 – R Bedford
R Sussex R
1105 – B Maiba
Tanganyika
1104 – O Aberinego
Uganda
1106 – R Gordon
Jamaica
1110 – E Odiase
Nigeria
1107 – WS Chisale
Malawi
1108 – ES Nichol
Gambia
1109 – S Kisine
Kenya
1111 – JA Brush
York & Lanc R
1112 – H Sherif
Libya
1113 – PA Cave
Barbados
1114 – Mohd Aondar
Bin Alaidin
Royal Malaya
Regiment

1967
1115 – SEM James
KSLI
1116 – D Mannifield
LGSM ARCM
RS
1117 – EK Acquah
Ghana
1118 – Gabriel Sandu
Tanganyika
1119 – F Onwoh
Nigeria

1967 cont.
1120 – Abdul Razak
Ibrahim
Iraq Army
1121 – JB Williams
ARCM
Jamaica Defence Force
1122 – J Gibson LTCL
Ldn R.
1124 – E Slater ARCM
SCLI

1968
1123 – BW Titley
13/18 H
1126 – TL Crichton
ARCM
1 Queens
1125 – GH Boynton
Worc R
1127 – Garib Ahamed
Mohamed
Kenya Police
1130 – Hamid
Osazawa
Nigerian Army
1128 – F Howlett
ARCM LGSM
16/5 L
1129 – J Bangura
Sierra Leone
Regiment
1131 – T Platts
ARCM
PWO
1134 – TG Cooper
4 R Anglian
1133 – JV Ayling
ARCM
Cheshire
1138 – RA Smith
ARCM
3 R Anglian
1135 – C Wood ARCM
King's Own Border
1132 – RI Woollcott
LGSM
Staffords
1139 – CJ Briggs
4/7 DG
1136 – HW Carter
ARCM
9/12 L
1137 – CT Pike ARCM
Green Howards
1141 – TB Domingue
LRSM ARCM LGSM
Mauritius Police
1140 – D Game LGSM
2 Queens
1143 – PB Smith
ARCM A(Mus)LCM
QRIH
1144 – J McToumey
1 RGJ

1968 cont.
1149 – Z Bowness
ARCM
WRAC
1142 – MA Butcher
LRAM ARCM LGSM
Royal Australian Air
Force

1969
1146 – ME Cadwal-
lader
2 LI
1145 – P Mallas
ARCM
4 Queens
1147 – RG Tomlinson
ARCM LGSM
A&SH
1150 – PD Conibear
17/21 L
1153 – J Angi
Sarawak Police
1154 – WD Allen
Sierra Leone
Police
1155 – P Osile
Nigeria Police
1148 – MC Scholfield
Glosters
1151 – P Hannam
BEM
3 RRF
1156 – A Chircop
A(Mus)LCMR
Malta Artillery
1158 – JT Boden
A(Mus)LCM
2 RGJ
1152 – A Gomersall
LGSM A(Mus)LCM
1 R Anglian
1161 – D Bisoni
Malay Police
1157 – M Alexander
A(Mus)LCMDWR
1163 – D Jones
A(Mus)LCM
D and D
1166 – AJW Khozi
Zambia
1159 – MS Hennis
ARCM
QOH
1169 – AJ Winter
King's Own Border
1162 – AW Healey
Loya R
1165 – FA Renton
ARCM
Gordons
1164 – CJ Petheram
14/20 H
1169 – N Anderton
R Irish Rang

1969 cont.

1167 – AR Jeffs
RH
1168 – L Gibson
Staffords

1970

1170 – H Yafai
South Yemen Army
1171 – WN Harris
1 Para
1172 – P Parsons
5 DG
1173 – RJ Parker ARCM
2 RRF

1971

1175 – E Raper ARCM
2 Para
1174 – JG McColl ARCM
QDG
1176 – Abu Bakar bin
Pun ARCM
Malaysian Army
1177 – ED Wade
LRAM ARCM A(Mus)LCM
Trinidad Regiment
1178 – C Mynns
ARCM
St Lucia Police
1179 – V Bale
Fiji Police
1180 – N Wasume
Kenya Army
1181 – NA Borlase
ARCM
DERR
1182 – CM Leverty
(Henry)
KOSB
1184 – J Wood
3 Queens
1183 – BEP Briggs-
Watson ARCM
RS
1185 – PR Evans LTCL
A(Mus)TCL1
5/19 H

1972

1186 – EA Mortlake
3 Para
1188 – L Chamberlain
A&SH
1187 – CJ French
R Hamp R
1189 – AS Leeming
LGSM A(Mus)LCM
3 RGJ
1190 – J Dott
1 RRF
1192 – P Standing
RSDG
1191 – JB Dawson
1 Kings

1972 cont.

1195 – MM Hassen
Ceylon Army
1194 – RA Martin
1 PWO
1193 – WJ Simpson
LTCL
RHF
1196 – AG Clarke
DWR
1197 – ED Tulloch
Jamaica Defence Force

1973

1199 – CL Teo
Singapore Army
1198 – GH Leask LTCL
QLR
1204D – Chikakuda
Malawi Maharaja Band
1205 – CRM Pearce
R Irish Rang
1200 – NM Rogerson
LLTCL
BW
1202 – DE Price
Cheshire
1201 – CJ Ross
King's Own Border
1203 – BA Hughes LTCL
RWF
1206 – GP Scott LRSM
LTCL
Trinidad Police
1207 – J Cherry
1 R Anglian
1209 – GE Joseph ARCM
2 R Anglian
1208 – AWK Melvin
LTCL
1 Queens
1210 – JG Lewis LRAM
LTCL A(Mus)LCM BBCM
RRW

1974

1211 – CRC Garrity
LTCL
D and D
1213 – SA Watts
3 R Anglian
1212 – AM Jarrey
Glosters
1214 – MJ Evans LTCL
3 LI
1215 – JPatrick
Tanzania Defence Force
1217 – J M'Wase
Uganda Air Force
1218 – AD Daud
Royal Malay Regiment
1216 – J Wright
Nigerian Army
1219 – SR Clarke
A&SH

1974 cont.

1222 – LAE Hopkin
MBE LRAM
WRAC
1220 – FW Matthews
LLCM
1 RGJ
1221 – KW Napier
1 LI
1223 – JE Simmonds
2 LI
1225 – A Dzokoto ARCM
Ghana Air Force
1224 – PC Road-Night
3 RRF
1226 – RG Swift LRAM
ARCM LTCL
QRIH
1227 – REW Maycock
LRAM ARCM LGSM LTCL
4/7 DG

1975

1228 – MJ Verrall1
6/5 L
1231 – BH Bignall
LRAM ARCM LTCL
*Australian Army
Corps*
1232 – KS Dill LRAM
ARCM
Bermuda Regiment
1229 – WC Gilpin LTCL
2 R Irish Rang
1230 – I Thompson
13/8 H
1233 – L Mhango
Zambia Police
1234 – A Ashworth
ARCM BBCM
1 Para
1235 – JT Royley
ARCM BBCM
1 QDG
1239 – M Jonit
*Royal Malasian
RECCE*
1236 – CR Donaldson
2 RGJ
1237 – MF Lee
Staffords
1238 – DJ Marshall
ARCM
WFR
1240 – R Wearne
ARCM
QOH
1241 – DF Wall
KOSB
1242 – JP Gbagla
Sierra Leone Regiment

1976

1243 – DJ Little
1 RGJ

1976 cont.

1244 – B Idowu
Nigerian Police
1246 – RJ Francis
2 Queen's
1247 – TDK Batham
Gordons
1248 – JH Dodd
2 RRF
1250 – P Esplin
15/19 H
1252 – JWJ Dawson
Green Howards
1253 – MJ Henderson
5 DG
1259 – GM Compson
QO Hidrs
E Lifa
Malawi Army
KH Callender
Jamaica Defence Forces
Tanmeopeau
Tonga Police

1977

1255 – P Renn
9/12 L
1256 – P Jackson
AABC
1257 – J Seddon
1 RGJ
1258 – RD Judd
17/21 L
1260 – CJ Reeves
R Scots
1261 – R Allsop
Cheshire
1262 – TP Mulkern
1 RRF

1978

1263 – ME Jobe
Gambia Police
1264 – TSK Alubaidi
Iraq Forces
1265 – JC Robinson
QLR
1266 – LP Tyler
3 Para
1267 – PE Hills
1 Queen's
1268 – TS Davis
3 Queen's
1269 – SPW Lines
1 R Anglian

1979

1270 – PG Butler
KOSB
1271 – P Judson
D and D
1272 – R Sands
14/20 H
1273 – JB Tyrer
RHF

1979 cont.

1274 – MB Pyne
AABC
1275 – L Bakar
*Royal Malaysian
Police*
1276 – E Okwampah
Ghana Army
1277 – Tazehrooh
Imperial Iran Forces
1278 – KA Moore
Barnados Police
1279 – F Slack
QRIH
1280 – GA Kingston
RWF
1281 – DW Wood
R Hamps
1282 – RA Ely
2 Para
1283 – GE Locker
13/18 H
1284 – MS Cammack
4/7 DG
1284 – TSK Alubaidi
Irak Army

1980

1285 – RG Sowerby
RH
1286 – RC Nother
DERR
1287 – D Phyall
16/5 L
1288 – RL Coomber
3 RRF
1289 – JZ Nicoo
Iranian Air Force
1289 – PG Smith
King's
1290 – MJ Pegram
RRW
1290 – S Hayi
Nigeria A B C
1291 – RC Darke
Gordons
1292 – PH Byrne
JLR
1293 – JF Winterflood
2 R Irish Rang
1294 – JW Baines
Staffords
1295 – BA Shaw
QDG
1296 – DB Catt
1 R Irish Rang
1299 – CR Dawe
Green Howards
1300 – KC Shell
PWO
1302 – AG O'Connor
RRW
A Thompson
*Royal Bahamas
Police*

1981
1297 – SJ Smith
3 RRF
1298 – MJ Torrent
KORB
1301 – M Lever *3 LI*
1303 – KA Cowley
WFR
1308 – Milne *AABC*
ID Yusof
Singapore Police

1982
1304 – TE Pickering
Cheshire
1305 – GWC Jarvis
QO Hldrs
1306 – K Taylor
DWR
1307 – B Cunningham
3 Queen's

1983
1309 – PK Kane
17/21 L
1310 – EM Anderson
AABC
1311 – D Thompson
RSDG
1312 – RJ Owen
QLR
1314 – I Harding
3 RGJ
1315 – NC Wallis
1 R Anglian

1984
1313 – AR Bennett
Glosters
1316 – D Burton
2 LI
1317 – KG Lamb
A&SH
1318 – D Knox
Gordons
1319 – RC Salisbury
1 RTR
1320 – McLean
AABC
1321 – EP Forster
WRAC
1322 – JR Farthing
2 RTR
1323 – McCrum
2 R Anglian
1324 – AJ Hodgetts
R Scots
1325 – A Liaquat
Pakistan Army
1325 – EG Mooney
RWF
1326 – C Nimako
Ghana Police
1328 – Ramis J Sabti
Royal Guard of Oman

1985
1327 – LF Lowe
Bermuda Regt
1329 – SG Khanganwa
Malawi Police
1330 – AR Chatburn
13/18 H
1331 – SA Thompson
PWO
1332 – PD Shannon
RRW
1333 – GO Jones
16/5 L
1334 – R Hatton
15/19 H
1335 – T Carlton
BW
1338 – I McElligott
RGJ (Normandy)
1339 – CC Attrill
St George's RRF

1986
1337 – RA Wade
Jamaica Defence Force
1340 – PF Cooper
5 Innis DG
1341 – I Stewart
QOH
1342 – GW Taylor
4/7 DG
1343 – DM Clarke
1 R Irish Rang
1344 – M Davidson
RH
1345 – C Hogg
Para (Falklands)
1349 – JW Taylor
Para (Pegasus)

1987
1346 – JM Kamsa
Kenya Police
1348 – IR Peaple
Queens (Albuhera)
1350 – JE Chapman
KOSB
1351 – Martin
KORB
1352 – PL Murrell
WFR
1353 – C Horth
DWR
1354 – CC Gray
R Hamps
1355 – TJ Parkinson
3 R Anglians
1356 – K Hatton
1 DERR
1357 – DW Cresswell
QRIH
1358 – PR Clark
Duke of Kent's RRF
1359 – CJ Gold
15/19 H

1987 cont.
1360 – CC A Bovello
Guyana Police
1361 – HS Hamood
Royal Oman Police
1362 – W Chinkombelo
Malawi Army
1363 – K Defour
Trinidad & Tobago Regt
1364 – St V Dill
Bermuda Regt
1365 – TW Whittingham
QO Hldrs

1988
1336 – G Lloyd
AABC
1366 – S Barnwell
QLR
1367 – K J Harrod
17/21 L
1368 – M Hardman
2 RTR
1369 – DD Robertson
Kings
1370 – G Cross *QDG*

1989
1347 – Z Othman
Royal Brunei Malay Regt
1371 – PA Pickett
AABC
1372 – AS Rosli
MalaysianArmy
1373 – C Meldrum
Staffords
1374 – GD Rodger
3 RTR
1375 – CE Hicks
14/20 H
1376 – SJ Applegate
9/12 L
1377 – DB Greer *RHF*
1378 – R Falshaw
RSDG
1379 – MA Perry
D and D
1381 – PM Manyeh
Sierra Leone Regt
1382 – PJ Mikundi
Malawi Army
1383 – M Dibba
Gambia National Army

1990
1380 – GJ Bright
9/12 L
1384 – JR Young
Queen's (Quebec)
1385 – PJ Hunt
A&SH
1386 – JAC Huggins
Cheshire
1387 – KN Crook
Glosters

1990 cont.
1388 – EH Keeley
LI (Corunna)
1389 – PM Greener
13/18 H
1390 – VF Eckerman
1 RTR
1391 – R Pennington
4/7 DG
1392 – P Goodwin
RWF
1395 – S Julaopas
Royal Thai Army
1396 – NA Villafana
Trinidad & Tobago Police
1397 – AH Habib
Royal Oman Police
1399 – TJ Cooper
Gordons
M Adel
Jordanian Armed Forces

1991
1398 – BM Taylor
LI (Salamanca)
1400 – BW Hopla
R Irish Rang
1401 – C Shearer
2 R Anglian
1402 – MJ Searle
Green Howards
1403 – NG Slater
D and D
1404 – IB MacPherson
RGJ (Penninsular)
1405 – G Eyas
Jordanian Armed Forces
1406 – GB Gurung
Bde Gurkhas
1407 – VB Heemans
Jamaica Regt
1408 – Al H Nasser
Royal Guard of Oman
1409 – EH Laini
Malawi Police
S Cline-Decker
Sierra Leone Police

1992
1410 – G Williams
R Scots
1411 – B Wassell
RGJ (Normandy)
1412 – L Sharpe
Para (Falklands)
1413 – D Milgate
KORB
1414 – M Al-Akhras
Jordanian Armed Forces
1415 – N A Oliech
Kenya Army
1416 – C S Loo
Singapore Armd Forces
1417 – V Pongpoonsub
Royal Thai Army

1992 cont.
1418 – SI Khondker
Bangladesh Army
1419 – CR Way
DWR
1420 – DJ Bertie
PWO
1421 – GE Clegg
Glosters
1422 – NF Morfill
Gibraltar Regt

1993
1432 – TL Peng
Singapore Armd Forces
1433 – A Mingmit
Royal Thai Army
1434 – A Amereen
Jordanian Armed Forces
1435 – M Sauka
Malawi Army
1436 – D Myers
St Lucia Police
1437 – S Alnoobi
Royal Guard of Oman

1994
1423 – MA Clarke
Lowland
1424 – TD Arnold
AAC
1425 – MJ Ainley
POW (Lucknow)
1426 – KFN Roberts
RTR
1427 – J Ridgway
Highland
1428 – NP Morgan
REME
1441 – DR Clarke
Jamaica Defence Force
1442 – KH Lee
Singapore Armed Forces
1443 – F Chaowalit
Royal Thai Army
1444 – NM Marcadia
Kenya Army
1445 – HS Holla
Malawi Police

1995
1429 – RD Gray
Gibraltar Regt
1430 – JD Brigden
Para
1431 – GC Henderson
Queens (Minden)
1439 – P Stredwick
Queens (Normandy)

1996
1438 – KL Davies
R Signals
1440 – A Knox
Gibraltar Regt

REGIMENT AND CORPS ABBREVIATIONS

4 DG	4th Dragoon Guards
4 H	4th Hussars
5 Innis DG	5th Royal Inniskilling Dragoon Guards
6 DG	Carabiniers (6th Dragoon Guards), The
7 DG	7th (Princess Royal's) Dragoon Guards
7 H	7th Hussars
8 H	8th Hussars
11 H	11th Hussars
12 L	12th Lancers
13 H	13th Hussars
14 H	14th King's Hussars
16 L	16th The Queen's Lancers
18 H	18th Royal Hussars (Queen Mary's Own)
21 L	21st Lancers (Empress of India's)
AAC	Army Air Corps
A&SH	Argyll and Sutherland Highlanders, The
ACC	Army Catering Corps
AGC	Adjutant General's Corps
AJSM (Bov)	Army Junior School of Music (Bovington)
AJSM (Pir)	Army Junior School of Music (Pirbright)
Albuhera	Albuhera Band, The Queen's Regiment
ASC	Army Service Corps
Bays, The	Queen's Bays, The
Bedf R	Bedfordshire Regiment, The
Bedfs & Herts R	Bedfordshire and Hertfordshire Regiment, The
Border R	Border Regiment, The
BAOR	British Army Of The Rhine
Buffs, The	Buffs, The
BW	Black Watch (Royal Highland Regiment), The
Cameronians	Cameronians, The
Camerons	Queen's Own Cameron Highlanders, The
Can LI	Princess Patricia's Canadian Light Infantry
Can Signals	Royal Canadian Corps of Signals
Cheshire	Cheshire Regiment, The
Coldm Gds	Coldstream Guards
Conn Rang	Connaught Rangers, The
D and D	Devonshire and Dorset Regiment, The
DCLI	Duke of Cornwall's Light Infantry, The
Derby R	Derbyshire Regiment, The
DERR	Duke of Edinburgh's Royal Regiment (Berkshire and Wiltshire), The
Devon R	Devonshire Regiment, The
Dorset R	Dorsetshire Regiment, The
Durham LI	Durham Light Infantry, The
DWR	Duke of Wellington's Regiment, The
E Kent R	East Kent Regiment, The
E Lan R	East Lancashire Regiment, The
Essex R	Essex Regiment, The
E Surr R	East Surrey Regiment, The
E York R	East Yorkshire Regiment, The
Foresters	Sherwood Foresters, The
Gds Depot (Pir)	Guards Depot Pirbright
GJ	Green Jackets, The
Glosters	Gloucestershire Regiment, The
Gordons	Gordon Highlanders, The
Green Howards	Green Howards (Alexandra Princess of Wales's Own Yorkshire Regiment), The
Gren Gds	Grenadier Guards
Greys, The	Scots Greys, The
HAC	Honourable Artillery Company, The
Hampshire R	Hampshire Regiment, The
Highland Bde	Highland Brigade, The
Highland R	Highland Regiment, The
HLI	Highland Light Regiment, The
IG	Irish Guards
Inniskilling Fus	Royal Inniskilling Fusiliers, The
JLR	Junior Leaders Regiment (Bovington)
JMW	Junior Musicians Wing (Pirbright)
KDG	1st King's Dragoon Guards
KH	Kneller Hall (Royal Military School of Music)
Kings	King's Regiment, The
Kings (Norm)	Normandy Band, The King's Division
Kings Own Border	King's Own Royal Border Regiment, The
King's Own R	King's Own Royal Regiment, The
Kings (Water)	Waterloo Band, The King's Division
KOSB	King's Own Scottish Borderers, The
KRH	King's Royal Hussars, The
KRRC	King's Royal Rifle Corps
KSLI	King's Shropshire Light Infantry
Lan Fus	Lancashire Fusiliers, The
LD	Light Dragoons, The
Leicester R	Leicestershire Regiment, The
Leins R	Leinster Regiment, The
LG	Life Guards, The
LI	Light Infantry, The
Lincoln R	Lincolnshire Regiment, The
Lowland Bde	Lowland Brigade
Lowland R	Lowland Regiment, The
Loyal R	Loyal Regiment, The
L'pool R	Liverpool Regiment, The
Manch R	Manchester Regiment, The
Midd'x R	Middlesex Regiment, The
MSC	Medical Staff Corps
N Lan R	North Lancashire Regiment, The
Norf R	Norfolk Regiment, The
North'd Fus	Northumberland Fusiliers, The
North'n R	Northamptonshire Regiment, The
N Stafford R	North Staffordshire Regiment, The
Ox & Bucks LI	Oxfordshire and Buckinghamshire Light Infantry, The
Ox LI	Oxfordshire Light Infantry, The
Para	Parachute Regiment, The
PoW (Clive)	Clive Band, The Prince of Wales's Division
PoW Div	Prince of Wales's Division Depot
PoW (Luck)	Lucknow Band, The Prince of Wales's Division

PPLI	Princess Patricia's Light Infantry of Canada
PWO	Prince of Wales's Own Regiment of Yorkshire, The
PWRR	Princess of Wales's Royal Regiment
QDG	1st The Queen's Dragoon Guards
QLR	Queen's Lancashire Regiment, The
QO Buffs	The Queen's Own Buffs, The Royal Kent Regiment
QOH	Queen's Own Hussars, The
QO Hldrs	Queen's Own Highlanders (Seaforth and Camerons)
Queens	Queen's Regiment, The
Queens (Alb)	Albuhera Band, The Queen's Regiment
Queens (Mind)	Minden Band, The Queen's Division
Queens (Norm)	Normandy Band, The Queen's Division
Queens (Queb)	Quebec Band, The Queen's Regiment
Queen's R	Queen's Royal Regiment, The
QRH	Queen's Royal Hussars, The
QRIH	Queen's Royal Irish Hussars, The
QRL	Queen's Royal Lancers, The
QR Surr	Queen's Royal Surrey Regiment, The
RA	Royal Artillery
RA(Alan)	Royal Artillery (Alanbrooke)
RA(BAOR)	Royal Artillery (BAOR)
RA(Gib)	Royal Artillery (Gibraltar)
RA(Mtd)	Royal Artillery (Mounted)
RA(N Cmd)	Royal Artillery (Northern Command)
RA(Plym)	Royal Artillery (Plymouth)
RA(Port)	Royal Artillery (Portsmouth)
RA(Sal Pl)	Royal Artillery (Salisbury Plain)
RA(Wool)	Royal Artillery (Woolwich)
RAC	Royal Armoured Corps
RAC Jnr Ldrs	Royal Armoured Corps, Junior Leaders Regiment
RAF	Royal Air Force
RAMC	Royal Army Medical Corps
R Anglian	Royal Anglian Regiment, The
RAPC	Royal Army Pay Corps
RASC	Royal Army Service Corps
RAVC	Royal Army Veterinary Corps
R Berks R	Royal Berkshire Regiment, The
R Canadian R	Royal Canadian Regiment, The
RCT	Royal Corps of Transport
RDG	Royal Dragoon Guards, The
R Dub Fus	Royal Dublin Fusiliers, The
RE(Ald)	Royal Engineers (Aldershot)
RE(Chat)	Royal Engineers (Chatham)
Recce	Reconnaissance Corps, The
REME	Corps of Royal Electrical and Mechanical Engineers
RFC	Royal Flying Corps, The
R Fus	Royal Fusiliers, The
RGA	Royal Garrison Artillery
R Gar R	Royal Garrison Regiment, The
RGJ	Royal Green Jackets, The
RH	Royal Hussars (Prince of Wales's Own), The
RHA	Royal Horse Artillery
R Hamps	Royal Hampshire Regiment, The
RHF	Royal Highland Fusiliers (Princess Margaret's Own Glasgow and Ayrshire Regiment), The
RHG	Royal Horse Guards
RHG/D	Blues and Royals (Royal Horse Guards and 1st Dragoons), The
R Highrs	Royal Highlanders, The
Rifle Bde	Rifle Brigade, The
R Innis Fus	Royal Inniskilling Fusiliers, The
R Ir Constab	Royal Irish Constabulary
R Ir Fus	Royal Irish Fusiliers, The
R Irish	Royal Irish Regiment, The (after 1992)
R Irish Rang	Royal Irish Rangers, The
R Ir R	Royal Irish Regiment, The (before 1922)
R Ir Rif	Royal Irish Rifles, The
R Lanc R	Royal Lancaster Regiment, The
RLC	Royal Logistic Corps
R Leic	Royal Leicestershire Regiment, The
RM	Royal Marines
RM(Chat)	Royal Marines (Chatham)
RM(Plym)	Royal Marines (Plymouth)
RM(Port)	Royal Marines (Portsmouth)
RM(Wool)	Royal Marines (Woolwich)
RMA(Sand)	Royal Military Academy (Sandhurst)
R Malta Artillery	Royal Malta Artillery
RM Art	Royal Marine Artillery
RMC(Sand)	Royal Military College (Sandhurst)
RMLI	Royal Marine Light Infantry
RMSM	Royal Military School of Music, Kneller Hall
R Mun Fus	Royal Munster Fusiliers, The
R Norfolk R	Royal Norfolk Regiment, The
R North'd Fus	Royal Northumberland Fusiliers, The
RNSM	Royal Naval School of Music.
Royals, The	Royal Dragoons, The
RRF	Royal Regiment of Fusiliers, The
RRW	Royal Regiment of Wales, The
RS	Royal Scots (The Royal Regiment), The
R S Fus	Royal Scots Fusiliers, The
R Signals	Royal Corps of Signals
R Sussex R	Royal Sussex Regiment, The
RTR	Royal Tank Regiment
RTR (Alamein)	Alamein Band of the Royal Tank Regiment
RTR (Cambrai)	Cambrai Band of the Royal Tank Regiment
RTR (Rhine)	Rhine Band of the Royal Tank Regiment
R U Rifles	Royal Ulster Rifles, The
RWAFF	Royal West African Frontier Force
R War R	Royal Warwickshire Regiment, The
RWF	Royal Welsh Fusiliers, The
R W Kent R	Royal West Kent Regiment, The
R W Surr R	Royal West Surrey Regiment, The
Sco Rif	Scottish Rifles, The
Scots DG	Royal Scots Dragoon Guards (Carabiniers and Greys), The
Scots Fus Gds	Scots Fusilier Guards
Seaforth	Seaforth Highlanders, The
SG	Scots Guards
Shrops LI	Shropshire Light Infantry, The
S Lan R	South Lancashire Regiment, The
Somerset LI	Somerset Light Infantry, The
S Stafford R	South Staffordshire Regiment, The
Staffords	Staffordshire Regiment (The Prince of Wales's), The
Suffolk R	Suffolk Regiment, The
S Wales Bord	South Wales Borderers, The
S Yorks	South Yorkshire Regiment, The
Welsh R	Welsh Regiment, The
WFR	Worcestershire and Sherwood Foresters Regiment, The
WG	Welsh Guards
Wilts R	Wiltshire Regiment, The
W India R	West India Regiment, The
Worc R	Worcestershire Regiment, The
WRAC	Women's Royal Army Corps
W Rid R	West Riding Regiment, The
W York R	West Yorkshire Regiment, The
York & Lanc R	York and Lancaster Regiment, The
York R	Yorkshire Regiment, The

BIBLIOGRAPHY

We are heavily indebted to the official diary kept at Kneller Hall and to the many musicians we have spoken to who have attended the School in differing capacities, but the following published sources have also been of particular significance.

BOOKS

Bevan, Clifford *The Tuba Family* (London, Faber and Faber, 1978)

Binns, Lieutenant Colonel P L *A Hundred Years of Military Music: Being the Story of the Royal Military School of Music, Kneller Hall* (Gillingham, Blackmore, 1959)

Cobbett, R S *Memorials of Twickenham: Parochial and Topographical* (London, Smith & Elder, 1872)

Farmer, Henry George *The Rise & Development of Military Music* (London, William Reeves, undated)

Gaunt, William *Court Painting in England from Tudor to Victorian Times* (London, Constable, 1980)

Grove's Dictionary of Music and Musicians ed. Eric Bloom (London, MacMillan, 5th edition, 1954)

Jacobs, Arthur *Arthur Sullivan: A Victorian Musician* (Oxford, Oxford University Press, 1984)

Kennedy, Michael *The Concise Oxford Dictionary of Music* (Oxford, Oxford University Press, 3rd edition, 1980)

Killanin, Lord *Sir Godfrey Kneller and His Times 1646-1723: Being a Review of English Portraiture of the Period* (London, B T Batsford, 1948)

Mackenzie-Rogan, J *Fifty Years of Army Music* (London, Methuen & Co, 1926)

Nalden, Charles *Half and Half: The Memoirs of a Charity Brat 1908 - 1989* (Wellington, New Zealand, Moana Press, 1989)

Ponting, Clive *Whitehall: Tragedy & Farce* (London, Hamish Hamilton, 1986)

Sandford, E G (ed.) *Memoirs of Archbishop Temple* (London, MacMillan, 1906)

Sandford, E G *Frederick Temple: An Appreciation* (London, MacMillan, 1907)

Sheppard, Edgar ed. *George, Duke of Cambridge: A Memoir of his Private Life* (London, Longmans & Green, 1906, two volumes)

St Aubyn, Giles *The Royal George 1819 - 1904: The Life of H.R.H. Prince George, Duke of Cambridge* (London, Constable, 1963)

Thorne, R G *The History of Parliament: The House of Commons 1790 - 1820* (London, Secker & Warburg/History of Parliament Trust, 1986)

Turner, Gordon & Alwyn W Turner *The History of British Military Bands Vol I: Cavalry & Corps* (Staplehurst, Spellmount, 1994)

Turner, Gordon & Alwyn W Turner *The History of British Military Bands Vol II: Guards & Infantry* (Staplehurst, Spellmount, 1996)

Turner, Gordon & Alwyn W Turner *The History of British Military Bands Vol III: Infantry & Irish* (Staplehurst, Spellmount, to be published)

Young, Percy M *Sir Arthur Sullivan* (London, J M Dent & Sons, 1971)

NEWSPAPERS, JOURNAL AND ARTICLES

Aldershot Command News

Army Quarterly

British Bandsman

British Musician

Daily Herald

Fanfare - The Journal of Kneller Hall

Farmer, Henry George 'Foreign Army Bandmasters: their rise and fall' *Journal of the Society for Army Historical Research* Vol XXVII, No.111, Autumn 1949

Leading Note, The

Lion and the Rose, The - The Regimental Journal of the King's Own Royal Regiment

Orchestral Times & Bandsman

Richmond And Twickenham Times

Times, The

INDEX

Illustrations indicated by bold type

INTO BATTLE series:

Across the Lines – An Account of Axis Intelligence and Sabotage in Italy 1943–1945 by Donald Gurrey OBE
And Maybe A Man – With the Royal Signals of the Sixth Airborne Division by Ramond Leeming
Bombs and Barbed Wire – My War in the RAF and Stalag Luft III by Geoffrey Wilatt
Came the Dawn – 50 Years an Army Officer by Brigadier Paul Crook CBE DSO
Dual Allegiance – From the Punjab to the Jordan (WW2) by Monty Green
Five Lives in One by Ralph Benjamin CB
HMS Glory by Peter Barrett
Haul Taut & Belay – Memoirs of a Flying Sailor by Rear Admiral Sir Donald Gibson KCB DSC JP
In The Trade of War by James R. Allan
Keep Your Head Down – Falklands Notes by Comdr Bernie Bruen MBE DSC
A Kriegie's Log – The Lighter Side of Prison Life by Stephen P.C. Johnson
Let Go Aft – The Indiscretions of a Salthorse Commander by Cmdr H.G. de Chair DSC*
Letters from the Front – Letters of Lt Brian Lawrence, Grenadier Guards (WW1) by Ian Fletcher
Ordinary Naval Airmen by Jim Spencer
Para Memories by Eric Barley and Yves Fohlen
The Perilous Road to Rome Via Tunis (WW2) by Edward Grace MC
Soldier On! by Brigadier Joe Starling CBE MC DL
Some Letters from Burma by Tom Grounds
They Gave me a Seafire by Comdr Mike Crosley DSC*
Triumph and Disaster – The Autobiography of a Naval Officer by Cmdr Victor Clark DSC*
Wren's Eye View – The Adventures of a Visual Signaller (WW2) by Stephanie Batstone